BY

GLORIA STEINEM

Outrageous Acts and Everyday Rebellions

Marilyn: Norma Jeane

Revolution from Within

Moving Beyond Words

As If Women Matter (India)

My Life on the Road

MY LIFE
ON THE ROAD

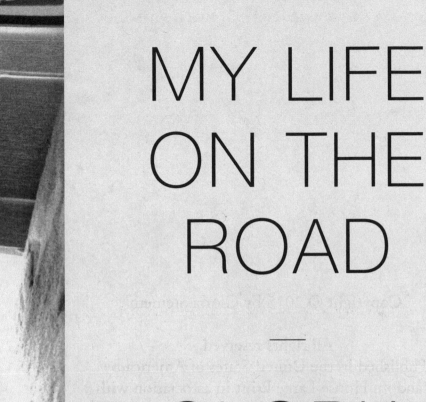

MY LIFE ON THE ROAD

—

GLORIA STEINEM

R A N D O M   H O U S E
LARGE PRINT

The Library of Congress has established a
Cataloging-in-Publication record for this title.

ISBN: 978-0-3995-6727-8

www.randomhouse.com/largeprint

FIRST LARGE PRINT EDITION

Printed in the United States of America

10 9 8 7 6 5 4 3 2 1

This Large Print edition published in accord with
the standards of the N.A.V.H.

Dr. John Sharpe of London, who in 1957, a decade before physicians in England could legally perform an abortion for any reason other than the health of the woman, took the considerable risk of referring for an abortion a twenty-two-year-old American on her way to India.

Knowing only that she had broken an engagement at home to seek an unknown fate, he said, "You must promise me two things. First, you will not tell anyone my name. Second, you will do what you want to do with your life."

Dear Dr. Sharpe, I believe you, who knew the law was unjust, would not mind if I say this so long after your death:

I've done the best I could with my life.

This book is for you.

"Evolution intended us to be travelers. . . . Settlement for any length of time, in cave or castle, has at best been . . . a drop in the ocean of evolutionary time."

—Bruce Chatwin,
ANATOMY OF
RESTLESSNESS

CONTENTS

—

PRELUDE

———

I board a plane for Rapid City, South Dakota, and see a lot of people in black leather, chains, and tattoos. Airline passengers usually look like where they're going—business suits to Washington, D.C., jeans to L.A.—but I can't imagine a convention of such unconventional visitors in Rapid City. It's the kind of town where people still angle-park their cars in front of the movie palace. My bearded seatmate is asleep in his studded jacket and nose ring, so I just accept one more mystery of the road.

At the airport, I meet five friends from different parts of the country. We are a diverse group of women—a Cherokee activist and her grown-up daughter, two African American writers and one musician, and me. We've been invited to a Lakota Sioux powwow celebrating the powerful place that women held before patriarchy arrived from Europe, and efforts now to restore that place.

As we drive toward the Badlands, we see an

acre of motorcycles around each isolated diner and motel. This solves the mystery of the leather and chains, but creates another. When we stop for coffee, our waitress can't believe we don't know. Every August since 1938, bikers from all over the world have come here for a rally named after Sturgis, a town that's just a wide place in the road. They are drawn by this sparsely populated space of forests, mountains, and a grid of highways so straight that it is recognizable from outer space. Right now about 250,000 bikers are filling every motel and campground within five hundred miles.

Our band of six strong women takes note. The truth is we are a little afraid of so many bikers in one place. How could we not be? We have all learned from movies that bikers travel in packs, treat their women like possessions, and may see other women as sexual fair game.

But we don't run into the bikers because we spend our days traveling down unmarked roads, past the last stand of trees, in Indian Country. We eat home-cooked food brought in trucks, sit on blankets around powwow grounds where dancers follow the heartbeat of drums, and watch Indian ponies as decorated as the dancers. When it rains, a rainbow stretches from can't-see to can't-see, and fields of wet sweet grass become as fragrant as gigantic flowers.

Only when we return late each night to our

cabins do we see motorcycles in the parking lot. While walking in Rapid City, I hear a biker say to his tattooed woman partner, "Honey, shop as long as you want—I'll meet you at the cappuccino place." I assume this is an aberration.

On our last morning, I enter the lodge alone for an early breakfast, trying to remain both inconspicuous and open-minded. Still, I'm hyperconscious of a room full of knife sheaths, jackboots, and very few women. In the booth next to me, a man with chains around his muscles and a woman in leather pants and an improbable hairdo are taking note of my presence. Finally, the woman comes over to talk.

"I just want to tell you," she says cheerfully, "how much Ms. magazine has meant to me over the years—and my husband, too. He reads some now that he's retired. But what I wanted to ask—isn't one of the women you're traveling with Alice Walker? I love her poetry."

It turns out that she and her husband have been coming to this motorcycle rally every year since they were first married. She loves the freedom of the road and also the mysterious moonscape of the Badlands. She urges me to walk there, but to follow the paths marked by ropes. During the war over the sacred Black Hills, she explains, Lakota warriors found refuge there because the cavalry got lost every time.

Her husband stops by on his way to the

cashier and suggests I see the huge statue of Crazy Horse that's being dynamited out of the Black Hills. "Crazy Horse riding his pony," he says, "is going to make all those Indian-killing presidents on Mount Rushmore look like nothing." He walks away, a gentle, lumbering man, tattoos, chains, and all.

Before she leaves, my new friend tells me to look out of the big picture window at the parking lot.

"See that purple Harley out there—the big gorgeous one? That's mine. I used to ride behind my husband, and never took the road on my own. Then after the kids were grown, I put my foot down. It was hard, but we finally got to be partners. Now he says he likes it better this way. He doesn't have to worry about his bike breaking down or getting a heart attack and totaling us both. I even put 'Ms.' on my license plate—and you should see my grandkids' faces when Grandma rides up on her purple Harley!"

On my own again, I look out at the barren sand and tortured rocks of the Badlands, stretching for miles. I've walked there, and I know that, close up, the barren sand reveals layers of pale rose and beige and cream, and the rocks turn out to have intricate womblike openings. Even in the distant cliffs, caves of rescue appear.

What seems to be one thing from a distance is very different close up.

I tell you this story because it's the kind of lesson that can be learned only on the road. And also because I've come to believe that, inside, each of us has a purple motorcycle.

We have only to discover it—and ride.

WITH ALICE WALKER NEAR THE BADLANDS, 1994.

FROM GLORIA STEINEM'S PERSONAL COLLECTION

Road Signs

WHEN PEOPLE ASK ME WHY I STILL HAVE HOPE and energy after all these years, I always say: **Because I travel.** For more than four decades, I've spent at least half my time on the road.

I've never tried to write about this way of life, not even when I was reporting on people and events along the way. It just seemed to have no category. I wasn't on a Kerouac road trip, or rebelling before settling down, or even traveling for one cause. At first I was a journalist following stories, then a sometime worker in political campaigns and movements, and most consistently an itinerant feminist organizer. I became a person whose friends and hopes were as spread out as my life. It just felt natural that the one common element in that life was the road.

When friends or reporters assumed that spending so much time away from home was a hardship, I often asked them to travel with me, hoping they would get as hooked as I was. Yet in all these years, only one took me up on it—for just three days.[1]

As decades passed, and the word **still** entered my life—as in "Oh, you're **still** traveling"—it dawned on me that I'd been writing least about what I was doing most.

So I sat down and began to make notes about many trips, past and present, that left me amazed by what is, angered by what isn't, and hooked on what could be. As I looked through old date books and schedules, letters and abandoned journals, suddenly I was awash in a sense memory of my father going through his tattered road maps and address books, trying to figure out how much gas money he needed to get from here to there, where to find trailer parks that would shelter his wife and two daughters, and what roadside dealers might buy the small antiques which he sold and bartered as we made our way across the country. It was so vivid that I could sense our conspiratorial whispering as we tried not to wake my mother, who was asleep in this house trailer that was our home for most of each year.

Until that moment, I would have sworn that I had rebelled against my father's way of life. I created a home that I love and can retreat to, though he wanted no home at all. I've never borrowed a penny, though he was constantly in debt. I take planes and trains to group adventures, though he would spend a week driving cross-country alone rather than board a plane. Yet in the way that we rebel, only to find ourselves in the midst of the familiar, I realized there was a reason why the road felt like home. It had been exactly that for the evocative first decade of my life. I was my father's daughter.

I never imagined starting this book with my father's life. Then I realized I had to.

More discoveries followed. For instance, I always thought of my road life as temporary, assuming that one day I would grow up and settle down. Now I realized that for me, the **road** was permanent, and **settling down** was temporary. Traveling had created my nonroad life, not the other way around.

Take public speaking: I spent all of my twenties and early thirties avoiding it. When I once asked a speech teacher about my aversion, she explained that dancers and writers were especially difficult to teach to speak in public, since both had chosen a profession in which they didn't have to talk—and I had been both.

Then in the late 1960s and early 1970s, the editors I'd been freelancing for were gigantically uninterested in the explosion of feminism across the country. I finally got angry enough and desperate enough to partner with a woman who was much braver than I, and to travel to campuses and community groups. Over time and far from home, I discovered something I might never otherwise have learned: people in the same room understand and empathize with each other in a way that isn't possible on the page or screen.

Gradually, I became the last thing on earth I would ever have imagined: a public speaker and a gatherer of groups. And this brought an even bigger reward: public listening. It was listening that taught me there would be readers for a national feminist magazine, no matter what publishing experts said.

Up to then, I'd been a freelance writer who never wanted to work in an office or be responsible for anything other than my own rent. But because of what I learned on the road, I invited writers and editors to explore starting a feminist magazine that was devoted, in the words of the great Florynce Kennedy, "to making revolution, not just dinner." When those women also said they had no place to publish what they cared about most, **Ms.** magazine was born.

From then on, I came home to a magnetic office full of journalists and editors. **Ms.** gave me not only an added reason to go on the road, but a chosen family to return to after every trip, my pockets full of scribbled notes about new events.

Altogether I might never have had the will or the way to do any of the things that matter most to me, had it not been for just being Out There.

Taking to the road—by which I mean letting the road take you—changed who I thought I was. The road is messy in the way that real life is messy. It leads us out of denial and into reality, out of theory and into practice, out of caution and into action, out of statistics and into stories—in short, out of our heads and into our hearts. It's right up there with life-threatening emergencies and truly mutual sex as a way of being fully alive in the present.

—

As you can see, the first reason for this book is to share the most important, longest-running, yet least visible part of my life. It's my chance to do more than come home saying to friends, "I met an amazing person who . . . ," or "Here's a great new idea for . . . ," or, most of all, "We have to stop generalizing about 'the American people,'" as if we were one homogeneous lump. I'm also now immune to politicians who say, "I've traveled the length and breadth of this great land, and I **know** . . ." I've traveled more than any of them, and I don't **know.**

What we're told about this country is way too limited by generalities, sound bites, and even the supposedly enlightened idea that there are two sides to every question. In fact, many questions have three or seven or a dozen sides. Sometimes I think the only real division into two is between people who divide everything into two, and those who don't.

Altogether, if I'd been looking at nothing but the media all these years, I would be a much more discouraged person—especially given the notion that only conflict is news, and that objectivity means being evenhandedly negative.

On the road, I learned that the media are not reality; reality is reality. For instance, Americans are supposed to cherish freedom, yet we imprison a bigger percentage of our people than any other country in the world. I talk to students who are graduating in crippling debt, yet don't connect this to state legislatures that are building prisons we don't need instead of schools we do need, and then spending an average of fifty thousand dollars a year per prisoner and way less per student. I love the entrepreneurial spirit of people who start a high-tech company or a hot dog stand, but our income and wealth gaps are the biggest in the developed world. I meet people in Indian Country who can trace their origins back a hundred thousand years, and survivors of sex and labor trafficking who arrived yesterday. Also, this country is transforming before our eyes. In thirty years or so, the majority will no longer be European Americans; the first generation of mostly babies of color has already been born. This new diversity will give us a better understanding of the world and enrich our cultural choices, yet there are people whose sense of identity depends on the old hierarchy. It may just be their fear and guilt talking: **What if I am treated as I have treated others?** But with all the power and money that is behind it, this backlash could imprison us in a hierarchy all over again.

As Robin Morgan wrote so wisely, "Hate generalizes, love specifies."[2] That's what makes going on the road so important. It definitely specifies.

MY SECOND PURPOSE IS to encourage you to spend some time on the road, too. By that, I mean traveling—or even living for a few days where you are—in an on-the-road state of mind, not seeking out the familiar but staying open to whatever comes along. It can begin the moment you leave your door.

Like a jazz musician improvising, or a surfer looking for a wave, or a bird riding a current of air, you'll be rewarded by moments when everything comes together. Listen to the story of strangers meeting in a snowstorm that Judy Collins sings about in "The Blizzard," or read Alice Walker's essay "My Father's Country Is the Poor." Each starts in a personal place, takes an unpredictable path, and reaches a destination that is both surprising and inevitable—like the road itself.

An addiction to the road can exist anywhere. The Sufi poet Rumi's caravan wandered through a dozen Muslim lands; the Roma people left India for Europe and never settled down; and Australia's aboriginals and Torres Strait Islanders go on walkabout to renew ancient songlines. I am writing this on-the-road-in-America book because it's the place I live and travel most, and most need to understand, especially given its outsize influence on the world. Also I'm not sure we can understand another country if we don't understand our own. In my twenties, I had the good luck to live for a year in Europe, and then for two years in India—yet in some ways, I was escaping more than being fully present. Secure Europe was a momentary way of leaving an insecure childhood behind. Faraway India helped to introduce me to the way most people live in the world, something way beyond anything I knew. I'm still thankful to that huge and struggling country for being impossible to ignore; otherwise I might have come home as the same person I was when I left.

My purpose here is to tempt you to explore this country. American travel seems to need an advocate. If I'm going to Australia or Zambia, people tell me how exciting it is, yet if I'm traveling anywhere in these United States, they sympathize and say how tiring it must be. In fact, there are many unique satisfactions here. One is that Americans seem to outstrip every nation for hope. Perhaps because so many of us came in flight from something worse, or rose from poverty here, or absorbed the fact and fiction of the "land of opportunity," or just because optimism itself is contagious—whatever the reason, hopefulness is what I miss the most when I'm not here. It's the thing that makes me glad to come home. After all, hope is a form of planning.

However, I'm not suggesting that you travel as much as I have. Like Sky Masterson, the wandering gambler in Damon Runyon stories, I've been in more hotel rooms than the Gideon Bible—and he didn't wash his hair with hotel soap, eat from vending machines, or sit up late organizing with the hotel maids. After my first two decades traveling as an organizer, I realized that the longest stretch I'd spent at home was eight days.

As you can see, I'd fallen in love with the road.

—

MY THIRD HOPE IS to share stories. For millennia, we have passed down knowledge through story and song. If you tell me a statistic, I'll make up a story to explain why it's true. Our brains are organized by narrative and image. After I joined the ranks of traveling organizers—which just means being an entrepreneur of social change—I discovered the magic of people telling their own stories to groups of strangers. It's as if attentive people create a magnetic force field for stories the tellers themselves didn't know they had within them. Also, one of the simplest paths to deep change is for the less powerful to speak as much as they listen, and for the more powerful to listen as much as they speak.

Perhaps because women are seen as good listeners, I find that a traveling woman—perhaps especially a traveling feminist—becomes a kind of celestial bartender. People say things they wouldn't share with a therapist. As I became more recognizable as part of a movement that gives birth to hope in many people's lives, I became the recipient of even more stories from both women and men.

I remember such serendipity as waiting out a storm in a roadhouse that just happened to have a jukebox and a stranded tango teacher who explained the street history of this dance; hearing Mohawk children as they relearned language and spiritual rituals that had been forbidden for generations; sitting with a group of Fundamentalists Anonymous as they talked about kicking the drug of certainty;

being interviewed by a nine-year-old girl who was the best player on an otherwise all-boy football team; and meeting a Latina college student, the daughter of undocumented immigrants, who handed me her card: CANDIDATE FOR THE U.S. PRESIDENCY, 2032.

There are also natural gifts of an on-the-road life. For instance, witnessing the northern lights in Colorado, or walking under a New Mexico moon bright enough to reveal the lines in my palm, or hearing the story of a solitary elephant in a Los Angeles zoo reunited with an elephant friend of many years before, or finding myself snowed into Chicago with a fireplace, a friend, and a reason to cancel everything.

More reliably than anything else on earth, the road will force you to live in the present.

MY LAST HOPE IS to open up the road—literally. So far it's been overwhelmingly masculine turf. Men embody adventure, women embody hearth and home, and that has been pretty much it.

Even as a child, I noticed that Dorothy in **The Wizard of Oz** spent her entire time trying to get back home to Kansas, and Alice in Wonderland dreamed her long adventure, then woke up just in time for tea.

From Joseph Campbell and his Hero's Journey to Eugene O'Neill's heroes who were kept from the sea by clinging women, I had little reason to think the road was open to me. In high school, I saw **Viva**

Zapata!, the Hollywood version of that great Mexican revolutionary. As Zapata rides to his destiny, his wife hangs on to his boot, dragging in the dust, imploring him to stay home. Since I couldn't yet admit to myself that I was more interested in going to sea and the revolution than in staying home as the mother or the wife, I just vowed silently that I would **never** become an obstacle to any man's freedom.

Even the dictionary defines **adventurer** as "a person who has, enjoys, or seeks adventures," but **adventuress** is "a woman who uses unscrupulous means in order to gain wealth or social position."

When women did travel, they seemed to come to a bad end, from the real Amelia Earhart to the fictional **Thelma and Louise.** In much of the world to this day, a woman may be disciplined or even killed for dishonoring her family if she leaves her home without a male relative, or her country without a male guardian's written permission. In Saudi Arabia, women are still forbidden to drive a car, even to the hospital in an emergency, much less for an adventure. During the democratic uprisings of the Arab Spring, both female citizens and foreign journalists paid the price of sexual assault for appearing in the public square.

As novelist Margaret Atwood wrote to explain women's absence from quest-for-identity novels, "there's probably a simple reason for this: send a woman out alone on a rambling nocturnal quest and she's likely to end up a lot deader a lot sooner than a man would."[3]

The irony here is that thanks to molecular archaeology—which includes the study of ancient DNA to trace human movement over time—we now know that men have been the stay-at-homes, and women have been the travelers. The rate of intercontinental migration for women is about eight times that for men.[4]

However, these journeys have often been unchosen one-way trips in cultures that were patriarchal and patrilocal; that is, women were under male control and also went to live in their husbands' households. In matrilocal cultures, men joined their wives' families—in about a third of the world they still do—but with equal status, since those cultures are and almost never were matriarchal.

In the face of all the dire and often accurate warnings of danger on the road for women, it took modern feminism to ask the rock-bottom question: **Compared to what?**

Whether by dowry murders in India, honor killings in Egypt, or domestic violence in the United States, records show that women are most likely to be beaten or killed at home and by men they know. Statistically speaking, home is an even more dangerous place for women than the road.

Perhaps the most revolutionary act for a woman will be a self-willed journey—and to be welcomed when she comes home.

———

As you will see, this book is the story not of one or even several trips, but of decades of travel leading out from the hub of home. You might say it's the story of a modern nomad.

Besides horizontal travel across the country, you will find two other kinds: vertical travel into the past of this North American continent that you and I are walking around on, and cultural travel between and among very different people and places.

Because this book is all about stories, I hope some here might lead you to tell your own and also to get hooked on the revolutionary act of listening to others.

I wish I could imitate the Chinese women letter writers of at least a thousand years ago. Because they were forbidden to go to school like their brothers, they invented their own script—called **nushu**, or "women's writing"—though the punishment for creating a secret language was death.[5] They wrote underground letters and poems of friendship to each other, quite consciously protesting the restrictions of their lives. As one wrote, "Men leave home to brave life in the outside world. But we women are no less courageous. We can create a language they cannot understand."

This correspondence was so precious to them that some women were buried with their letters of friendship, yet enough survive for us to see that they wrote in a slender column down the center of each page, leaving wide margins as spaces for a correspondent to add her own words.

"There have been great societies that did not use the wheel," as Ursula Le Guin wrote, "but there have been no societies that did not tell stories."

If I could, I would leave an open space for your story on every page.

MY LIFE ON THE ROAD

My father, Leo Steinem, in his favorite
photograph, 1949.

I.

My Father's Footsteps

I COME BY MY ROAD HABITS HONESTLY. There were only a few months each year when my father seemed content with a house-dwelling life. Every summer, we stayed in the small house he had built across the road from a lake in rural Michigan, where he ran a dance pavilion on a pier over the water. Though there was no ocean within hundreds of miles, he had named it Ocean Beach Pier, and given it the grandiose slogan "Dancing Over the Water and Under the Stars."

On weeknights, people came from nearby farms and summer cottages to dance to a jukebox. My father dreamed up such attractions as a living chess game, inspired by his own love of chess, with costumed teenagers moving across the squares of the dance floor. On weekends, he booked the big dance bands of the 1930s and 1940s into this remote spot. People might come from as far away as Toledo or

Detroit to dance to this live music on warm moonlit nights. Of course, paying the likes of Guy Lombardo or Duke Ellington or the Andrews Sisters meant that one rainy weekend could wipe out a whole summer's profits, so there was always a sense of gambling. I think my father loved that, too.

But as soon as Labor Day had ended this precarious livelihood, my father moved his office into his car. In the first warm weeks of autumn, we drove to nearby country auctions, where he searched for antiques amid the household goods and farm tools. After my mother, with her better eye for antiques and her reference books, appraised them for sale, we got into the car again to sell them to roadside antique dealers anywhere within a day's journey. I say "we" because from the age of four or so, I came into my own as the wrapper and unwrapper of china and other small items that we cushioned in newspaper and carried in cardboard boxes over country roads. Each of us had a role in the family economic unit, including my sister, nine years older than I, who in the summer sold popcorn from a professional stand my father bought her.

But once the first frost turned the lake to crystal and the air above it to steam, my father began collecting road maps from gas stations, testing the trailer hitch on our car, and talking about such faraway pleasures as thin sugary pralines from Georgia, all-you-can-drink orange juice from roadside stands in Florida, or slabs of salmon fresh from a California smokehouse.

Then one day, as if struck by a sudden whim rather than a lifelong wanderlust, he announced that it was time to put the family dog and other essentials into the house trailer that was always parked in our yard, and begin our long trek to Florida or California.

Sometimes this leave-taking happened so quickly that we packed more frying pans than plates, or left a kitchen full of dirty dishes and half-eaten food to greet us like Pompeii on our return. My father's decision always seemed to come as a surprise, even though his fear of the siren song of home was so great that he refused to put heating or hot water into our small house. If the air of early autumn grew too chilly for us to bathe in the lake, we heated water on a potbellied stove and took turns bathing in a big washtub next to the fireplace. Since this required the chopping of wood, an insult to my father's sybaritic soul, he had invented a wood-burning system all his own: he stuck one end of a long log into the fire and let the other protrude into the living room, then kicked it into the fireplace until the whole thing turned to ash. Even a pile of cut firewood in the yard must have seemed to him a dangerous invitation to stay in one place.

After he turned his face to the wind, my father did not like to hesitate. Only once do I remember him turning back, and even then my mother had to argue strenuously that the iron might be burning its way through the ironing board. He would buy us a new radio, new shoes, almost anything rather than retrace the road already traveled.

At the time, I didn't question this spontaneity. It was part of the family ritual. Now I wonder if seasonal signals might be programmed into the human brain. After all, we've been a migratory species for nearly all our time on earth, and the idea of a settled life is very new. If birds will abandon their young rather than miss the moment to begin a flight of thousands of miles, what migratory signals might our own cells still hold? Perhaps my father—and even my mother, though she paid a far higher price for our wanderings—had chosen a life in which those signals could still be heard.

My parents also lived off the land—in their own way. We never started out with enough money to reach our destination, not even close. Instead, we took a few boxes of china, silver, and other small antiques from those country auctions, and used them to prime the process of buying, selling, and bartering our way along the southern route to California, or still farther south to Florida and the Gulf of Mexico. It was a pattern that had begun years before I was born, and my father knew every roadside dealer in antiques along the way, as a desert traveler knows each oasis. Still, some shops were always new or under new management, and it must have taken courage to drive up in our dusty car and trailer, knowing that we looked less like antique dealers than like migrants forced to sell the family heritage. If a shop owner treated us with too much disdain, my father was not above letting him think we really were selling our possessions. Then he would regain his dignity by elaborating on his triumph once he was back in the car.

Since my parents believed that travel was an education in itself, I didn't go to school. My teenage sister enrolled in whatever high school was near our destination, but I was young enough to get away with only my love of comic books, horse stories, and Louisa May Alcott. Reading in the car was so much my personal journey that when my mother urged me to put down my book and look out the window, I would protest, "But I just looked an hour ago!" Indeed, it was road signs that taught me to read in the first place—perfect primers, when you think about it. COFFEE came with a steaming cup, HOT DOGS and HAMBURGERS had illustrations, a bed symbolized HOTEL, and graphics warned of BRIDGE or ROAD WORK. There was also the magic of rhyming. A shaving cream company had placed small signs at intervals along the highway, and it was anticipating the rhyme that kept me reading:

> **If you**
> **don't know**
> **whose signs**
> **these are**
> **you can't have**
> **driven**
> **very far.**
> **Burma Shave**

Later, when I read that Isak Dinesen recited English poems to her Kikuyu workers in Kenya—and they requested them over and over again, even though they didn't understand the words—I knew exactly what they meant. Rhyming in itself is magic.

In this way, we progressed through rain and sandstorms, heat waves and cold winds, one small part of a migration of American nomads. We ate in diners where I developed a lifetime ambition to run one with blue gingham curtains and bran muffins. In the car during the day, we listened to radio serials, and at night, to my father singing popular songs to stay awake.

I remember driving into the pungent smell of gas stations, where men in overalls emerged from under cars, wiping their hands on greasy rags and ushering us into a mysterious and masculine world. Inside were restrooms that were not for the queasy or faint of heart. Outside were ice chests from whose watery depths my father would pluck a Coke, drink it down in one amazing gulp, and then search for a bottle of my beloved Nehi Grape Soda so I could sip it slowly until my tongue turned purple. The attendants themselves were men of few words, yet they gave freely of their knowledge of the road and the weather, charging only for the gas they sold.

I think of them now as tribesmen along a trading route, or suppliers of caravans where the Niger enters the Sahara, or sailmakers serving the spice ships of Trivandrum. And I wonder: Were they content with their role, or was this as close to a traveling life as they could come?

I remember my father driving on desert roads made of wired-together planks, with only an occasional rattlesnake ranch or one-pump gas station to break the monotony. We stopped at ghost towns that had been emptied of every living soul, and saw sand dunes pushing against lurching buildings, sometimes shifting to reveal a brass post office box or other treasure. I placed my hands on weathered boards, trying to imagine the people they once had sheltered, while my parents followed the more reliable route of asking the locals. One town had died slowly after the first asphalt road was laid too far away. Another was emptied by fear when a series of mysterious murders were traced to the sheriff. A third was being repopulated as a stage set for a western movie starring Gary Cooper, with sagging buildings soaked in kerosene to make an impressive fire, and signs placed everywhere to warn bystanders away.

Ever challenged by rules, my father took us down the road to a slack place in the fence, and sneaked us onto the set. Perhaps assuming that we had permission from higher-ups, the crew treated us with deference. I still have a photo my father took of me standing a few feet from Gary Cooper, who is looking down at me with amusement, my head at about the height of his knee, my worried gaze fixed on the ground.

As a child who wanted too much to fit in, I worried that we would be abandoned like those towns one day, or that my father's rule-breaking would bring down some nameless punishment. But now I wonder: Without those ghost towns that live in my imagination longer than any inhabited place, would I have known that mystery leaves a space for us when certainty does not? And would I have dared to challenge rules later in life if my father had obeyed them?

Whenever we were flush, we traded the cold concrete showers of trailer parks for taking turns at a hot bath in a motel. Afterward, we often went to some local movie palace, a grand and balconied place that was nothing like the warrens of viewing rooms today. My father was always sure that a movie and a malted could cure anything—and he wasn't wrong. We would cross the sidewalk that sparkled with mica, enter the gilded lobby with fountains where moviegoers threw pennies for luck and future return, and leave our cares behind. In that huge dark space filled with strangers, all facing huge and glowing images, we gave ourselves up to another world.

Now I know that both the palaces and the movies were fantasies created by Hollywood in the Depression, the only adventures most people could afford. I think of them again whenever I see subway riders lost in paperback mysteries, the kind that Stephen King's waitress mother once called her "cheap sweet vacations"—and so he writes them for her still. I think of them when I see children cramming all five senses into virtual images online, or when I pass a house topped by a satellite dish almost as big as it is, as if the most important thing were the ability to escape. The travel writer Bruce Chatwin wrote that our nomadic past lives on in our "need for distraction, our mania for the new."[1] In many languages, even the word for **human being** is "one who goes on migrations." **Progress** itself is a word rooted in a seasonal journey. Perhaps our need to escape into media is a misplaced desire for the journey.

Most of all from my childhood travels, I remember the first breath of salt air as we neared our destination. On a California highway overlooking the Pacific or a Florida causeway that cut through the Gulf of Mexico like Moses parting the Red Sea, we would get out of our cramped car, stretch, and fill our lungs in an ontogeny of birth. Melville once said that every path leads to the sea, the source of all life. That conveys the fatefulness of it—but not the joy.

Years later, I saw a movie about a prostituted woman in Paris who saves money to take her young daughter on a vacation by the sea. As their train full of workers rounds a cliff, the shining limitless waters spread out beneath them—and suddenly all the passengers begin to laugh, throw open the windows, and toss out cigarettes, coins, lipstick: everything they thought they needed a moment before.

This was the joy I felt as a wandering child. Whenever the road presents me with its greatest gift—a moment of unity with everything around me—I still do.

——

ANOTHER TRUTH OF MY EARLY WANDERINGS is harder to admit: I longed for a home. It wasn't a specific place but a mythical neat house with conventional parents, a school I could walk to, and friends who lived nearby. My dream bore a suspicious resemblance to the life I saw in movies, but my longing for it was like a constant low-level fever. I never stopped to think that children in neat houses and conventional schools might envy me.

When I was ten or so, my parents separated. My sister was devastated, but I had never understood why two such different people were married in the first place. My mother often worried her way into depression, and my father's habit of mortgaging the house, or otherwise going into debt without telling her, didn't help. Also, wartime gas rationing had forced Ocean Beach Pier to close, and my father was on the road nearly full time, buying and selling jewelry and small antiques to make a living. He felt he could no longer look after my sometimes-incapacitated mother. Also, she wanted to live near my sister, who was finishing college in Massachusetts, and now I was old enough to be her companion.

We rented a house in a small town, and spent most of one school year there. It was the most conventional life we would ever lead. After my sister graduated and left for her first grown-up job, my mother and I moved to East Toledo and an ancient farmhouse where her family had once lived. As with all inferior things, this part of the city was given an adjective while the rest stole the noun. What once had been countryside was crowded with the small houses of factory workers. They surrounded our condemned and barely habitable house on three sides, with a major highway undercutting its front porch and trucks that rattled our windows. Inside this remnant of her childhood, my mother disappeared more and more into her unseen and unhappy world.

I was always worried that she might wander into the streets, or forget that I was in school and call the police to find me—all of which sometimes happened. Still, I thought I was concealing all this from my new friends. Most were quiet about their families for some reason, from speaking only Polish or Hungarian at home, to a father who drank too much or an out-of-work relative sleeping on the couch. By tacit agreement, we tended to meet on street corners. Only many years later would I meet a high school classmate who confessed that she had always worried about me, that my mother was called the Crazy Lady of the neighborhood.

During those years, my mother told me more about her early life. Long before I was born, she had been a rare and pioneering woman reporter, work that she loved and had done so well that she was promoted from social reporting to Sunday editor for a major Toledo newspaper. She had stayed on this path for a decade after marrying my father, and six years after giving birth to my sister. She was also supporting her husband's impractical dreams and debts, suffering a miscarriage and then a stillbirth, and falling in love with a man at work: perhaps the man she should have married. All this ended in so much self-blame and guilt that she suffered what was then called a nervous breakdown, spent two years in a sanatorium, and emerged with an even greater feeling of guilt for having left my sister in her father's care. She also had become addicted to a dark liquid sedative called chloral hydrate. Without it, she could be sleepless for days and hallucinate. With it, her speech was slurred and her attention slowed. Once out of the sanatorium, my mother gave up her job, her friends, and everything she loved to follow my father to isolated rural Michigan, where he was pursuing his dream of building a summer resort. In this way, she became the mother I knew: kind and loving, with flashes of humor and talent in everything from math to poetry, yet also without confidence or stability.

While I was living with her in Toledo, my father was driving around the Sunbelt, living almost entirely in his car. Once each summer, he drove back to the Midwest for a visit, his timing always dependent on his mysterious deals. He once wrote me about a short story whose principal character was always waiting for the Big Deal, a story he said could have been about him. Between visits he sent postcards signed "Pop," fifty-dollar monthly money orders tucked into various motel envelopes, and letters written on his idea of business stationery, a heavy ragged-edge paper without address or his first name—which was Leo—just at the top in big exploding red letters, "It's Steinemite!"

This way of life ended when I was seventeen, and our Toledo house was sold as a teardown for a parking lot, a sale my mother had long planned so I would have money to pay for college. My sister came during my father's visit that summer because she had a plan: if he would take responsibility for our mother for a year, I could live with my sister in Washington, D.C., where she was a jewelry buyer in a department store. This would give me a carefree senior year of high school.

I told my sister that our father would never do it—and when the three of us went out for a breakfast together, this was exactly what he said. After she stormed out in anger, my father drove me to my summer job as a salesgirl. Opening the car door to go to work, I surprised us both by starting to cry. I had no idea that a ray of hope had crept in. Because he couldn't bear to see anyone cry, certainly not the daughter he'd known mostly as a child, he reluctantly said okay—but only if we synchronized our watches to exactly one year.

Somehow my father did manage to take care of my mother, even while driving around California, from one motel to the next. I had a glorious year finishing high school, getting sympathy for being without my parents and secretly feeling free.

When our father brought our mother to Washington to live with my sister and me—and after I left for college in the fall—my sister realized she couldn't both work and be a full-time caregiver. Instead, she found a kindhearted doctor at a mental hospital near Baltimore, who admitted our mother as a resident and began to give her some of the help she should have had years before.

When I visited her there on weekends from my summer job and then on college vacations, I slowly began to meet someone I'd never known. I discovered that we were alike in many ways—something I either hadn't seen or couldn't admit out of fear that I would share her fate. I learned that the poems I remembered her reciting by heart were by Edna St. Vincent Millay and Omar Khayyam; that teaching me to fold a sheet of typing paper into three columns for note-taking had been sharing a tool of her journalistic trade; and that she had wanted with all her heart to leave my father and go with a girlfriend to try their luck as journalists in New York. As I looked into her brown eyes, I saw for the first time how much they were like my own.

If I pressed and said, "But why didn't you leave? Why didn't you take my sister and go to New York?" she would say it didn't matter, that she was lucky to have my sister and me. If I pressed hard enough, she would add, "If I'd left, you never would have been born."

I never had the courage to say: **But you would have been born instead.**

—

AT COLLEGE I LIVED in a dormitory, happy to be responsible for no one but myself. I think my classmates were mystified by my wall-to-wall cheerfulness and mistook it for some odd midwestern trait. I spent an undergraduate year in Europe, pretending to study while actually traveling, because I was sure I would never get to Europe again. After graduation I lived for a summer with my mother, who was well enough to live first in a rooming house, then with my sister, who had married and created an apartment for our mother in her home. Then I went to India on a fellowship, and spent nearly two years there wandering and writing.

But at home again, I couldn't find a job that used what I had learned there. I wandered more, worked in student politics, and finally began to make a freelance living as a writer in New York, always in the familiar land of the temporary. I found an apartment and a roommate but kept on living out of boxes and suitcases. In city streets, I often looked into lighted windows and repeated the mantra of my childhood: **Everybody has a home but me.**

Meanwhile my mother worked part time in a gift shop near where she lived with my sister, and pursued interests that included Eastern philosophy and an Episcopalian church she loved because it allowed the homeless to sleep in its pews. She would never be able to live on her own, but when she visited me in

New York, she seemed both proud and scared that I was where she had once wished to be.

I learned from my father's postcards that he had revisited his show business dreams by buying the contract of a young Italian pop singer. He drove the singer and his wife to gigs at bars and roadhouses, but the singer got few callbacks, made no records, and, according to my father, ate a lot, as did his wife. My father sent him back to his job at an aircraft factory and became a solitary traveler again.

When he heard that semiprecious stones could be bought on the cheap in Latin America, he financed a trip by selling his car. However, when he arrived in Ecuador, he encountered an earthquake, few bargains, and a woman from Germany who wanted to marry a U.S. citizen in order to enter this country, something he didn't confide in me until after they were divorced. He also made the sole personal comment of our lifetime together: "You know how people say you lose interest in sex after sixty? Well, it isn't true." When he discovered he would be financially responsible for his ex-wife in this country, he urged her to return and come back on her own—which he was lucky she was willing to do. Altogether, he ended his Latin American adventure more broke than when he began.

Later, this woman who was so briefly my stepmother called to ask me where she could send my father a birthday card. I'd lived apart from him so long that I'd forgotten my childhood training to never, ever, say more than "Daddy isn't home." After all, the caller might be a bill collector. It's amazing how fast one can learn a way of life, and how fast one can forget it. I actually told her where to write him. This caused my usually softhearted father to shout at me from a faraway pay phone, "How could you?" He was sure she only wanted money.

Yet on his annual trips east, my father was his usual cheerful, good-hearted self. He worried about only two things: avoiding the IRS (he hadn't paid taxes or even filed a return in years) and dealing with minor health problems that plagued him. At over three hundred pounds, he had what he jokingly called "very-close veins," plus difficulty moving anywhere outside his car, like a whale out of water. Nonetheless, he never stopped patronizing the best ice cream places and every all-you-can-eat restaurant from coast to coast, or driving even to the corner to mail a letter. And he never gave up on his dreams and deals.

Once he swore me to secrecy about his idea for a roadside chain called Suntana Motels. Each unit would have a retractable roof that guests could crank back, and sunbathe in privacy. Another time he told me about a highly confidential formula for an orange drink that would rival Orange Julius. Mostly he sent slogans to ad agencies—by registered mail so no one could steal them—for example, "You

Can Bet Your Bottom Dollar on Scott Tissue," or
"If You're a Chain Smoker, Make Every Link Old
Gold." When his ideas weren't accepted, he just
thought of more.

After I graduated from college with a Phi Beta
Kappa key, he worried about my fate as an over-
educated woman. He thought a college degree was
nice but unnecessary, for either one of us. He once
sent me an ad from **Variety,** his show business bible,
that called for women under twenty-four, over five
foot seven, with a Phi Beta Kappa key, to dance in a
Las Vegas chorus line to be called the Hi Phi Betas.
Scrawled across the clipping, he had written in red,
"Kid"—which was the way he always addressed
me—"this is perfect for you!"

After I went off to India instead, he had another
idea. He sent me eight hundred dollars to buy a
star sapphire on my return trip through Burma. He
would meet me when my boat docked in San Francisco, and sell the stone for a profit that would sub-
sidize our drive back east in style. When I emerged
along with three hundred Chinese immigrants from
steerage—the cheapest way home—he met me
with his jeweler's loupe. Right away he saw that I'd
picked a lopsided star. When I was in college, he
had improved on my short-lived engagement ring
by dipping it in water made bluish by swishing an
indelible pencil, thus making a yellowish diamond
look white. Yet this star problem was something he
couldn't fix. He knew he would be lucky to get his
money back.

Rolling with the punches, he offered to introduce me to a friend who made aerosol cans and might employ me to sell this new invention on the road. I would get paid for traveling—in my father's eyes, the best of all worlds. When I didn't say yes to that either, he said he had enough gas and food money to get us to Las Vegas. I asked worriedly what would happen then, and he said, "Then you'll be lucky at the one-armed bandits—beginners always are—and you can help me sell jewelry on the road back east."

In a windowless Las Vegas casino filled with silent gamblers and noisy slot machines, he staked me to a fifty-dollar bucket of coins. After a couple of hours of twirling fruits and no idea what I was doing, I'd multiplied our money by five. Only then did he confess this had been his last fifty dollars. To celebrate, we stuffed ourselves with the food kept cheap to attract gamblers, saw a free show by his tried-and-true method of walking in after it was well under way, and set off on the road again.

Since I'd won only enough money to get us out of Nevada, his next plan was to sell jewelry to small-town stores along the route east. He was sure that if I wore, say, a ring and a pin or a bracelet when we went into a jewelry store, the store owners would assume they were making a killing at the expense of a down-on-our-luck father and daughter. It was the same technique he had used on condescending antique dealers in my childhood. Besides, as my father pointed out, the stores really were getting a bargain. This tactic worked well enough to pay for gas, food, and motels all the way to Washington, D.C., where my mother and sister waited.

Much later, when I saw the father-and-daughter team in **Paper Moon**, this trip came back in all its precarious optimism. So did my father's joy at defeating fate. Only then did I realize that we really **were** a down-on-our-luck father and daughter. He had turned our plight into a game we could win.

My father's nomadic life continued until he was almost sixty-four. "If we're ever in an accident on a freeway," he had said to me as a child, "get out and run—the cars are coming too fast to stop." On a freeway in the urban sprawl of Orange County, California, this was exactly what happened to him. My father's car was sideswiped with such force that the driver's door was staved in, he was pinioned beneath the steering wheel, and the car was spun into the oncoming traffic. Unable to move, much less get out and run, he was hit by another car.

From a hospital that was little more than a battle station by the freeway, a doctor left a message for me in New York. My father must have given him my number, knowing that my sister couldn't leave her young children, my mother couldn't travel alone, and I was the most logical helper. But I was also my father's daughter. I was out of the country, traveling, unreachable.

By the time I got home days later, the doctor had reached my sister. She suggested I fly out a week later, when my father would be ready to leave the hospital and would need help in his furnished room.

I think I sensed that I should go right away, yet somehow the accident seemed like a normal part of my father's life on the road, nothing to be too alarmed about. Also I felt a cold stab of fear that if I went to California, I would become my father's care-taker, as I had been my mother's—and never come back to my own life.

A few days before I was to leave, the doctor called my sister to say that our father had taken a turn for the worse due to internal bleeding. I got on the first flight to Los Angeles, but when I changed planes in Chicago, I heard myself being paged. It was my sister. The doctor had called again. There had been a massive internal hemorrhage—our father had died.

When I arrived at that hospital, I found only a manila envelope with my father's few belongings, and a doctor who seemed barely able to control his anger that no family member had been present. My father had succumbed to gushing traumatic ulcers, he said, more lethal than his crash wounds. I don't know whether I was listening with a daughter's ears or hearing a fact, but I thought he was saying that this fatal bleeding had been caused not by the crash itself, but by trauma, stress, despair.

It was something I could never find the courage to tell my sister. It was something I would never forget.

Still, I thought I could get through the hospital procedures without breaking down. And I did—until I held my father's worn wallet in my hands, its leather shaped to the curve of his body by years in his back pocket as he drove the road. I can feel it still.

I will never stop wishing I had been with him. I will always wonder: Alone in a hospital within sound of the freeway, would he have traded the freedom of the road for the presence of family and friends? Having lived his life in the belief that something great could be just around every corner, did he realize for the first time that no more corners could be turned?

Did he regret having raised a traveling daughter?

IN MY CHILDHOOD, I think my father and I often felt as if we were alone on our journey. My mother was lying down in the trailer behind us, and my sister was often away at school. As the captain of a very fragile ship, he looked to me for companionship, just as he had when I helped him wrap and unwrap antiques. Yet I wasn't with him in the end. Was this a fate created by his choices? By mine? By both?

I am left without answers. There are only questions I must answer for myself. What is the balance between home and the road? Hearth and horizon? Between what is and what could be?

I only know that I can't imagine my father living any other life. When I see him in my mind's eye, he is always the traveler, eating in a diner instead of a dining room, taking his clothes out of a suitcase instead of a closet, looking for motel VACANCY signs instead of a home, making puns instead of plans, choosing spontaneity over certainty.

Even his argument for persuading my mother to marry him was "It will only take a minute." Going to a movie wasn't planned. Instead of checking newspaper listings, he got in his car and drove around to look at every theater marquee within miles. It was years before I learned that other people didn't just walk into a movie and stay until the story reached the same point again.

I remember him choosing the fastest highway, not the scenic route my mother was always arguing for. When he swung through a state where he had friends, he never called in advance; he just dropped in. He didn't even make plans for the poker and chess games he loved so much, but found them by happenstance. He took comfort in not knowing about the future. As he always said, "If I don't know what will happen tomorrow, it could be wonderful!"

When I imagine the sound of his voice on the phone, it's only after I hear the words of a long-distance operator saying, "Please deposit . . . ," and the sound of coins dropping.

He was a sailor, not a sailmaker. He wouldn't stay behind in a port or an oasis while ships or caravans passed by. He was always moving on.

I was twenty-seven when he died. I had lived and traveled in other countries, but hadn't yet made traveling in this country my own. I think he knew that I was still regretting our wanderings. He could only have remembered me as a child with my head in a book, refusing to sing along with his cheerful renditions of World War I songs, asking him to drive slowly past pretty houses and wishing aloud that we lived there. I fear he knew my childhood hope that I was adopted and that my real parents would come and take me to a home with a canopied bed and a horse to ride.

In college, I tried to avoid the embarrassment of our atypical family by mining our odd life for stories like these:

• My father was unable to resist swearing, and my mother had asked that he not swear around his daughters, so he named the family dog Dammit. When he felt something stronger was needed, he made up his own long composite word that he said at top speed: GoshdarnCaloramorbusAntonioCanovaScipio AfricanustheYoungertheEldertheMiddleaged. Later when I discovered that Antonio Canova was a nineteenth-century Italian sculptor, Scipio Africanus the Elder had defeated Hannibal, and Scipio Africanus the Younger had sacked Carthage, I was impressed. But when I asked why he had chosen those names, he said, "I just liked their sound."

• At home in rural Michigan, we were missing our favorite nighttime programs due to a broken radio, and my father bet my mother that he could replace it, even though there were no stores within miles and all would be closed anyway. He got in his car—and was back in an hour with a huge brand-new model. He never told us how he did it.

• As a connoisseur of extra-thick malteds, he knew all the best roadside sources from coast to coast. He also knew that if two customers came in together, each got half the contents of one tall malted mixer, in which two servings fit exactly. However, a solitary customer got the dividend in the bottom of the can. That's why he gave me money as we sat in the car, and told me to go in, to order my own malted, and when he followed a few minutes later, to pretend I didn't know him. Then we both got the dividend, though I doubt we were fooling anybody. If there was anything more delicious to a five- or six-year-old than a malted, it was pretending not to know your own father, and playing a part in a grown-up game.

• In an elevator or any other public space, he coached me in routines like these:

MY FATHER: "If you're not a good girl, you
  won't go to heaven."
ME: "I don't want to go to heaven, Daddy. I
  want to go with you."

Or his all-time favorite:

ME: "And then what happened, Daddy?"
MY FATHER: "So I told the guy to keep his
fifty thousand dollars!"

• When I was about five and we were in a
country store, I asked my father for a nickel. He
asked me what for. By his account, I said, "You
can give it to me, or not give it to me, but you
can't ask me what it's for." He not only gave me
the nickel but told me I was right. He loved to
tell this story as proof of my spirit. In reality, it
was his cherishing of a child's spirit that was the
gift.

In college, I told these and other stories as a
source of entertainment, yet all the while I was hoping against hope that my father wouldn't turn up on
campus in his food-stained suit and dusty car full of
boxes, his great weight causing the driver's side to list
downward like a ship. I was glad he was too far away
to come to Fathers' Weekend, where he would have
been too different from the other fathers. I could
imagine him falling into a snoring sleep after eating,
or getting sentimental tears in his eyes when talking
about money, or uttering cheerfully naïve comments
like "Where there's smoke, there's fire" about the
McCarthyite accusations being leveled at two of my
professors, though bravely ignored by the college.
From my classmates, I belatedly discovered that
even outside the movies, families really did live in
neat houses, take naps, have nine-to-five jobs, pay

bills on time, and eat at a table instead of standing up next to a refrigerator. Just as my father had
rebelled against the orderly life of his immigrant parents who had fled insecurity, I regretted insecurity
and became vulnerable to the siren song of the conventional.

In the years after college, my father's influence
became ever clearer in the choices I made—for
instance, to go to India instead of seeking a regular job—but I still wasn't admitting it. Like many
children, I had been drawn to the needier parent.
Like many daughters especially, I was living out the
unlived life of my mother. Like my father, I inhabited the future, the land of possibilities, but that was
something we never talked about. There wasn't time
or place to explore what I think we both knew: that
in our small family, we were the most alike.

For reasons of work and geography, we saw each
other less and less in the years before he died. I never
told him that I could see myself in him, and vice
versa. I never thanked him for, say, stopping at endless horse farms, pony rides, and every palomino in
a pasture, all to please a horse-crazy daughter. One
summer he even bought me a horse of my own,
though I was much too young and the horse was
much too old. With the help of a neighboring farmer
who told us what to do, my father helped me feed
and groom him—until that farmer took pity on all
three of us and gave the horse a retirement home.

I never told my father how grateful I was that he
was different from my best friend's father. I had just

witnessed my first humiliating clean-your-plate-or-you-can't-have-dessert incident at her house. When I came home, I tested my father. We were eating in our usual haphazard way in the living room—never on the debris-covered dining room table that was used only on national holidays—and he asked me if I wanted dessert. I pointed out that I hadn't finished my dinner. "That's okay," he said as he went into the kitchen for ice cream. "Sometimes you're hungry for one thing and not another." I loved him so much at that moment.

He listened to all my complaints about not going to school like other kids, yet years after his death, I realized that I'd also been spared the Dick and Jane limitations that school then put on girls. Nor was he around when I finally understood that having a loving and nurturing father made a lifetime difference. Only after I saw women who were attracted to distant, condescending, even violent men did I begin to understand that having a distant, condescending, even violent father could make those qualities seem inevitable, even feel like home. Because of my father, only kindness felt like home.

It's true that my father's idea of childrearing was to take me to whatever movie he wanted to see, however unsuitable; buy unlimited ice cream; let me sleep whenever and wherever I got tired; and wait in the car while I picked out my own clothes. Salespeople were shocked to see a six- or eight-year-old with cash and making her own choices, but this resulted in such satisfying purchases as a grown-up ladies' red hat, Easter shoes that came with a live rabbit, and a cowgirl jacket with fringe.

All I knew was that my father enjoyed my company, asked my opinion, and treated me better than he treated himself. What more could any child want?

Once I became a freelance writer, I also realized the value of his ability to live with and even love insecurity. He had two points of pride: he never wore a hat, and he never had a job—by which he meant he never had a boss. I knew I was my father's daughter when I took a part-time editing job to pay the rent. It was work I could do at home, but when suddenly I was expected to spend two days a week in the office, I quit, bought an ice cream cone, and walked the sunny streets of Manhattan. My father would have done the same—except for the walking.

It's said that the biggest determinant of our lives is whether we see the world as welcoming or hostile. Each becomes a self-fulfilling prophecy. My mother had performed the miracle of creating a welcoming world for my sister and me, even though she herself grew up in a hostile one. But her broken spirit could not help but let the darkness in—and I absorbed it during our long years together. My father and I lived together for far less time, but his faith in a friendly universe helped balance my mother's fear of a threatening one. He gave me that gift. He let in the light.

As DECADES PASSED AFTER his death, my father seemed so improbable that I sometimes wondered if I'd made him up. My mother died peacefully of heart problems just before her eighty-second birthday. I wrote a long essay about her called "Ruth's Song: Because She Could Not Sing It." I mourned her unlived life. Still, my father's chosen life was less understandable. My sister was the only other witness—and she had left home when she was seventeen. My father's friends were as spread out as his life, and were strangers to me.

When I got two letters about my father out of the blue, I was older than he had been when he died. These generous correspondents had known my father when they themselves were boys.

The first letter came from John Grover, by then a retired obstetrician. In high school, he had a summer job as a trombone player with the house band at Ocean Beach Pier. One Saturday night, the bandleader took all the cash the band had earned, leaped over the side of the pier, and swam away, leaving Grover and another teenage band member stranded.

"Your father saved the summer for us by offering us a place to stay and enough cash to help us get food," Grover wrote. "In return, we acted as 'guardians' of the pier at night. We slept on a mattress placed on a dance floor under the stars . . . and he found day jobs for us in a cement-block manufacturing plant. . . . I also played third trombone with several bands as they passed through on weekends, providing a little more cash."

Before the end of the summer, Grover and his friend had found jobs as musicians with a traveling circus. Then they went home to finish high school.

Grover, by then in his seventies, wrote: "I've always remembered your father's solicitude in helping two homeless and broke West Virginia boys that summer. . . . It is interesting that I, too, went into a field important to women and women's rights. I spent a large part of my professional career helping to make the care of pregnant women and women in labor more humane. I was also deeply involved with the birth control and legal abortion movements in the state of Massachusetts during the 1960s."

At last, I had a witness to my father's kindness. Though his solution to unjust rules was to ignore them, not change them, it was no accident that a young man he helped had grown up to help others. My father knew a good heart when he saw one. He himself was often dependent, in the timeless phrase of Tennessee Williams, "on the kindness of strangers."

A few years later, I got a letter from Hawaii and another physician. Dr. Larry Peebles had grown up in Los Angeles, where his own late father, also a doctor, had been my father's best friend. He was writing because he had just vacationed in Latin America, bought a few gemstones, and had a Proustian memory of my father that set him to reminiscing on paper. He kindly wrote to give me an unknown part of my father's life.

I think I was Leo's youngest pal. He was in his sixties when he died, and I was fifteen. My father, William Peebles, was his chief pal. I never saw my dad happier than when he was around Leo. I knew I was a lesser pal, but being a pal of Leo's was the best. He treated everyone equally, he was not pretentious nor condescending. He was kind. And best of all, he was fun. He had lots of stories.

My father gave the appearance of being sophisticated, but he was still a farm boy from Grande Prairie, Alberta. He ran away from home and an abusive father when he was fourteen and spent his formative years on the road.

I think he and Leo, who was a salesman of sorts, liked being out in the world. They shared the awareness that's only developed by being outside in a strange environment, anytime, day or night. I guess you'd call it street sense. When Dad came into money, he spent it. Leo helped him. He and Leo were constantly scheming to make money. Their mantra was "Never work for anyone else." It was a game, and life was the playing field.

While my dad was practicing medicine, they would plot between patients and after work. Saturdays I would ostensibly go to work. I would put pills in pillboxes and label them or develop X-rays. Sometimes I got to assist during minor surgeries. When Leo was there, I pretty much hung out with him in a small anteroom to my father's office, with a private entrance.

Leo was larger than life. He was a big man, over three hundred pounds. We would always start out the same way: I would call him "Mr. Steinem," and he would look a little pained and say, "Call me Leo." Not "Uncle Leo" or anything like that, just Leo. It was how I knew we were pals.

When he told me to sit down, he always patted the couch next to him, looking furtively around the room. What was going to happen next was not for just anyone to see. He would start searching around in his suitcoat pockets, eventually coming out with gems. Diamonds, rubies, sapphires. Big ones, little ones. They were not in boxes, no wrappings of any kind. No settings, just loose in his pockets. He loved them. I loved them. We would carefully examine them. We would talk about them. Many times we would just admire them in silence, take our time, we both had lots of time. . . . Invariably, he would reach into another pocket and pull out a roll of money and ask if I needed any. Somehow, I never did.

I never could figure out why he carried all that money and those precious gems on his person. It was all very mysterious and dangerous.

My favorite time was going to lunch across the street at the Radar Room. It was painted black outside, with a single neon sign that you could hardly see during the day but at night was a spectacular green, blinking and spelling Radar in both directions. Inside, it was also black, with red leather bar stools and booths and a large mirror behind the bar. We sat in my dad's favorite booth in the dark. I would always have a cheeseburger, my dad would always have one martini with his lunch, and Leo would eat but never drink.

For entertainment, Leo and my dad would get customers to bet that I couldn't name a particular bone or muscle in the body. This worked better when I was eight, but anytime I was stumped, I would just say, "sternocleidomastoideus." The customer would look amazed and pay his dime, but I knew I had to know the real answer by the time my father and I went home. Leo didn't care if I was right or wrong, we were just having fun. He didn't sweat the small stuff. I wanted to be like Leo.

One sunny morning my father told me that Leo hadn't been around because he'd been in a serious car accident. We drove down to Orange County, where he was in intensive care. My dad talked to the staff, then we went in to see Leo. He was breathing oxygen through a clear mask, the sheet was around his massive waist, and he didn't have a shirt on. This was the first time I'd ever seen him without his gray suit. He was breathing heavily, obviously working hard, and sweating profusely. His entire upper body was bruised. Even though he was laboring, he was calm. I imagine he was getting lots of morphine, but he talked to us, and we talked to him. We told him we'd be back in the morning to see him. We'd been told his family was on the way. I wish I could remember all that was said. But I guess it doesn't matter. The main thing was he knew he wasn't alone.

Before we got to the car, my dad told me matter-of-factly that Leo wouldn't make it through the night. I was already planning the return visit. I was irritated he told me. I was already miserable, I didn't feel like being a good soldier. But I knew he was right. The sunny morning had given me optimism. Now I got a dose of reality. Maybe I was learning street sense.

After Leo died, my father practiced for another year. He got into trouble, went to jail for a while, then retired. . . . I've been working for myself for almost thirty years.

I've become a general surgeon and often
times, especially when I see gemstones, I
remember my pal, Leo.

I wonder: If you think of someone you
love, do you become a little more like them?
I would like to think so.

I wrote back to the generous Dr. Peebles—who
asked me to call him Larry in my father's spirit—and
thanked him with all my heart. For the first time, I
knew that my father had seen two familiar faces in the
hospital before he died. When I explained that I had
arrived too late—something he hadn't known—he
wrote back to say that, years later, he arrived too late
for his own father's death. He assured me that my
father "seemed to be okay with all of it. Like someone who had a good run."

Each of us knew we were comforting the other.

IF EVERYONE HAS A full circle of human qualities
to complete, then progress lies in the direction we
haven't been. My father's clear case of **horreur du
domicile** was a fear of home so common, especially
among men, that Baudelaire called it "La Grande
Maladie." My father had grown up in an apartment
with meals served at the same time and no sound
except a ticking clock on the mantelpiece. When
psychologist Robert Seidenberg studied women in
such changeless homes, he named the result "the
trauma of eventlessness." As a boy, I think my father

suffered from this, too. That's why he pushed his own life's pendulum to the opposite extreme.

Of course, his quixotic nature played a role, as did his optimism and his gift for excess, yet I doubt he would have chosen such a risky life if he hadn't been fleeing an orderly one.

My mother was also adventurous by nature. She had rebelled against a mother who thought that creating guilt in her two daughters was the path to their good behavior, and then rebelled against a church so strict that dancing was forbidden. She told me stories of wearing her father's overalls to play basketball at a time when girls did neither, and learning to drive before anyone else on her block. She then worked her way through university by embroidering for a fancy linen shop and by teaching calculus. On campus, she met my devil-may-care father, the son of an upper-middle-class Jewish family. He made her laugh and was full of dreams—the very opposite of her unforgiving mother, and a father who was often away, working on the railroad. She married my father for his refusal to worry, then was left to worry alone.

Both my mother and my father paid a high price for lives out of balance. Yet at least my father had been able to choose his own journey. He never realized his dreams, but my mother was unable even to pursue hers.

In my heart, I know that if I were forced into an either/or choice between constancy and change, home and the road—between being a **hazar,** a dweller in houses, and an **arab,** a dweller in tents—I, too, would choose the road.

I sometimes wonder if I am crisscrossing my father's ghostly paths and we are entering the same towns or roadside diners or the black ribbons of highways that gleam in the night rain, as if we were images in a time-lapse photograph.

We are so different, yet so much the same.

WITH SPEAKING PARTNER FLORYNCE KENNEDY
ON CAMPUS IN THE 1970S.

COURTESY OF GLORIA STEINEM/RAY BALD

II.

Talking Circles

BECAUSE I SAW MY FATHER AS A ROOTLESS WAN-derer, my first solution was to become the opposite. I was sure my peculiar childhood would give way to an adulthood with one job, one home, and one vacation a year. Indeed, I probably longed for that life more than people who had grown up in it. I could have had a sign on my forehead, HOME WANTED, but I just assumed a real home would have to wait until I had a husband and children, a destiny I both thought was inevitable and couldn't imagine. Not even in a movie had I ever seen a wife with a journey of her own. Marriage was always the happy end, not the beginning. It was the 1950s, and I confused growing up with settling down.

It would take two years of living in India, where I went right after college—to avoid my engagement to a good but wrong man—to show me that my father's isolated way of traveling wasn't the only one. There was a shared road out there, both ancient and very new.

I.

WHEN I FIRST ARRIVED IN NEW DELHI, I LONGED for the "memsahib travel" of a car and a driver, something every local official and tourist seemed able to afford. I couldn't imagine any other way of navigating streets jammed with slow oxcarts, fast motorcycles, yellow and black taxis that looked like bumblebees, swarms of bicyclists, a wandering cow or two, ancient buses stuffed with passengers inside and festooned with freeloaders outside, and peddlers who darted up to sell food and trinkets at every stop.

It would take two months as a rare foreigner living in Miranda House, the women's college at the University of Delhi, and kindhearted students teaching me how to wear saris and take buses, for me to realize that in a car by myself, I wouldn't really be in India.

I wouldn't see women leaning out of bus windows to buy strings of jasmine for their hair, or men and women being endlessly patient with crying babies, or male friends unselfconsciously linking fingers as they talked, or skinny kids in patched and starched school uniforms memorizing by chanting out loud from copybooks. I wouldn't hear political arguments in the Indian English that bridges fourteen languages, or witness the staggering variety of newspapers that Indians read. Nor would I have known how hard it is for the average Indian just to get to work, or that "Eve teasing," the sexual harassment and touching that women may suffer in public, was what my college friends traveled in groups to avoid. Certainly I would never have come to share the calm of people in crowds that would have signaled an emergency anywhere else.

I never did ride in one of the tongas pulled by skinny bicyclists. Friends assured me they were an advance over the barefoot runners who had been outlawed in independent India, though some could still be seen in the poorest neighborhoods. Being pulled by another human being just seemed colonial and a mark of shame. This made it especially ironic many years later, when I saw Indian bicycle tongas imported into Manhattan, and pulled by athletic, well-fed young men who charged by the minute.

But even after group travel in New Delhi, it would take one very long trip down the east coast of India to change my homegrown notion that private is always better than public, something American carmakers had preached as gospel.[1]

In the way that youth plunges in where age would think twice, I had decided to travel from Calcutta to Kerala on my own, stopping at villages and temples on my way to the oldest part of India at its southern tip. My student friends urged me to take one of the women-only railway cars that were still a feature of trains crisscrossing the subcontinent as a legacy of the British.

When I climbed into that ancient third-class car, I found myself in a dormitory on wheels. Women of different ages and sizes were sitting in groups to talk or nurse babies or share meals from the tiered brass food carriers known as tiffins. As a foreigner in a sari, I soon inspired curiosity, kindness, and a lot of advice, all in our few shared English and Hindi words, plus a lot of gesticulating. Since this was a two-day journey with stops at many small stations, women bargained on my behalf with peddlers who sold hot chai, bright-colored cold drinks, kebabs and chapatis—plus an addictive ice cream known as **kulfi**—all through train windows at every station. In between stops, they offered me their own curries, rice, and homemade breads, taught me more ways to tie a sari than I had imagined possible—including one for playing tennis—and discussed varieties of mangoes with all the nuance that Westerners reserve for wines.

I soon learned there was a very Indian habit of asking personal questions. It must have driven the reticent English crazy. "Why hasn't your family found you a husband?" "All Americans are rich, so why are you with us in third class?" "Does everyone in America carry a gun?" "If I came to your country, would I be welcome?" And once we got to know each other: "How do American women keep from having too many babies?"

Later I would listen to Indira Gandhi describe her

youthful travels in these women-only railway cars as her best preparation for becoming prime minister. She was the daughter of Jawaharlal Nehru, the first prime minister of India, yet she felt she learned more from these women, whose view was personal. They knew that **khadi,** India's hand-spun, handwoven cloth, was being driven out of business by machine-made cloth from England—even if they didn't know this was the familiar colonial pattern of taking raw material from a colony, transforming it in England, and selling it back at a profit. They could see why Mahatma Gandhi himself had adopted the spinning wheel as his symbol of Indian independence.

Also, despite the belief of population experts that uneducated women wouldn't use birth control, these women knew very well when their own bodies were suffering from too many pregnancies and births. That's why as prime minister, Indira Gandhi took on the controversy of creating the first national family planning program. Her early journeys in those women-only cars had taught her that ordinary women would use it, even if in secret, and literacy had little to do with it.

For myself, I remember not only the learning but the laughing. I was asked to sing an American song—everybody in India seems to sing as part of everyday life—but even they had to admit I wasn't a singer. They taught me how to squeeze my hands and slip on glass bangles hardly bigger than my wrist, and explained that **cholis,** the tight blouses worn under saris, are the Indian equivalents of bras. They introduced me to fresh lychees, though I'd never seen one out of a can, and warned me about Indian men who would try to marry an American just to get a visa and a job.

Decades later, these women still live in my memory. As their first close-up foreigner, perhaps I still live in theirs. Had I been isolated in a car, this talking circle could never have happened.

After we said our good-byes, I boarded a rickety bus inland, headed to an ashram of Vinoba Bhave, the leader of a land reform movement inspired by Gandhi. He had been assassinated a decade before, but Bhave was still walking from village to village, asking landowners to give a small percentage of their acreage to the landless. I'd written to a former American missionary who was part of this movement, and he had arranged for me to stay in a guesthouse nearby.

But when I got to Bhave's ashram, almost everyone was gone. An elderly man explained that caste riots had broken out in nearby Ramnad, a large rural area of the southeast, and government leaders in far-off New Delhi had ordered the area cordoned off in the hope of containing the burnings and killings. Not even reporters were allowed in. Nonetheless, teams of three or four from the ashram had walked around the roadblocks and were going from one village to the next, holding meetings, letting people know they were not abandoned, and dispelling rumors that were even worse than reality—an on-the-ground organizing effort to reverse the spiral of violence.

Each team had to include at least one woman. Men couldn't go into the women's quarters to invite women to meetings, and if there was no woman present, other women were unlikely to come anyway. But the ashram had no women left.

That's how I was persuaded that a foreigner in a sari would seem no more out of place than someone from New Delhi, and why I found myself leaving behind all my possessions except a cup, a comb, and the sari I had on, and getting on a rickety bus. As my companion, the elderly man from the ashram, explained to me, if the villagers wanted peace, they would feed and house the peacemakers. If they didn't want peace, no outsiders could help anyway. As we started on our journey, I noticed that without possessions, I felt oddly free.

After hours on that ancient bus that seemed to stop everywhere, we arrived at the place where police barriers had blocked the dusty road into Ramnad. Without a car or even an oxcart, we just bypassed the road altogether and walked into this large area so traumatized by caste riots.

Thus began a week unlike any other. We walked between villages in the heat of the day, stopping to cool off in shallow streams or find shade in groves where chai and steamed rice cakes called **idlis** were sold from palm-roofed shelters. At night, I watched as villagers slowly came out of their small earthen houses and compounds to sit around a kerosene lamp in circles of six or twenty or fifty. I listened as villagers told stories of burnings and murders, thefts and

rapes, with fear and trauma that needed no translation. It was hard to imagine anything that could
slow this cycle of violence, yet villagers took comfort from neighbors who had ventured out of their
compounds, too. People seemed relieved to see one
another, talk, be heard, separate truth from rumor,
and discover that any outsiders knew or cared.

To my surprise, these long nights often ended
with pledges to keep meeting, to sort out what was
true and what was not, and to refuse to be part of
vengeful cycles that only endangered them more.
Sometimes it was almost dawn before we went home
with families who fed us and gave us straw mats
or charpoys, wooden frames strung with hemp, to
sleep on.

It was the first time I witnessed the ancient and
modern magic of groups in which anyone may speak
in turn, everyone must listen, and consensus is more
important than time. I had no idea that such talking
circles had been a common form of governance for
most of human history, from the Kwei and San in
southern Africa, the ancestors of us all, to the First
Nations on my own continent, where layers of such
circles turned into the Iroquois Confederacy, the
oldest continuous democracy in the world. Talking
circles once existed in Europe, too, before floods,
famines, and patriarchal rule replaced them with
hierarchy, priests, and kings. I didn't even know, as
we sat in Ramnad, that a wave of talking circles and
"testifying" was going on in black churches of my
own country and igniting the civil rights movement.

I certainly didn't guess that, a decade later, I would see consciousness-raising groups, women's talking circles, giving birth to the feminist movement. All I knew was that some deep part of me was being nourished and transformed right along with the villagers.

I could see that, because the Gandhians listened, they were listened to. Because they depended on generosity, they created generosity. Because they walked a nonviolent path, they made one seem possible. This was the practical organizing wisdom they taught me:

> If you want people to listen to you, you have to listen to them.
> If you hope people will change how they live, you have to know how they live.
> If you want people to see you, you have to sit down with them eye-to-eye.

I certainly didn't know that a decade or so after I returned home, on-the-road organizing would begin to take up most of my life.

IT WOULD BE ALMOST twenty years before I visited India again. By then, in the late 1970s, the civil rights and anti–Vietnam War movements at home had inspired more change, including among women who loved and were crucial to those movements, yet were rarely equal within them.[2] They realized the need for an independent and inclusive feminist movement that would take on the personal and global politics of gender.

This contagion was going on in many countries. Altogether, a new consciousness was spreading as women met or read about one another, whether in small meetings and underground feminist publications or at global events like the UN Conference on Women in Mexico City in 1975. The dry tinder of inequality was everywhere, just waiting to be set on fire.

Devaki Jain, a Gandhian economist and a friend from my earlier time living in India, invited me back toward the end of the 1970s to talk with some of these new women's groups. It was as if she and I had been having the same realizations by long-distance telepathy. We could finish each other's sentences. Inspired by our different paths to a shared place, we had the idea of collecting Gandhian tactics into a pamphlet for women's movements everywhere. After all, Gandhi's tactic of satyagraha, or nonviolent resistance, would be well suited to women, and so would his massive marches and consumer boycotts.

As part of our research, we interviewed Kamaladevi Chattopadhyay, a rare woman leader during the independence struggle. She had worked with Gandhi, led his national women's organization, warned him against agreeing to the partition of India and Pakistan as the price of independence, and then led a renaissance of Indian handicrafts that used the talents of millions of refugees displaced by partition.

As we explained our idea of teaching Gandhian tactics to women's movements, she listened to us patiently, sitting and rocking on her veranda, sipping tea. When we were finished, she said, "Well, of course, my dears. We taught him everything he knew."

She made us laugh—and she explained. In India under the British, Gandhi had witnessed a massive women's movement organizing against suttee, the immolation of widows on their husbands' funeral pyres, and much more. In England as a young man studying to be a barrister, Gandhi also saw the suffrage movement, and he later urged activists working for self-rule in India to emulate the courage and tactics of the Pankhursts, England's most famous and radical suffragists. After his return to India from South Africa, where he organized against the discrimination that Indians were subjected to, he was alarmed to find an independence movement with almost no roots in the villages and the daily lives of ordinary people. He began to live like a villager himself, to organize mass marches and consumer boycotts, and to measure success by changes in the lives of the poorest and least powerful: village women.

As Kamaladevi explained kindly, Devaki and I had the Great Man theory of history, and hadn't known that the tactics we were drawn to were our own. She made us both laugh again—and learn. As Vita Sackville-West wrote:

I worshipped dead men for their strength,
Forgetting I was strong.

WHEN I WENT HOME after that second India visit, I saw my own past differently.

I had walked in Indian villages in the 1950s, sure that they had no relevance to my own life. But now a women's revolution was springing from talking circles of our own. At home, I had been going to everything from battered women's shelters and freestanding women's clinics to women's centers on campuses and protests by single mothers trying to survive on welfare. My becoming an itinerant feminist organizer was just a Western version of walking in villages.

Though I had imagined my life would be that of a journalist and observer, sure that I didn't want to be responsible for the welfare of others as I had been for my mother, I found myself committed to colleagues and a magazine that made me lie awake at night wondering if we could make the payroll. Yet this responsibility had become a community, not a burden.

I had wanted to escape my traveling childhood, yet I was traveling and making the discovery that ordinary people are smart, smart people are ordinary, decisions are best made by the people affected by them, and human beings have an almost infinite capacity for adapting to the expectations around us—which is both the good and the bad news.

Finally, I could see that the love of independence and possibilities that I absorbed from my father now had a purpose. All movements need a few people who can't be fired. When you're dependent, it's very hard not to be worried about the approval of whoever and whatever you're dependent on. For me, a mix of freedom and insecurity felt like home and allowed me to become an itinerant organizer.

This is not a calling you will learn about from a career counselor, or get recruited for, or even see in a movie. It's unpredictable and often means patching together a livelihood from speaking fees, writing, foundations, odd jobs, friends, and savings. But other than becoming a rock musician or a troubadour, nothing else allows you to be a full-time part of social change. It satisfies my addiction to freedom that came from my father, and my love of community that came from seeing the price my mother paid for having none. That's why, if I had to name the most important discovery of my life, it would be the portable community of talking circles; groups that gather with all five senses, and allow consciousness to change. Following them has given me a road that isn't solitary like my father's, or unsupported like my mother's. They taught me to talk as well as listen. They also showed me that writing, which is solitary, is fine company for organizing, which is communal. It just took me a while to discover that both can happen wherever you are.

II.

IN 1963 I WAS MAKING A LIVING AS A FREELANCE journalist, writing profiles of celebrities and style pieces—not the kind of reporting I had imagined when I came home from India. I read that Martin Luther King, Jr., was leading a March on Washington, a massive campaign for jobs, justice, new legislation, and federal protection for civil rights marchers who were being beaten, jailed, and sometimes murdered in the South, all with police collusion. However, I couldn't get an assignment to write about it.

True, I did have a long-sought assignment to write a profile of James Baldwin—who would be speaking at the march—but following him around amid multitudes seemed impossible, intrusive, or both. Plus I could see and hear his speech better on television. Also the press was full of dire warnings about too few people and failure, or too many people and violence. This march was being called too dangerous by a White House worried that it could turn off moderates in Congress who were needed to pass the Civil Rights Act, and too tame by Malcolm X, who said that asking for help from Washington was too needy, not self-sufficient, and unlikely to succeed.

For all those reasons, I decided not to go to the march—right up until I found myself on my way. All I can say years later is: If you find yourself drawn to an event against all logic, go. The universe is telling you something.

On that hot August day, I was just one person being carried slowly along in a sea of humanity. I washed up next to "Mrs. Greene with an e," an older, plump woman wearing a straw hat, who was marching with her grown-up, elegant daughter. As Mrs. Greene explained, she had worked in Washington during the Truman administration, in the same big room as white clerks, but segregated behind a screen. She hadn't been able to protest then, so she was protesting now.

As we neared the Lincoln Memorial, she pointed out that the only woman seated on the speakers' platform was Dorothy Height, head of the National Council of Negro Women, an organization that had been doing the work of racial justice since the 1930s, yet even she hadn't been asked to speak. Mrs. Greene wanted to know: **Where is Ella Baker? She trained all those SNCC young people. What about Fannie Lou Hamer? She got beaten up in jail and sterilized in a Mississippi hospital when she went in for something else entirely. That's what happens—we're supposed to give birth to field hands when they need them, and not when they don't. My grandmother was dirt poor and was paid seventy-five dollars for every live birth. The difference between her and Fannie Lou? Farm equipment. They didn't need so many field hands anymore. These are black women's stories, who will tell them?**

I hadn't even noticed the absence of women speakers. Also I'd never thought about the racist reasons for controlling women's bodies. I felt a gear click into place in my mind. It was like India, where high-caste women were sexually restricted and women at the bottom were sexually exploited. This march was magnetic because living in India had made me aware of how segregated my own country was. But only Mrs. Greene made me understand the parallels between race and caste—and how women's bodies were used to perpetuate both. Different prisons. Same key.

Mrs. Greene's daughter rolled her eyes as her mother told me about complaining to their state delegation leader. He had countered that Mahalia Jackson and Marian Anderson were singing.[3] **Singing isn't speaking,** she told him in no uncertain terms.

I was impressed. Not only had I never made any such complaints, but at political meetings, I had given my suggestions to whatever man was sitting next to me, knowing that if a man offered them, they would be taken more seriously. **You white women,** Mrs. Greene said kindly, as if reading my mind, **if you don't stand up for yourselves, how can you stand up for anybody else?**

As streams of people surged toward the Lincoln Memorial and the speakers' platform, the three of us got separated. I used my press credentials to climb the steps, hoping to see them. But when I turned around, all I could see was an ocean of upturned faces. It was a scene I will never forget. Stretching over the expanse of green, past the reflecting pool, past the Washington Monument, all the way to the Capitol, there were a quarter of a million people.

The sea of humanity looked calm, peaceful, not even pressing to come closer to the speakers, as if each one felt responsible for proving that the fears of violence and disorder were wrong. We were like a nation within a nation. From nowhere, a thought rose up: **I wouldn't be anywhere else on this earth.**

Martin Luther King, Jr., read his much-anticipated speech in a deep and familiar voice. I'd always imagined that if I were present at the creation of history, I would know it only long afterward, yet this was history in the moment.

As King ended his speech, I heard Mahalia Jackson call out, "Tell them about the dream, Martin!" And he did begin the "I have a dream" litany from memory, with the crowd calling out to him after each image—**Tell it!** What would be most remembered had been least planned.

I hoped Mrs. Greene heard a woman speak up— and make all the difference.

FIFTY YEARS LATER I stood again with thousands who gathered at the Lincoln Memorial to celebrate the anniversary of that first march—and this time there were women's voices. Bernice King, who had been an infant at home when her father gave that first speech, spoke about the absence of women in 1963. There was also Oprah Winfrey, who had been a nine-year-old girl in Mississippi when Dr. King spoke, and Caroline Kennedy, the daughter of John F. Kennedy, the president who the marchers had hoped would disobey his political advisers, leave the White House, and just appear—but he never did. Finally, there was President Barack Obama, twice elected president of the United States, a possibility even Dr. King hadn't dreamed of.

This was huge progress, yet nothing can make up for truths untold. As Dr. King once said, "Justice too long delayed is justice denied." If Rosa Parks and Fannie Lou Hamer and others had been heard fifty years ago—if women had been half the speakers in 1963—we might have heard that the civil rights movement was partly a protest against the ritualistic rape and terrorizing of black women by white men.[4] We might have known that Rosa Parks had been assigned by the NAACP to investigate the gang rape of a black woman by white men—who had left her for dead near a Montgomery bus stop—before that famous boycott. We might have known sooner that the most reliable predictor of whether a country is violent within itself—or will use military violence against another country—is not poverty, natural resources, religion, or even degree of democracy; it's violence against females. It normalizes all other violence.[5] Mrs. Greene knew that. She also knew it was all about keeping women from controlling their own bodies. It has been part of the history of this country ever since Columbus captured Native women as sex slaves for his crew, and expressed surprise when they fought back.[6]

I knew Mrs. Greene couldn't possibly be alive to see women speaking a half-century later, but I hoped her daughter was watching. Back then, she had been impatient with her mother's complaints, but I bet now she would be proud.

After these fiftieth anniversary speeches, I found myself standing with a group of young African American women, some wearing Smith College T-shirts. Yolanda King, Martin and Coretta King's daughter, had gone there, and these women knew I had, too. We took photos with our cell phones. I told them that my class of 1956 included not one African American student—or Negro girl, as everyone then would have said—and when I asked a man in the Smith admissions office why, he said, "We have to be very careful about educating Negro girls because there aren't enough educated Negro men to go around."

The young women laughed at this sexist/racist double whammy—and hugged me with sympathy, as if I had been the wronged one—and in a way, they were partly right. White people should have sued for being culturally deprived in a white ghetto. When humans are ranked instead of linked, everyone loses.

These young women were not looking to Washington, as Malcolm X might have feared, nor were they waiting to be asked to speak. They were complete unto themselves, as in the line from one of Alice Walker's poems in **Revolutionary Petunias:**

Blooming Gloriously
For its Self

Malcolm X would have been proud of them, too. I knew the oldest of his six daughters, Attallah Shabazz, an elegant and experienced version of those self-possessed young women. She was a writer, speaker, activist, and, by then, a grandmother herself. Getting to know her had been a gift of the road.

When we talked again, she told me something I'd never heard or read. Malcolm X had been in Washington for that historic 1963 march. He stayed in the hotel suite of actor and activist Ossie Davis, who spoke at the march, and made sure Dr. King knew he was there in support. But as his daughter explained, "He also knew his presence would have disrupted or split the focus—and he was a supporter of the big picture."

Somehow I found this little-known fact very moving. These two men seemed to be growing toward each other. Dr. King was becoming more radical by speaking out on issues like the Vietnam War, and Malcolm X was beginning to talk about a bloodless revolution. Some tragedies become more tragic. They might have become part of the same talking circle.

III.

THANKS TO MRS. GREENE—AND MANY OTHERS brave enough to stand up for themselves and other women—I began to understand that females were an

out-group, too. That realization solved such mysteries as why the face of Congress was male but the face
of welfare was female; why homemakers were called
women who "don't work," though they worked longer, harder, and for less pay than any other class of
worker; why women did 70 percent of the produc-
tive labor in the world, paid and unpaid, yet owned
only 1 percent of the property; why **masculinity**
meant leading and **femininity** meant following in
the odd dance of daily life.

More than ever, I found myself wanting to report
on this new view of the world as if everyone mattered. But it was still the 1960s, and even my most
open-minded editor explained that if he published
an article saying women were equal, he would have
to publish one next to it saying women were not—in
order to be objective.

I had retreated into writing profiles of Mar-
got Fonteyn, the dancer I couldn't be, or Dorothy
Parker, Saul Bellow, and other authors I admired—
which seemed as close as I would ever get to being
an author myself. Then two women from a lecture
bureau wrote to ask if I would speak to groups who
had expressed curiosity about this new thing called
women's liberation. I'd recently written a piece for
my column in **New York** magazine, "After Black
Power, Women's Liberation." It had been triggered
by my own click of consciousness—namely, that I
had been silent and silenced about an abortion I'd
had years before. Like many women, I'd been made
to feel at fault, not realizing there were political

reasons why female humans were not supposed to make decisions about our own bodies.

I was intrigued by the offer, but I had a big problem: I was terrified of public speaking. I'd so often canceled at the last minute when magazines booked me on television to publicize this or that article—as writers were often expected to do—that some shows had blacklisted me. Fortunately, I had a friend named Dorothy Pitman Hughes, a pioneer of nonsexist, multiracial child care in New York, a fearless speaker, a mother, and a member of an extended black family in rural Georgia—all things I was not.

We had met when I wrote about her community child care center for **New York** magazine.[7] As we sat on child-size chairs, sharing lunch on paper plates, her one assistant, a young Italian radical, told us he was sad: the girl he loved wouldn't marry him because he wouldn't allow her to work after marriage. Dorothy and I didn't know each other, but we went to work pointing out parallels between equality for women and the rest of his radical politics. It actually worked.

Since we had been successful one on one, Dorothy suggested we speak to audiences as a team. Then we could each talk about our different but parallel experiences, and she could take over if I froze or flagged.

Right away we discovered that a white woman and a black woman speaking together attracted far more diverse audiences than either one of us would have done on our own. I also found that if I confessed my fear of public speaking, audiences were not only tolerant but sympathetic. Public opinion polls showed that many people fear public speaking even more than death. I had company.

We started in school basements with a few people on folding chairs, and progressed to community centers, union halls, suburban theaters, welfare rights groups, high school gyms, YWCAs, and even a football stadium or two. Soon we discovered the intensity of interest in the simple idea that each person's shared humanity and individual uniqueness far outweighed any label by group of birth, whether sex, race, class, sexuality, ethnicity, religious heritage, or anything else. That's why my first decade or so on the road wasn't spent going to meetings of the Business and Professional Women or the American Association of University Women or even the National Organization for Women. I was traveling to campuses, meetings of the National Welfare Rights Organization, the United Farm Workers, 9-to-5, which was a new group of and for clerical workers, lesbian groups sometimes excluded both by mainstream feminists and by gay men, and the political campaigns of anti–Vietnam War and new feminist candidates.

We came to see our job as creating a context in which audiences themselves could become one big talking circle, and discover they were neither crazy nor alone in their experiences of unfairness or efforts to be both their unique selves and to find a community. As in India all those years earlier, they told their own stories. Often, these talking circles went on twice as long as our talks.

When we first started speaking at the very end of the 1960s, the war in Vietnam was the main cause of activism. Buildings were being occupied and draft cards burned. At the same time, the gay and lesbian movement was moving out of the underground and into a public arena, and the Native American movement was trying to stop the purposeful obliterating of their languages, culture, and history. As always, the idea of freedom was contagious.

A few years earlier in the 1960s, women a decade or so older than I had begun to reject the "feminine mystique" of the suburbs, as brilliantly and lethally described by Betty Friedan in her best seller, and to demand women's rightful place in the paid workforce. Friedan had dared to name this glorified consumer role that women's magazines were forcing on readers—though to be fair, advertisers were forcing it on editors—but younger and more radical women didn't want just a job and a piece of the existing pie. They wanted to bake a new pie altogether.

Eventually these more conservative women came to agree that feminism had to include all women—lesbians, women on welfare, the intertwining of sex and race for women of color; everyone—and the more radical women of diverse races and classes no longer turned up their noses at the idea of making change from inside the system as well as outside. Though the starting places of these various activist groups had been very different and had created pain and misunderstanding, by the end of the 1970s they came together as fractious, idealistic, diverse, and effective parts of the same movement.

Given my age of just over thirty, I was in between these two groups of women—one trying to integrate and the other to transform. But because of my experience, I was drawn to the more radical and younger ones. I wasn't married and living in the suburbs. I'd always been in the workforce, but the gender ghetto in journalism was not just a glass ceiling, it was a glass box. Also India had taught me that change grows from the bottom, like a tree, and that caste or race can double or triple women's oppression.

Soon feminism became a brushfire that spread coast to coast—and some people viewed it with the same alarm. To the religious right wing and much of the mainstream, we were defying God, family, and the patriarchy they decreed. To the left wing and some in the mainstream, bringing up bias against females was a distraction from struggles over class, race, and other issues that were taken more seriously, because they also affected men. Nonetheless, the idea of equality was so contagious that the right wing would soon rate feminism as a danger right up there with secular humanism and godless Communism. The American mainstream began to support issues of equality in public opinion polls, even when some of those issues were still thought of simply as "life"—think of sexual harassment or domestic violence.

After Dorothy had a baby and decided to travel less, my partners became friends and colleagues like Margaret Sloan, a black feminist poet and activist from Chicago's South Side, and Florynce Kennedy, a civil rights lawyer and an infinitely quotable and charismatic speaker. Flo especially took me in hand. When I felt I had to prove the existence of discrimination with statistics, for instance, she pulled me aside. "If you're lying in the ditch with a truck on your ankle," she said patiently, "you don't send somebody to the library to find out how much the truck weighs. You get it off!"

I always spoke first—especially after Flo, I would have been an anticlimax—and we each talked about our own experience of seeing talent wasted by imaginary limits of race, gender, class, sexuality, and so on—including the prison of "masculinity" that limits men. To make a balance between speakers and audience, we did our best to split the time equally between our talk and an audience free-for-all. I knew this was working when, say, someone on one side of the hall asked a question, and someone on the other side answered it. People stood up and spoke about ideas and experiences they might never have brought up even with a friend.

Together and separately, we as speakers disproved another description used to disqualify feminists: that we were all "whitemiddleclass," a phrase used by the media then (and academics who believe those media clippings now) as if it were a single adjective to describe the women's movement. In fact, the first-ever nationwide poll of women's opinions on issues of gender equality showed that African American women were twice as likely as white women to support them.[8] If the poll had included Latinas, Asian Americans, Native Americans, and other women of color, the result might well have been even more dramatic. After all, if you've experienced discrimination in one form, you're more likely to recognize it in another. Also racism and sexism are intertwined—as Mrs. Greene and millions of others experienced—and cannot be uprooted separately.

Traveling in an interracial team taught me some important and unsettling truths about this country. Though we were both speaking about women's liberation, for instance, reporters would ask me questions about women, and then ask Dorothy or Flo or Margaret about civil rights. This was true even though Flo was eighteen years older than I and had been very public as a feminist lawyer. We learned to let this effort to divide us go for a while before naming it—whether with anger and humor, as in Flo's case, or with history, as in the case of Margaret, who recited Sojourner Truth's "But Ain't I a Woman?" This was a small taste of a general problem: the invisibility in the media of the many women of color who pioneered the women's movement. In the way that image can overwhelm reality, nothing but struggle for decades would keep this from becoming a self-fulfilling prophecy.

Sometimes sexual politics took petty and odd forms. For example, I had been called a "pretty girl" before I was identified as a feminist in my mid-thirties. Then suddenly I found myself being called "beautiful." Not only was I described by my appearance more than ever before, but I was told that how I looked was the only reason I got any attention at all. In 1971 **The St. Petersburg Times** headlined, "Gloria's Beauty Belies Her Purpose."[9] It took me a few years to figure out this sudden change in response to the same person. I was being measured against the expectation that any feminist had to be unattractive in a conventional sense—and then described in contrast to that stereotype. The subtext was: **If you could get a man, why would you need equal pay?**

This grew into an accusation that I was listened to **only** because of how I looked, and a corollary that the media had created me. Though I'd been a freelance writer all my professional life without being told that my appearance was the reason I got published, it now became the explanation for everything, no matter how hard I worked. Never mind that the opposite was sometimes the case, as when my literary agent had sent me to an editor at a major national magazine, who dismissed me by saying, "We don't want a pretty girl—we want a writer." The idea that whatever I had accomplished was all about looks would remain a biased and hurtful accusation even into my old age.

Fortunately, traveling and speaking took me to audiencess full of down-home common sense. When a reporter raised the question of my looks as more important than anything I could possibly have to say, for example, an older woman rose in the audience. "Don't worry, honey," she said to me comfortingly, "it's important for someone who could play the game—and win—to say: 'The game isn't worth shit.'"

I also learned from my speaking partners. When we were in the South especially, some man in the audience might assume that a black woman and a white woman traveling together must be lesbians. Florynce Kennedy modeled the perfect response: "Are you my alternative?"

If someone called me a lesbian—in those days all single feminists were assumed to be lesbians—I learned just to say, "Thank you." It disclosed nothing, confused the accuser, conveyed solidarity with women who were lesbians, and made the audience laugh.

I also came to appreciate this two-way understanding that happens only when we're all in the same space. It gradually made me less reluctant to go out on my own. Nervousness might still return, like malaria, but mostly I'd learned that audiences turn into partners if you just listen to them as much as you talk.

After I joined with a group of writers and editors to start **Ms.** magazine, I was traveling not only for stories, but also to sell ads to reluctant makers of cars who were convinced that men made that buying decision; to explain to makers of women's products why **Ms.** didn't publish fashion, beauty, or cooking articles that praised and promoted the products of advertisers; and to persuade newsstand dealers to carry a new kind of women's magazine whose cover looked nothing like the others. I remember going from city to city, buying doughnuts and coffee for men who loaded boxes of magazines onto the trucks at dawn, hoping they would persuade newsstand dealers to at least open our boxes.

Soon I was also traveling state by state to campaign for the Equal Rights Amendment, or for new women candidates who represented women's majority needs and views, or for male candidates who were doing this, too, or to fund-raise for various parts of this movement that I cared about so much.

In the 1980s, I published my first real book, **Outrageous Acts and Everyday Rebellions,** and discovered the author's tour as a new kind of road trip. There were actually author's escorts—often freelancers themselves—who knew each city and schlepped authors around to book signings and media appearances. That plus two more books and tours in the 1990s made me realize that bookstores were the great community centers. Anybody could come, whether they could afford a book or not, and the spaces reserved for talks and signings invited talking circles. Since no computer can provide this companionship, the more personal the store, the more likely it is to survive.

I know that some authors hate book tours—and maybe I would, too, if I had to keep repeating the plot of one novel—but I grew to love these spontaneous gatherings in shopping malls, university bookstores, and specialty bookshops that couldn't be replaced by the big chains, all the spaces with coffee, comfortable chairs, and the presence of books that allow people to browse and discover interests they didn't know they had. Recently when a book of mine was published in India,[10] I did a tour of bookstores from Jaipur and New Delhi to Kolkata. Those, too, range from big cheerful chains to small, discussion-filled, art-filled shops. Altogether, if I had to pick one place to hang out anywhere, from New York to Cape Town and Australia to Hong Kong, a bookstore would be it.

Every author also creates a world of her or his own. I watched Bette Midler signing every last book for her hundreds of fans lined up around the block, all while wearing a perky hat made to look like a piano. Oliver North of the Iran-Contra arms scandal had two guards carrying poorly concealed guns, took no questions, and signed copies of **Under Fire: An American Story—The Explosive Autobiography of Oliver North.** Ai-jen Poo, who won a MacArthur "genius" award for her organizing of domestic workers, turned book signings into rallies. No one left one of her events without knowing that living longer is not a crisis, it's a blessing, that the twelve million Americans over eighty-five will double in number by 2035, that many more home care workers will be needed, and that these workers deserve the same legal rights as workers anywhere else.

Altogether, I can't imagine technology replacing bookstores completely, any more than movies about a country replace going there. Wherever I go, bookstores are still the closest thing to a town square.

IV.

THERE ARE EVENTS THAT DIVIDE OUR LIVES INTO before and after. I notice that most people, when asked to name such an event, cite something that gave them a feeling of emotional connection, whether it was witnessing a birth, or walking New York streets after 9/11, or viewing a photo of our fragile planet from space.

Mine was an event you may never have heard of: the 1977 National Women's Conference in Houston. It may take the prize as the most important event nobody knows about. In three days, plus the two years leading up to them, my life was changed by a new sense of connection—with issues, possibilities, and women I came to know in the trenches. The conference also brought a huge and diverse movement together around shared issues and values. You might say it was the ultimate talking circle.

I'm not alone in being a different person after Houston. In the years since then, I've met diverse women who were there, and every one has told me of some way in which she, too, was transformed; her hopes and ideas of what was possible—for the world, for women in general, and for herself. Because eighteen thousand observers came to Houston from fifty-six other countries, and because delegates were chosen to represent the makeup of each state and territory, it was probably the most geographically, racially, and economically representative body this nation has ever seen—much more so than Congress; not even close. Issues to be voted on in Houston also had been selected in every state and territory. It was a constitutional convention for the female half of the country. After all, we had been excluded from the first one.

If you wonder why you haven't heard about this event—I'm glad. It all began in 1972, when the United Nations declared that 1975 would be International Women's Year—right up there with the Year of the Child or the Year of the Family Farm. In 1974, President Gerald Ford appointed a thirty-nine-member delegation to represent U.S. women, and named a man from the State Department to head it.

But the one who took on this task of finding out what issues and hopes really **did** represent the female half of this country was Congresswoman Bella Abzug, a woman who never thought small. She enlisted Congresswoman Patsy Mink as coauthor and Congresswoman Shirley Chisholm as coconspirator in writing a revolutionary piece of legislation. It called for federal funding for fifty-six open, economically and racially representative conferences over two years, one in every state and territory. Delegates elected and issues selected at each meeting would then go to a national conference in Houston. There, a National Plan of Action would be voted on. The purpose was to represent U.S. women not only to the rest of the world, but also to our own leaders in Washington and in state legislatures. At last, there would be democratic answers to the classic question: **What do women want?**

I couldn't think of anyone but Bella who could dream up such a massive series of events, much less have the chutzpah to ask Congress to pay for them. Though I'd campaigned with her in a Manhattan that loved her, a Washington that feared her, and a women's movement that depended on her, I'd never seen her try anything this huge. Women in every state and territory would be invited to debate and decide such contentious issues as reproductive freedom and abortion, welfare rights, lesbian rights, domestic violence, and the exclusion of domestic workers from labor laws. Her request for $10 million was actually a bargain at twenty-eight cents per adult American woman, but Congress went into shock. It delayed voting until a year after the first state conference was supposed to start; then it slashed the appropriation in half to $5 million. Still, money was approved, and the National Women's Conference was scheduled for Houston in November 1977.

To organize this mammoth undertaking, President Jimmy Carter appointed a new group of IWY commissioners. I was one, which is why I and about three dozen other members of this new commission ended up spending two years crisscrossing the country to help organize fifty-six conferences of two days each.

I CONFESS THAT I was as scared as I had ever been. This organizing challenge was a little like a presidential campaign, with a fraction of the resources. It meant helping to create a representative planning body in each state and territory, including groups that probably had never been together before. I would learn the big difference between protesting other people's rules and making one's own—between asking and doing.

Our election process for delegates was so open as to be terrifying. Anyone sixteen years old or over could be elected if the result, as a group, represented the state racially and economically.

Success can be as disastrous as failure—and it almost was. As if we had tapped some underground spring of desire, women came to conferences in such numbers that they overflowed the campuses and government buildings where our shoestring budget put them.

In Vermont, more than a thousand women slogged through ice and snow to create the biggest women's conference ever seen there. If most hadn't supplied their own brown-bag lunches and child care, our organizing goose would have been cooked at this first of all the state conferences.

In Alaska, an auditorium designed for six hundred

had to make way for seven thousand. Fortunately, most of the women good-naturedly sat on the floor.

In Albany, the capital of New York State, more than eleven thousand women—four times more than we planned for—lined up outside government buildings in the sweltering July heat, then waited most of the night in an airless basement to cast ballots for delegates and issues. I'd stopped in Albany for the opening ceremony—and then I was going home to write and make a living, but I ended up staying for two days and two nights without bed or toothbrush, helping with the voting lines.

Events in some other states made us realize that we'd been living in a fool's paradise. To represent majority views was definitely not everybody's goal. For instance, only about 2 percent of the population of Washington state was Mormon, but nearly half the women attending that state's conference were. Such disproportion also turned up in Michigan and Missouri, part of a massive Mormon effort to head off the Equal Rights Amendment, then in its ratification process and sure to be voted on in Houston.[11] Though over 60 percent of Americans supported it, one Mormon woman was about to be excommunicated for campaigning for the ERA.[12] Some said this opposition came from a fear that the ERA would take women out of a traditional role by offering them equality outside the home; others pointed out that Mormon-owned insurance companies would lose money if gender-rated actuarial tables were outlawed, as race-rated ones had been. (For instance, a woman who didn't smoke often paid higher premiums than a man who did smoke. Why? Because on the average, women live longer.) Opposition literature also said the ERA could mean integrated restrooms, women in combat, husbands who no longer had to support wives, and more—none of which was accurate.

On the theory that exposure cures many ills, Bella called a press conference to disclose this attempt to overrepresent one religious group. Congress members from states where Mormons had political power accused Bella of religious bias, demanding she apologize in public—and she had to. It was the only time I ever saw her give in to power.

Some other religious groups were just as opposed to representative conferences. In Missouri, church buses brought five hundred or so Christian fundamentalist women and men to the state conference—in time to vote but not long enough to be tainted by open discussion. In many states, Catholic groups brought anti-abortion and anti-birth-control pamphlets and picket signs, even though—or perhaps because—Catholic women were at least as likely as non-Catholics to use both. In Oklahoma, Christian fundamentalists voted to call homemaking "the most vital and rewarding career for women" and then to end the meeting. I began to see that for some, religion was just a form of politics you couldn't criticize.

In Mississippi, the Ku Klux Klan grew so alarmed at a multiracial conference that its members called in reinforcements and elected an almost totally white delegation in a state that was at least a third African American."[13]

Finally we ruled what we should have in the first place: registrants for the conferences had to sign up individually in advance, not at the door by the busload.

Koryne Horbal, a founder of the Feminist Caucus of the Democratic-Farmer-Labor Party in Minnesota, saw that anti-equality groups were distributing lists of issues to oppose in Houston, but pro-equality groups were giving out no lists of what to support. She put all the pro-equality issues into one National Plan of Action, made buttons that said I'M PRO-PLAN, and spent weeks phoning delegates to explain why each issue was important. Once in Houston, her work in creating clarity would save the day. I'M PRO-PLAN buttons would help women to recognize allies they didn't know, just as anti-equality delegates recognized each other by wearing red STOP ERA buttons.

THIS LONG, HARD, HUMOROUS, educational, angering, unifying, improvised, and exhausting two-year process probably shortened all our lives.

But it was worth it. On a hot November day in 1977, two thousand elected delegates and about eighteen thousand observers began to fill the biggest arena in Houston. With issue areas from the arts to welfare, and three days to vote on them, there was a feeling of urgency, excitement, and even a little fear that we couldn't pull it off. Also hundreds of anti-ERA, anti-abortion, and other pickets were marching outside the arena in the hope of making sure that we couldn't. Across town, a right-wing and religious counterconference—led by Phyllis Schlafly—was getting equal media coverage for accusing the National Women's Conference of being antifamily, anti-God, and otherwise unrepresentative; never mind that those counterconference participants had been elected by no one.

All I could hope was that Bella's tactics—for instance, including every democratic symbol she could think of—would convey the difference. There were First Ladies, Girl Scout Color Guards, and even relay runners: women athletes who set out from Seneca Falls, New York, where the fight for suffrage began, carrying a lighted torch all the way. Right-wing radio hosts attacked the First Ladies for showing up at all, and Phyllis Schlafly's supporters in Alabama persuaded local athletes to refuse to run a crucial stretch of highway on the way to Houston. Despite dangers, a young Houston woman had flown to Alabama to fill in.

As thousands of delegates-plus-alternates began to arrive, several business conventions were late in checking out of Houston hotels. Our delegates were lined up for hours waiting to check in.

I walked up and down the lobby lines, trying to be reassuring. Observers from faraway countries were camped out next to women who'd never left their states before; Title IX athletes shared water bottles with women disability advocates in wheelchairs; Native Hawaiians compared long flights with Native Alaskans; and high-powered women leaders in the corporate or political worlds stood in line like everybody else. Despite a few meltdowns, most women seemed to be getting to know each other in a kind of celebratory chaos. If I hadn't been so anxious about the combination of counterdemonstrations and crucial goals, I would have felt celebratory, too. As it was, I just longed to go home, put my head under a pillow, and forget this event that I cared about too much—and feared would fail.

In the midst of this chaos, about twenty women delegates from Indian Country were taking matters into their own hands. They had found each other by putting a hand-lettered notice in the lobby. When no meeting room was available, they gathered for their own talking circle in a fancy anteroom of the ladies' lounge. Rarely had these women from different and distant parts of Indian Country been able to meet together. When they told me this, I had my first flash of organizer's pride: **If only this happens, it will be enough.**

In the cavernous Coliseum, young women officials in red T-shirts began admitting delegates to the floor. Groups slowly filled up its acres of chairs arranged by states, as in a presidential convention. Outside, picketers were still chanting angry slogans, but they were soon drowned out by the buzz from the floor and from bleachers filling up with observers.

Up the center aisle, two young women runners

brought the lighted torch from Seneca Falls, miraculously just in time for Maya Angelou to read the poem she had composed for the occasion. I watched from behind the big stage as two past First Ladies and the wife of the current president—Lady Bird Johnson, Betty Ford, and Rosalynn Carter—greeted the delegates. The three women were applauded by activists who probably had demonstrated against all their husbands. Groups of observers holding signs from Mexico, India, and Japan cheered for a speech by Barbara Jordan, the African American congresswoman from Texas, as, in her elegant rhetoric, she called for "a domestic human rights program." Later teenagers led a standing ovation for an antinuclear speech by anthropologist Margaret Mead, though I knew many had no idea who this feisty old lady was.

With twenty-six multi-issue planks that had emerged from the states on subjects from child care to foreign policy, there was both fervent debate and an undercurrent of worry about the time it would take to debate them all. As the hours went on, the chairs and parliamentarians rotated, each one looking like Toscanini conducting a huge and unruly orchestra. I listened to disputes over arcane points of order, and also to heartfelt speeches, demonstrations that interrupted everything, and much caucusing on the floor. I couldn't believe that, somehow, process and a sense of humor were prevailing.

Despite fervent protests from all the women wearing anti-ERA buttons and American flags, the controversial "sexual preference" or sexual orientation plank passed. The conference had supported the right of lesbians to equal treatment in employment and child custody. Most surprising, Betty Friedan spoke from the floor in its support, marking the end of her decade-long stand that including lesbians—the "Lavender Menace," in her famous phrase, which was then adopted with humor and defiance by lesbians themselves—would damage or doom the women's movement. At last, a majority agreed that feminism meant all females as a caste, and that anti-lesbian bias could be used to stop any woman until it could stop no woman.

Up to then, I had feared that our opposition was more unified than we were. For instance, the same groups that opposed contraception and abortion also opposed sexual relationships between two people of the same sex. It was irrational on the surface, but the religious right wing was against **any** sex that couldn't end in conception. Now a representative majority was united, too, in recognizing that human sexual expression was not only a way to reproduce if we chose to, but also a way of pleasuring and bonding.

By the end of the first day's marathon, Bella got laughter and cheers when she broke the tension by saying, "Good night, my loves!"

MY SURPRISE DUTY AT the conference was a last-minute request from the various women-of-color caucuses to be a kind of scribe. I was to go from one hotel room to the next, one meeting to the next, writing down concerns that were shared by all, combining language for their approval, and appending issues that were unique to each. The goal was to compose a substitute for the so-called Minority Women's Plank that had come up from individual state conferences, yet women of color hadn't been able to meet as a group. Asian Americans were spread from Hawaii to New York. The Hispanic Caucus was mainly Chicanas on one coast and Puerto Ricans on the other. African Americans came from everywhere, and members of the American Indian and Alaskan Native Caucus were the most spread out of all. Houston was their first and only chance to meet and come up with a plank that included their shared and specific issues. Yet if they met during the day, they would miss crucial floor votes. As usual, double discrimination meant double the work.

I was to be what they referred to cheerfully as "our token," that is, the only one who wasn't a woman of color, going early in the morning or after hours at night from one drafting group to the next as they met in different hotel rooms. I would combine language where possible and list unique issues, then give the result back for the approval of all. This was an honor, but it also upped my already high anxiety level. I was afraid I would mess up. I wasn't even sure I could physically get to each meeting in the midst of conference chaos.

As I went from one caucus to the next, I saw women camped out on every surface around breakfast or late-night snacks, from Houston's idea of bagels to Tex-Mex pizzas. Among the three hundred African American delegates were legislators skilled in parliamentary procedure and women who'd never been to a conference before, Deltas in silk dresses and students in army boots, radicals with no faith in voting and civil rights veterans like Dorothy Height, who had worked for voting rights since she was a young woman meeting Eleanor Roosevelt.

While the African American women raised umbrella issues of racism and poverty, the Asian and Pacific American Caucus added language barriers, sweatshops, and the isolation of women who came to this country as servicemen's wives. The Hispanic Caucus spoke about Chicanas being deported away from their American-born children, Puerto Ricans who were treated as if they were not American citizens, and Cubans cut off from families by tensions with their home country. Somehow, this all had to go into one substitute Minority Plank that could come to the floor and be voted on by all delegates.

Still, nothing prepared me for the American Indian and Alaskan Native Caucus. These delegates from Indian Country had the most educating to do. For instance, when Native women spoke passionately against "termination," meaning of treaties, others in the Minority Caucus thought they meant "termination," as in pregnancies. While other women of color fought for equality **inside** the mainstream, Native women fought for that plus tribal sovereignty and self-determination **outside** the mainstream.

By treaty, Native nations were supposed to have government-to-government status with Washington, yet in reality they weren't even allowed to teach their own languages in schools. As one Native delegate said, "Other Americans have histories and families and gene pools in their home countries. If French or Arabic is forgotten in America, it's still being spoken somewhere. We have no other country. If our languages are wiped out, they can't come back. If we disappear here, that's it."

From listening, I began to realize there were major cultures in my own country of which I knew nothing, and these cultures were struggling to keep or restore a balance—between males and females, humans and nature—that modern social justice movements thought they had invented. Even the familiar term **Indian Country** meant not just self-governing territories within the United States, but also a sense of community that exists within big cities and small towns—wherever First Peoples live. As a Cherokee activist said to me, "**Indian Country** has become a shorthand for our home, reservation or city. It is where we are known, where we are safe."

I also noticed that humor was even more of a survival tactic here than in most women's groups. As one asked: **What did Columbus call primitive?** Answer: **Equal women.**

It was my first glimpse of how little I knew—and how much I wanted to learn.

———

FINALLY, URGENT ISSUES WERE reduced to phrases short enough for a plank to substitute for the original Minority Plank. Minutes before it was to be presented on the floor, a spokeswoman from each of the women-of-color caucuses gathered in an empty coatroom to give the final okay to the text, then rushed out on the floor to surround a mike in the huge Coliseum.

First, Maxine Waters read the preamble on the discriminatory impact of sex and race combined. It was an honor that this young California assemblywoman had earned by her organizing skill in bringing all three hundred diverse members of the Black Caucus together.

Then Billie Nave Masters, a Cherokee educator and activist, spoke on behalf of the Native American and Alaskan Native Caucus, citing their unique issues of sovereignty, and calling on "Earth Mother and the Great Spirit." Those words didn't seem to belong in a political plan of action, but I had asked the other caucuses if I could leave them in. An older woman in the Black Caucus had agreed. "Those are the only words my grandmother would give a damn about," she said. "Issues are the head; those words are the heart." When Billie read them, I saw delegates standing on their chairs to see who was speaking poetry.

Next came Mariko Tse, a young Japanese American actor, who cited the struggles of Asian and Pacific Americans against language barriers, cultural bias, the realities of sweatshops, and the stereotypes of being "a model minority," one supposedly without rebellion or problems.

For the Hispanic Caucus, three delegates—Mexican American leader Sandy Serrano-Sewell; Ana Maria Perera, a Cuban American; and Celeste Benitez from the Puerto Rican senate—came to the mike together. This was the first time that different Spanish-speaking groups had unified in public across national boundaries as Hispanics, something they were encouraging male counterparts to consider. They took turns reading, and stood together on everything from immigrant rights and a minimum wage for migrant workers to reminding the media that Spanish-language reporters were not foreign press.

Last came Coretta Scott King, standing with her bodyguard, a reminder of past tragedies and present danger. She cited the unemployment rate for young black women that was even higher than that for young black men, as well as housing bias against black families, black children in need of adoption, and more.

Then she spoke for all the caucuses when she called for "the enthusiastic adoption of this substitute resolution on behalf of all the minority women in this country!" There were cheers, but her voice rode over them: "Let this message go forth from Houston and spread all over this land. There is a new force, a new understanding, a new sisterhood against all injustice that has been born here. We will not be divided and defeated again!"[14]

With chants, applause, and tears, the two thousand delegates accepted the new so-called Minority Plank by acclamation. It was the high point of the conference. I was as proud of my facilitating role as anything I had ever done in my life.

In the back of this cavernous Coliseum, someone began to sing "We Shall Overcome." Like waves of an ocean, people stood to sing, too. I saw a white man and woman from the Mississippi delegation, the group that had been elected as a state conference partly taken over by the Klan, reach across neighbors to hold hands and stand.

By the second chorus, the observers in the bleachers and media were standing and singing, too. Even after the singing was over, people raised clasped hands above their heads and chanted, "It's our movement now!" No one seemed to want this moment to end.

I was surprised to find myself in tears. Because these women had trusted me to help as a writer, I began to see a way of bringing together two things—writing and activism—that until then had torn me apart in everyday life.

From those two years on, I divided my life into Before and After.

Before Houston, I had voted to pay some of our scarce funds to retired policemen, who would know how to protect the conference from hostile demonstrators.

After Houston, I realized that the young women volunteers with red T-shirts and movement experience had kept security far better than the retired cops. My lack of belief in them had been a lack of belief in myself.

Before Houston, I had known that women in small groups could be courageous and loyal to each other and respect each other's differences.

After Houston, I'd learned that women could do this in large numbers, across chasms of difference, and for serious purpose.

Before Houston, I had said that women could run huge public events at least as well as men.

After Houston, I believed it.

At the end of an emotional closing ceremony that left all the delegates plus observers singing and chanting, clusters of women lingered for hours on the convention floor—talking, exchanging addresses, pledging to stay in touch. They seemed reluctant to leave this space that had been our only reality for three days and nights. Then at last I found myself standing alone amid the litter and empty chairs, feeling my adrenaline draining away and exhaustion rushing in.

I wondered: Would anybody in the future know or care what had happened here? From my own college history courses, I knew that a century of abolitionists and suffragists had been reduced to a few textbook paragraphs. Magnetic people could be made to seem distant, boring, irrelevant. In newspaper coverage, the Houston conference was far overshadowed by a brief and symbolic visit to Israel by President Sadat of Egypt.[15]

As if summoned by my doubt, three young Native

women were walking toward me across the Coliseum floor. One was carrying a red-fringed shawl with a ribbon-work border of purple and gold. Another held a long beaded necklace with a large blue and white medallion. They put the shawl around my shoulders, explaining that I could wear it while dancing at powwows. "And you will dance at powwows," said one with a smile. They put the flower medallion around my neck, explained it was beaded in the style of the Woodlands people, and told me it would keep me safe. "You'll need it if you keep supporting us," said one with a hug. Then they left as mysteriously as they had come.

I WOULD INDEED WEAR my shawl while dancing at powwows in the future. I wore the necklace whenever I had to do something I was afraid of, like appearing before an Establishment group that made me feel as if I'd just emerged from East Toledo, a trailer park, or both. I wore it so often that I had to preserve the remaining beads in a bowl.

After I came home from Houston, I slept for days. Then I began to read what other women were writing about it. One account was from Billie Nave Masters, who had read the Native American resolution from the floor, the part with poetry. "If people do not take you seriously when it is a question of survival," she wrote, "Indians accept this as another loss in a history of many losses, and just walk away. But those ways were set aside in Houston . . . the most intense and meaningful experience I will have in my lifetime."[16]

We came from such different lives, yet we felt the same way about Houston. For Billie, it was rare to find a public event with any inclusion of Indian Country at all. For me, it was a glimpse of a way of life in which the circle, not a hierarchy, was the goal.

Without this glimpse of what once was—and so could be again—I wouldn't have traveled in the same way, seen the same country, or become the same person.

STARTING OUT ON ANOTHER TRIP, NEW YORK CITY,
1980.

© MARY ELLEN MARK

III.

Why I Don't Drive

WHY AM I WRITING AN ON-THE-ROAD BOOK when I don't have a driver's license, much less own a car? I'm so used to traveling as I do that I didn't anticipate this question.

I was once as obsessed as anybody else with driving as a symbol of independence. I signed up for a driver's ed course in my senior year of high school, though I had no car or access to one. I wasn't looking so much to be a driver as to symbolize the difference between my mother's life and mine. She was a passive passenger, so a driver's license would begin my escape. In the words of so many daughters who don't yet know that a female fate is not a personal fault, I told myself: **I'm not going to be anything like my mother.** When I was in college and read Virginia Woolf's revolutionary demand for "a room of one's own," I silently added, **and a car.**

But by the time I came home from India, communal travel had come to seem natural to me. I had learned that being isolated in a car was not always or even usually the most rewarding way to travel: I would miss talking to fellow travelers and looking out the window. How could I enjoy getting there when I couldn't pay attention? I stopped making excuses for being the rare American who didn't want to own a car. I even stopped citing environmental excuses, or explaining that Jack Kerouac didn't drive either. As he said, he didn't "know how to drive, just typewrite." I did sometimes quote public opinion polls that rated New Yorkers as the happiest of Americans. Why? Because in the nondriving capital of the nation, we actually see each other in the street instead of being isolated in speeding tin cans.

But the truth is, I didn't decide on not driving. It decided on me. Now when I'm asked with condescension why I don't drive—and I am still asked—I just say: **Because adventure starts the moment I leave my door.**

I.

I AM IN A TAXI ON MY WAY WITH A FRIEND TO JFK, AN airport named after a president who was assassinated only six years before. Our older driver is like a rough trade character from a Tennessee Williams play—complete with an undershirt revealing tattoos, and an old Marine Corps photo stuck in the frame of his hack license. Clearly, this is his taxi and his world.

My friend and I are acting a lot like lovers, which we are. We are also hyperaware that the driver is looking at us in the rearview mirror. That's because, while we waited with our luggage in a darkening street, a low-slung car full of white teenagers sped by, leaving behind in the evening air the lethal word "Nigger!" Now I can feel us struggling to forget that surreal attack and stay ourselves.

When we reach the airport, the driver slides open the divider between the front and back seat. Both my friend and I grow tense. I always think that talking into that opening makes me feel as if I'm ordering French fries, but this time, I am grateful for the barrier. We have no idea what the driver thinks of us.

The driver thrusts something through the opening. It turns out to be an old battered photo of a young man in a suit, standing with his arm around a plump and smiling young woman who is clutching her purse with both hands. "That's me and my wife when we got married," he says. "Except for when I was in Korea, we haven't spent a night apart for forty years. She's my best friend, my sweetheart—but believe me, we weren't supposed to get married. Her family is Jewish from Poland, mine is Sicilian Catholic—they wouldn't even speak to each other until after their first grandchild was born.

"I'm telling you this because today is our wedding anniversary—and if you don't mind my saying so, you two kind of remind me of us. If you wouldn't be offended, I'd like to give you a free ride—so I can go home and tell my wife I helped another young couple like us."

Surprised and touched, we say his words are enough, but we end up accepting because it matters so much to him. At the airport, we all stand outside his taxi, shaking hands—a little awkward with emotion.

"You know," the driver says, "me and my wife and you two, we're what this country is all about."

Later my friend and I will agree that the worst punishment of that racist shout in the street was making us mistrust this man when we first got into his taxi.

Years pass. My friend and I are carried into different lives. He lives on the West Coast, has children, grandchildren, and a life I cannot know. We are only sure that we wish each other well.

When I run into him again almost thirty years later, the first thing he says to me is, "Do you remember that taxi driver?"

And I do.

WHEN I ENTER A TAXI, I find myself in someone's life. Kids' photos on the dashboard, religious or other decorations hanging from the rearview mirror, name and perhaps ethnicity evident from the hack license on display—plus the sensory hit of the driver's physical self in a small space—all plunge me into a mobile world. In what writer Pete Hamill calls a "common strategy against loneliness, a fleeting intimacy with their passengers,"[1] drivers tell you stories and are happy to listen to yours.

I discovered these worlds on wheels when I was first living in New York. After I began writing "The City Politic," a weekly column for **New York** magazine, I depended on cabbies not only to get me to my destination but to give me tips on public opinion and elections. They tend to be shit-free guides to the state of social issues, and are often better political predictors than most media pundits. After all, they spend more time listening to random strangers than any public opinion poll could afford; they overhear more private conversations than a wiretapper; and they often are themselves new immigrants or work with those who are. This makes them treasure troves of information on what's really going on, not only here but in other countries.

An example came only ten days after the 9/11 terrorist attacks felled the Twin Towers in Manhattan. I was haunted by the televised scenes of office workers diving to their deaths rather than be immolated in that inferno, images so terrible that television stations soon stopped showing them. Downtown streets were covered with surrealistic gray ash and debris, and gutters were filled with the bodies of birds that had been incinerated in flight.

My driver was a quiet young white guy with a gravity that I sensed as soon as I got into his cab. We drove past construction fences covered with photos and notices posted by people who were still searching for missing relatives or friends or coworkers. There were also anonymous graffiti that had appeared as if by contagion all over New York with the same message: **Our grief is not a cry for war.**

"That's how New Yorkers feel," the driver said. "They know what bombing looks like, and they know the hell it is. But outside New York, people will feel guilty because they weren't here. They'll be yelling for revenge out of guilt and ignorance. Sure, we all want to catch the criminals, but only people who **weren't** in New York will want to bomb another country and repeat what happened here."

He was right. Even before it was clear that Iraq and Saddam Hussein had nothing to do with 9/11—despite false claims made by President George W. Bush, who seemed to have his eye on oil more than on facts—75 percent of New Yorkers opposed the U.S. bombing of Iraq. But a national majority supported it.

I also noticed the political smarts of taxi drivers in other cities. When I was in the Twin Cities of Minneapolis and St. Paul in the early 1990s, for instance, a driver with a Swedish name predicted that Sharon Sayles Belton would be the first African American woman to be elected mayor of Minneapolis. I had campaigned for her when she was a candidate for city council, and even that office was supposed to be a stretch. No professional politician or pollster gave Sharon a chance of winning in this overwhelmingly white city. Nonetheless, my taxi pundit, as blond and blue-eyed as the children in **Village of the Damned,** said, "If I'm voting for her, and my family is voting for her, and my passengers are voting for her, then she's going to win." He had his own test group. He was right.

In rural America, small-town drivers warned me about the growing power of such neofascist groups as the Posse Comitatus in the Midwest and the Aryan Nation in the Northwest. Local banks were afraid to foreclose on their farms, and police hesitated to help repossess farmhouses and barns when they knew their occupants to be well armed. When I carried this news back to New York, my friends dismissed it as an exaggeration or a few crazies.

However, driving is a loner profession that attracts rebels of many kinds, and one was an extremist himself. In Billings, Montana, a rancher moonlighting as a driver told me that the United Nations was using black helicopters to spy on Americans and was planning to establish a world government. I also dismissed him as one crazy guy—but a year later, newspapers carried reports of rural militia members in Montana who gathered on the ranch of one of them, threatened to shoot down all helicopters, and had the weapons to do it. I wondered if my driver was among them.

Still, when I came back to New York and said, "You know, there are ultra-right-wing groups out there, and they're well armed," urbanites would reply, "Just a few nuts, nothing to worry about."

Only later did the media begin to take extremist groups seriously. By then they had committed racist murders in several cities—starting with the liberal Jewish talk show host Alan Berg, who was shot down in his driveway by a white nationalist group—then also bombing a government building in Oklahoma City, shooting Jewish children in a child care center in Los Angeles, and attempting to bomb a Martin Luther King parade in Spokane.

I still don't see reports in newspapers about white supremacists who are trying to establish an armed and separatist homeland in the rural Northwest and parts of Canada, yet when I ask drivers or gas station attendants or other down-home authorities, they are quite matter-of-fact about the local Aryan Brotherhood, or methamphetamine labs operating with impunity in small towns, or certain rural areas where it's best not to go.

Since drivers have time and a captive audience, they can also be vectors of modern myths. In Boulder, for example, I learned that Jack Kennedy was the Lindbergh baby. A Salt Lake City driver told me that "godless Communists created the women's movement," and a Dallas driver said feminism was "a Jewish plot to destroy the Christian family," something I would hear a lot from right-wing Christian fundamentalists. Because it's a long ride to the Denver airport, I got the entire story of the Trilateral Commission as part of an international Jewish conspiracy that stretched all the way from the killing of Jesus Christ to David Rockefeller, the founder of this private group of leaders who came from the United States, Europe, and Japan. I thought he had won the

Conspiracy Prize—until another driver picked me up at Newark Airport and was sure that the Trilateral Commission was behind the destruction of the World Trade Center on 9/11. No kidding.

I can also tell which new immigrant groups are going to what cities, since driving is so often a first job. In Washington, I always get a disproportionate number of drivers from African countries. They may not know the fastest route, but they instruct me on more important issues. From the late 1960s to the present, drivers from Ethiopia and Eritrea kept me up to date on the armed conflict between those two countries. The United States, the Soviet Union, and Castro's Cuba all supported Ethiopia in a thirty-year war—assuming that this much larger country would defeat Eritrea. But according to drivers, it was always clear that Eritrea would prevail. Drivers from that country were proud of their independence fighters in the mountains, yet I never met an Ethiopian driver who wanted to fight for Emperor Haile Selassie or for the militaristic governments that followed. On the other hand, Eritrean drivers told me with pride that a third of their army was made up of women, some of them generals; that fighters had built schools and a hospital in mountain caves that were invulnerable to bombs; and that musicians in their "cultural troops," as they called them, performed for the fighters and even toured Europe. "When an Ethiopian general is killed, the troops are in disarray," one Eritrean driver explained to me. "When an Eritrean general is killed, every fighter becomes a general."

Tiny Eritrea did win the war. However, its revolutionary leaders broke the hearts of taxi drivers from Eritrea by taking over all the media and otherwise betraying the revolution. When another border war broke out between those two countries, I noticed that neither side wanted to go home and fight.

Recently, an Ethiopian and several Kenyan drivers have sounded a bigger alarm. As one said, "I never thought I would see a second wave of colonialism, but there is one and it's Chinese. Our countries are becoming wholly owned subsidiaries of China."

Maybe U.S. policy makers should talk to taxi drivers.

II.

AS MY FATHER'S DAUGHTER, I KNOW THAT BEING one's own boss is the reason taxi driving attracts free spirits, philosophers, and people who are too independent to do anything else. The hours are flexible enough for students and even the occasional homemaker, though women drivers are still rare. Whenever I have one, I tell her how glad I am to see her. Altogether, getting to know the human being **inside** the driver is an adventure, too.

• I'm glad to get a lifetime taxi driver in Manhattan. This one tells me he's been at it so long that he's writing a book called **Behind My Back**.

I tell him it's an inspired title. His book has already made him the rare American who feels equal to the rich and famous, and he spends the ride telling me about his subjects. "Robert Redford is much shorter than you think. . . . Cher is down-to-earth and a big tipper, but she's had too much plastic surgery. . . . Donald Trump has such an ego, he even tried to impress me. . . . Toni Morrison is more queenly than Queen Elizabeth. . . . I told Caroline Kennedy she should run for office. . . . Just from listening to bankers, I knew the subprime mortgage market would crash. . . ."

I can't decide whether I like this guy or not. He's so celebrity-obsessed that I wonder about his attitude toward ordinary passengers. Just then a homeless woman wheeling a shopping cart—probably holding all her life's possessions—darts out in front of us, and the driver almost sideswipes a bus while trying not to hit her. I'm expecting a string of expletives, but instead, he just calls out to her, "Be careful, sweetheart!"

After a quiet moment, he says, as if to excuse himself for being a softie, "Well, she's somebody's sweetheart."

• Another lifetime driver offers to photograph my hands, make a drawing of them, and deliver it to my door—all for thirty dollars. There are samples of his artwork plastered around his dashboard and on the passenger door, like ghostly hands applauding. He used to set up his easel in Central Park with other street artists, he explains, but here, he has air-conditioning in summer and heat in winter. I tell him I don't want a drawing but would like to contribute thirty dollars to his mobile art studio. First he declines, then says he'll take twenty-five because that's the entrance fee at the Metropolitan Museum—he goes there to look at paintings and copy just the hands. I tell him he's one of the happiest people I've ever met.

• I'm not surprised to get a taxi driver who is moonlighting as a film extra. Manhattan is one big movie set, and cops, firefighters, and homeless people sometimes try to make a little money as extras. But this guy is also an expert on taxi stories as a genre. He repeats, as if from something he read, "The combination of intimacy and anonymity make a great dramatic device." He also gives me a filmography that starts with Martin Scorsese's **Taxi Driver** and ends with **Taxicab Confessions,** a cheap-to-produce reality show in which drivers elicit voyeuristic sexual stories from passengers who are caught on a hidden camera. I can't believe people let their private lives go public, but when I say this, he tells me I'm a sucker if I think **any** reality show is real. "Hollywood people, a bunch of phonies in ripped jeans and thirty-thousand-dollar

Rolexes . . . not one of them could survive in Bed-Stuy or Harlem. . . . They just pay people to tell phony sex stories. . . . They don't give a damn about drivers getting robbed or shot, that's reality. . . . They should all go home to L.A."

Chastened, I pay my fare. On the front seat is a pile of eight-by-ten glossies of the driver, bare-chested and as sexy as an athlete, with a little Bob Marley thrown in. "Do you know anybody at **Law and Order?**" he asks me anxiously. "My kid is sick—I need the gig."

Suddenly I guess why he's so angry. All those shows tell the stories of passengers, not drivers. When I ask him, he says, "Exactly! This country thinks people with money are interesting, not people who need money like me."

I think he's right. I'd rather watch a show called **Taxi Drivers' Confessions.**

• I'm being driven by a woman with bottle-red hair who could be anywhere between thirty-five and sixty. When I say I'm glad to have a woman driver, she tells me that an Orthodox rabbi refused to get into her taxi at all, and her garage has so many male drivers that it's like a locker room. Then she lists her previous jobs—house painter, school bus driver, and welder of decorative iron—as if to prove that she doesn't need my help. She also yells expletives at drivers who try to cut her off, knits a row on an afghan square while we're waiting at a tollbooth, and, altogether, is as in command of her small ship as a pirate on the high seas.

To make up for underestimating her independence, I ask about the five male photo booth images on her dashboard, below a statue of the Virgin Mary and a blue Krishna. "Those are my old lovers—anyway, the ones I remember," she says. "I find the path to spirituality lies through ecstatic sex—and the path to ecstatic sex lies through spirituality—don't you?"

Thankful that this is a rhetorical question, I just keep quiet while she goes on. "I had kids with two of them, a rock band with one of them, and they're all still my best friends. Why? Because I taught them about sex, that's why. Not just sex-sex, but stay-in-bed-all-weekend sex, Tantric sex, go-to-a-place-otherwise-only-music-and-drugs-take-you sex."

Trying to be cool, I ask why she has the Hindu god Krishna. "Because he's the only male god who's into Tantric sex. That's why he's always surrounded by women. I told my old lovers to pass that kind of sex on to their girlfriends and wives. Do you know, one guy's wife called last year to thank me?"

She pulls in at the airport, beating a limousine to the last open space, then lifts my bag filled with books out of the trunk as if it were a feather. "You should write about take-no-shit women like me. Girls need to know they can break the rules. If the nuns had told me that, I could have saved twenty years."

As I'm walking away, she calls after me, "You pushy broads helped—even a loner like me." From her, this is high praise.

• I leave home for Newark Airport and end up sitting behind a heavy older driver who looks like an angry Buddha. He brakes and careens his way through midtown traffic, muttering in Russian over the sound of Howard Stern's talk show on the car radio. Stern is surpassing even his shock jock self by making jokes about two white teenage boys who have just shot and killed their classmates and teachers in Littleton, Colorado. He is suggesting they should have had sex with their girl victims first.

I ask the driver to turn the radio off, but he's too busy yelling expletives at people crossing the street. "Dirty, lazy peoples!" he shouts out the window, "You ruin this fucking country!" This last is aimed at three teenage Latino boys. "Dirty criminals!" This is flung at a young black couple. "I crush you!" This threat is for a bicycle messenger in a Jamaican T-shirt.

"Please stop yelling," I say.

This only causes him to add "black" to his epithets, and make it even more clear **why** he is yelling.

I think: **Okay, I'm not going to change him between here and Newark, but if I don't call** him on this bullshit, I'm saying it's okay. On the other hand, if I really get angry, I'll cry, and that's embarrassing.

"You know, some people here think bad things about immigrants from Russia, too, and they're wrong—"

"You crazy?" he explodes. "I from Ukraine, no Russia! Ukraine good place. Everybody white! No dirty peoples!"

Clearly, calling him a Russian is almost as bad as saying he has anything in common with the people he's yelling at.

I begin again: "Since there are no black or brown people in Ukraine, how can you know—?"

"Bitch!" he breaks in. "You know nothing! Black peoples ruin this fucking country!"

I'm a person who can admit only on Friday that I was angry on Monday, yet this time I get up the courage to tell him that he's giving Ukraine a bad name—but then, suddenly, he's screaming at a young black woman with a stroller, as if she were crossing the street just to get in his way, "Fucking bitch!"

Her startled face is the last straw.

I hurl at him a few words dangerously close to "Go home to Russia where you belong," and think, **I mean Ukraine.** I get out in the middle of traffic and slam the door.

The drama of my exit is marred when he starts yelling for a cop to arrest me. I realize I haven't paid my fare. I'm reduced to the ignominy of throwing money in his window and standing there while he counts every bill and coin. My only comfort is seeing the stroller woman give him the finger.

After throwing myself on the mercy of another taxi driver, I manage to get to Newark, run through the airport until my lungs hurt, and make my plane—barely. All the way to San Francisco, I think of devastating things I should have said. **Mots d'escalier** become **mots d'avion.**

The next day, I learn that Howard Stern has blown himself out of the water—if not off the air—with his horrific comments. They were too much even for his fans and his boss is forced to apologize for him. Somehow I feel this is a defeat for the taxi driver, too. I have a happy fantasy that anger plus overweight will do him in.

I add up the score: I've seen the racist bullshit that still goes on in the streets. I've learned that Russia and Ukraine are not the same country. I've expressed anger at the time I was feeling it—and I didn't cry.

Not bad for one taxi ride.

• I'm headed to the airport for the third time in a week, trying to hail a taxi in the pouring rain. I'm late, I'm grouchy, and when a driver finally picks me up, I'm in no mood to talk to this scruffy white kid in his twenties. The only personal thing I see is a drawing of a gigantic eye propped up on the front seat next to him. I suppress my curiosity.

After a long time of quiet, he asks what I do. I offer just three words—**I'm a writer**—hoping brevity won't invite conversation.

"Then I wouldn't know you," he says seriously, "because I don't read."

Assuming he's a smart-ass, I don't answer. "I also don't watch television," he goes on. "I don't look at the Internet or read newspapers or books or play video games. I haven't done any of those things in almost a year. I don't want anything to interpret the world for me. I'm mainlining life."

My resolve is slipping. He has made me think of a classics professor who told us to read Plato or Shakespeare or Dante as if we found their books in the street and had no idea who they were. I always loved his trust in the work itself—and also his trust in us.

Finally, I can no longer resist asking this guy why he is shutting out all the usual signals. He explains that his girlfriend was taking courses like women's studies and black studies, so she put tape over the names of authors and told him to judge without knowing the identity of the author. He found this so disorienting that he started to count the filters that were telling him what to think. "Filters let in a cup of water," he says, "but keep out the ocean."

It turns out that driving a taxi is just part of a year he's planned, working his way cross-country, doing odd jobs like repairing cars and picking fruit to support himself, all the while going cold turkey on media. He is seeing America without being told first what he's seeing.

I tell him he has a lot in common with organizers. We're trying to create spaces where people can listen and talk, without first putting each other in categories. After his year is up, I suggest he take what he's learned and teach it to others.

"You see?" he says seriously as we pull into LaGuardia, "This is what happens with no filters."

Instead of a tip, he asks for a bargain. "Write about my experiment," he says. "Explain that you met this recovering media addict who used to dream about people in movies instead of real people. I never read a book unless some reviewer told me to. I was such a news junkie, I went to sleep with my headset on. I even worried about missing email while I was making love to my girlfriend. I had media-itis, but now I'm trying to see life unmediated.

"I've been clean for eight months," he says seriously. "I'm just beginning to believe I exist."

Finally, I ask about that drawing of a huge

eye. "My girlfriend made that," he says, "to remind me to see with my own eyes."

I learned from him. I'm trying to see with my own eyes, too.

• In Kyle, Texas, driving is a way of life. Taxis are mostly for people too drunk or too old to drive, on welfare with no car, or visitors like me going to the Austin airport. I see that my Chicana driver has turned her taxi into a world. She has a baby in a laundry basket on the seat next to her and a mobile toy secured by the glove compartment. When I remark on this inventiveness, she explains that this way, she makes a living without being separated from her baby daughter. Since it's six a.m. on what is going to be a very hot day, I ask if this is hard. "No," she says firmly. "What's hard is worrying about my older daughter coming home from school by herself. Driving with each of my girls has been the happiest part of my life."

• I notice that a tough-looking, youngish white driver in Detroit is dressed in a shirt, bow tie, and suit jacket, like a Mormon missionary. He says it's his wife's birthday, and asks my advice about buying her a gift of lingerie. Gradually, his questions about panties grow ever more detailed. I begin to realize there is no wife. Even his pronouns switch from **she** to **I**. Then he's off on the relative merits of string bikinis, and trying to get me to talk about my own under-wear.

It's like a dirty phone call on wheels. Not only that, but he seems to be enjoying my esca-lating discomfort. I bet I'm not the first female passenger who's been left with the choice of get-ting out or letting him reach what is clearly his climactic destination.

Since we're speeding along a highway with no place to find another taxi, I try for a third option. With all the stern authority I can mus-ter, I tell him that if he doesn't stop laying his fantasies on me and passengers, I'll report his name and taxi number to his boss and to the cops.

He apologizes frantically, swears he'll never do it again, and even promises to go into therapy. Then all is quiet. Too quiet. We're at our des-tination and I'm almost out the door when he says with suspicious calm and an air of release, "I'm so glad you were severe with me. Thank you for punishing me."

I'm on the sidewalk before I realize: **I've done exactly what he had in mind.**

Years pass, and I forget this weird guy. Then I'm in Detroit again and I get a rare woman dri-ver in her forties, overly made up and drenched in perfume. As usual, I tell her I'm glad to have a woman driver. She says not a word. Only at the

end of the ride does she ask: "Do you remember a young man who drove you long ago and
wanted advice about lingerie?"

I say yes, I definitely do.

"Well, I was that miserable man," she says.
"Now I've had tops and bottoms done, and I'm
a happy woman."

I congratulate her on what has become a
choice. A growing number of people have been
able to match their inner sense of self with a
place on the continuum of gender that wasn't
assigned to them at birth. But hearing the same
voice, I have a sense memory of sitting in the
same position and feeling this driver's pleasure
in dominating me. One can change gender, but
what about character?

• As I get into a taxi to Friendship Airport, not
far from Annapolis, the driver puts a textbook
back on the stack next to him. Clearly, he's
been using every moment to study. He's moonlighting from his food service job at the Naval
Academy, as he explains, and is studying to be
an engineer.

For me, this is a big déjà vu. Long ago, in
1972, one of my first lectures with my speaking
partner, Dorothy Pitman Hughes, was to the
more than four thousand cadets at the Naval
Academy. We were the only women in a lecture
series that otherwise included a quarterback
from the Dallas Cowboys, the novelist Her-

man Wouk, and a deputy secretary of defense. The cadets themselves were all male, and only about eighty of the four thousand were other than white. We did our best to introduce the women's movement to this huge crowd seated far away from us in regimented rows, but we couldn't tell whether the roar of response was approval or disapproval. Some cadets carried oranges from dinner and tossed them at the stage. We weren't sure whether this was the equivalent of roses or rotten eggs.

Just before that lecture, there had been a seated dinner at the home of Admiral James Calvert, the Naval Academy superintendent. Dorothy and I were surprised that only Filipino men were serving us. For many years, assigning this domestic role to male Filipinos had been the navy's way of getting women's work done without women, yet I thought the 1960s and the civil rights movement would have changed all that. When we asked, Admiral Calvert assured us that Filipinos were happy to get these jobs. Dorothy replied, "Like my folks in Georgia were happy to be picking cotton?" I could see the admiral was relieved when we returned to arguing about Vietnam.

During dessert, the naval cadet sitting next to me whispered that one of the Filipino servers must not be all that happy. He had asked to borrow that cadet's engineering books.

Now I tell my Annapolis driver about my

memory. "I can't believe it," he says. "I think that guy serving you was my older brother. He did become an engineer—and he helped build the Folk Art Theater, one of the biggest arenas in Manila."

As I head into the airport, I look back to see the driver in his taxi, overhead light on, studying. If you travel long enough, every story becomes a novel.

My two longest-lasting taxi stories are ones that I owe to friends as well as drivers.

• In our co-lecturing days, Flo Kennedy and I were sitting in the back of a taxi on the way to the Boston airport, discussing Flo's book **Abortion Rap.** The driver, an old Irish woman, the only such cabbie I've ever seen, turned to us at a traffic light and said the immortal words, "Honey, if men could get pregnant, abortion would be a sacrament!"

Would she have wanted to own her words in public? I don't know, but I so wish we had asked her name. When Flo and I told this taxi story at speeches, the driver's sentence spread on T-shirts, political buttons, clinic walls, and protest banners from Washington to Vatican Square, from Ireland to Nigeria. By 2012, almost forty years after that taxi ride, the driver's words were on a banner outside the Republican National Convention in Tampa, when the party nominated Mitt Romney for president of the United States on a platform that included criminalizing abortion. Neither Flo nor the taxi driver could have lived to see him lose—and yet they were there.

• Years ago, when I was often staying with a friend in Brooklyn, I began to use Black Pearl, a car service in that oldest borough where residents are more than a third African American. Because Yellow cabs in Manhattan often avoid black neighborhoods and also refuse long trips to other boroughs—though by law they are required to take passengers wherever they want to go—many gypsy cabs and car services have sprung up. Among the oldest is Black Pearl. Its slogan has always been "We're Not Yellow, We'll Go Anywhere."

Every time I called the dispatcher, a driver showed up within minutes, always in a big old low-slung American car with such comforts as incense, seats covered in fake fur, surround-sound music, and no safety barrier to interfere with talking to the driver. It was like riding in a placenta with Marvin Gaye, Aretha Franklin, or Chaka Khan—listening to anything from the oldest blues and reggae to the newest dance or rap music.

The first time I thanked a driver for this peak experience—I'd been blissed out and unaware of traffic—he just smiled. "One day I turned around," he said, "and a couple on the backseat were—dancing."

I discovered from drivers just how important this car service was. Not only did many Yellow cabs bypass black people on the street—or say, "Sorry, I don't go to Brooklyn"—but black women close to giving birth couldn't count on a taxi to take them to the hospital, and had to find a car service in advance. Then an African American man named Calvin Williams returned to Brooklyn after serving in the Korean War and invented Black Pearl. It became so popular that voters elected him to the New York State Assembly, where he served two terms.

Within Black Pearl, every driver has a story. After getting the same one on a couple of trips, I asked why he had the only venetian blinds I'd ever seen in a car.

"Around here," he says, gesturing to the streets of Brooklyn's Bedford-Stuyvesant neighborhood, "money is easier to come by than privacy. You can borrow or steal money, but you can't find a private place. When I was coming up with seven brothers and sisters, I met my girlfriend under the stairs, dodging rats and winos, or I froze my ass off on street corners with my buddies. Even when I went to the Brooklyn Fox to see Little Stevie Wonder—he was a little kid then—security guards would shine flashlights up and down the aisles. All I wanted was to be cool in summer, warm in winter, and listen to music—to have just a little private space for happiness.

"So when I retired from my city job and started driving for Black Pearl, I thought, **This is it! I'm a rescuer! I'm a Black Knight in Silver Armor!** I always make sure nobody has guns, drugs, or alcohol in my car. Then I turn up the music, turn down the blinds, and drive around for as long as my customers want."

Among his regulars were girls from a local Catholic school who rode around with the boyfriends they weren't supposed to have, a Black Muslim father of five whose wife wouldn't let him listen to sinful music, two male firefighters who rode home together after work in the most famously homophobic agency in the city, a single mother who needed time away from her job and kids, and an elderly unmarried couple who held hands where their children and grandchildren couldn't see them.

"Only food and water are more important than music and privacy," he says seriously. "I'm a rescuer."

III.

TAXI DRIVERS ARE ENTREPRENEURS OF THE ROAD. Like my father, they drive and dream. But flight attendants experience work as a group.

When I first began flying a lot in the early 1970s, planes meant only mindlessness, escape from phones, maybe a movie, and most of all, sleep. Even if I took work on board, I nodded off as soon as we were aloft. Like a flying version of Pavlov's dog, just being carried through space made me feel I needed to make no further effort.

Once when I stayed awake long enough to admire the olive twill pants of a flight attendant's uniform, she let me order a pair at her discount, thus combining shopping with travel. It was the beginning of a lifetime of finding girlfriends in the sky.

I noticed that stewardesses were all young—and all female—but I assumed they wanted a few years of travel before doing something else, or this was an entry-level job and a pipeline for airline executives. I only began to pay attention when I was shuttling constantly between the start-up of **Ms.** magazine in New York and the organizing of the National Women's Political Caucus in Washington. Once when exhaustion caused me to fall asleep with my credit card in my hand, a kindhearted stewardess removed the card, ran it through the onboard ticket machine—the way one paid for the shuttle in those days—and put it back in my hand without waking me. Neither she nor others knew who I was or why I was such a frequent-flying oddity among the mostly male passengers going to our nation's capital, but we seemed to share a sense of being outsiders.

On longer trips with various airlines, I began to hang out in the galley, where I could ask questions and listen. I learned that the first stewardesses had been registered nurses hired to make passengers feel safe at a time when flying was new, airsickness was frequent, and passengers were fearful. Some pilots resented this female invasion of their macho air space so much that they quit. Like the first American astronauts who compared sending a Soviet woman into space with sending up a monkey, the presence of any woman devalued a masculine domain.

Once male business travelers became the airlines' bread and butter, everything changed. Stewardesses were hired as decorative waitresses with geishalike instructions. There were even "executive flights" for men only, complete with steaks, brandy, and cigars lit by stewardesses. Though they still had to know first aid, evacuation procedures for as many as seventy-five kinds of planes, underwater rescue, emergency signaling, hijacking precautions, and other skills that took six weeks of schooling—not to mention how to handle passengers and fend off some—their appearance was prescribed down to age, height, weight (which was governed by regular weigh-ins), hairstyle, makeup (including a single shade of lipstick), skirt length, and other physical requirements that excluded such things as "a broad nose"—only one of many racist reasons why stewardesses were overwhelmingly white. They had to be single as well as young, and were fired if they married or aged out at over thirty or so. Altogether the goal of airline executives seemed to be to hire smart and ornamental young women, to use them as advertising come-ons, to work them hard, and to age them out soon. Flight schedules were so merciless that on some airlines, the average stewardess lasted only eighteen months. As one United executive famously said, "If a flight attendant was still on the job after three years . . . I'd know we were getting the wrong kind of girl. She's not getting married."[2]

Back in the galley, stewardesses were only too glad to tell me about the indignities, from ad campaigns with slogans like "I'm Sandy, Fly Me," and "She'll Serve You—All the Way," to an "Air Strip" in which they were required to walk up and down the aisles while stripping to hot pants. Passengers were influenced by this image of stewardesses, and made them second only to farmers' daughters as objects of sex jokes. This image was publicized by such X-rated pornographic movies as **Come Fly with Me** and **The Swinging Stewardesses.** Some pilots expected to be serviced sexually on layovers, and though the answer from stewardesses was overwhelmingly no, passengers assumed they must be saying yes. Airlines fended off sex discrimination lawsuits for refusing to hire male stewards by maintaining that the care and feeding of passengers was so peculiarly "feminine" that it amounted to a "BFOQ"—a bona-fide occupational qualification—otherwise reserved for wet nurses and sperm donors. Stewardesses could be "written up" for any infraction of the rules, including talking back to an obnoxious drunk passenger or refusing to sell more drinks to an already inebriated one. They were made to share rooms on layovers while male crew had private rooms, and they were definitely not on a job ladder to the executive suite.

But pilots, on whose physical condition much more depended, got away with many fewer physical requirements and weigh-ins, a fact visible in red faces and potbellies. They also earned an average of 400 percent more than flight attendants, and had a lock on piloting because the air force, which paid and trained almost all of them, hadn't trained a woman pilot since World War II. Then, WASPs ferried planes across the Atlantic, but after the war, no Amelia Earharts needed apply.

The more I listened to all this, the more I admired the degree to which this group of women maintained their humanity, despite being regulated right down to getting demerits if they didn't smile constantly. As one said to me, "Even my face is not my own."

Of course, punished people sometimes pass punishment downward, especially to members of their own devalued group. Flying to Kansas for a campus speech with my speaking partner Dorothy Pitman Hughes and her newborn baby, a stewardess ordered Dorothy, who was nursing her daughter, into the lavatory, as if nursing were an obscene act. Only Dorothy's fierce objection, my threat to write about it, and the anger of a nearby white woman passenger dissuaded her. When I was traveling with Flo Kennedy, a stewardess insisted that the plane couldn't take off until Flo's purse was stashed in the overhead bin. Flo pointed out similar purses on white women's laps, flat out refused to remove hers, and asked the stewardess why she was oppressing other women when she herself was oppressed. In solidarity with Flo, I took my satchel out of the overhead, though it really was luggage, and put it on my lap. Neither Flo nor I would budge. Finally, the plane took off anyway.

We laughed about such scuffles later, and Flo kept reminding me that they gave us an opportunity to teach, though each one was also punishing to the soul.

Mostly, though, stewardesses were a revolution waiting to happen. When I was on a plane from St. Louis, long the airport nearest home for Phyllis Schlafly—a creation of the Fairness Doctrine, because she was the rare woman the media could find who opposed the Equal Rights Amendment—a flight attendant whispered to me, "I had Phyllis Schlafly on my flight, and I put her in a middle seat!" I knew things were changing when I got on a flight from San Francisco, and found a stewardess wearing a button, I'M LINDA, FLY YOURSELF. Then some flight attendants rebelled against having just first names on their identifying pins. Why should they be Susie or Nan while the pilots were Commander Rothgart or Captain Armstrong? (Eventually they also demanded last names preceded by **Ms.** so they wouldn't be identified by marital status.) Their name demand was right up there with salary and safety. As Elizabeth Cady Stanton wrote, "When the slave leaves bondage, his first act is to name himself."

By the mid-1970s, a newly minted group called Stewardesses for Women's Rights opened a small office in Rockefeller Center. I visited it and found women from many different airlines holding joint press conferences, pressuring in and outside their company unions, protesting their image in airline ads, and exposing such hazards as recirculated air that endangered them and their passengers. Knowing that the job would be more honored if men were doing it, too, they were making the integration of men into this all-female workforce as much a priority as integrating female pilots into the all-male cockpit. They pushed to change **stewardesses** to **flight attendants,** since even **steward** would mark a job description by gender.

As I learned from listening to these smart women who were treated as not smart, stewardesses of the 1960s had filed a complaint with the Equal Employment Opportunity Commission (EEOC), trying to change the "no men, no marriage" policy of their job. Aileen Hernandez, the only female or African American on the EEOC, supported them. Years later they finally won, but the airlines called the ruling "improper" because Hernandez, after leaving the EEOC, had become president of the National Organization for Women. A judge actually agreed. That's why discrimination was still okay when I started flying a lot—and remained okay until 1986.

When corporate raider Carl Icahn took over TWA, he expected flight attendants to both take a pay cut and accept a work increase—unlike the (almost totally male) machinists and pilots. In 1986, flight attendant Vicki Frankovich led a strike of unprecedented length and unity—and campaigned for a public boycott of TWA because of its discrimination. **Ms.** magazine named her one of our Women of the Year. Icahn had the support of the pilots and machinists and more or less won, but he was forced to admit that the striking flight attendants had cost him $100 million.[3] When I met him quite accidentally, I discovered he was furious about the **Ms.** article supporting Frankovich. He told me he didn't discriminate against women. As proof, he said that if he needed one of his top male executives on a national holiday—and that executive spent the holiday with his family instead—he would fire him, too.

I could see what flight attendants were up against. By then, I'd been flying so much and listening to so many that I had to resist saying **we** when I talked about job problems. I also began to get the other end of women's stories whose first chapters I had seen on earlier flights.

In the 1970s, on a flight to Milwaukee, for instance, a stewardess told me she resented feminists for saying that men could do her job, and that women could be pilots. "That isn't the way the world works," she said with energy. "You're telling people to fight what's in our nature and biology. You're only making women discontent by telling them to do the impossible." At the end of the 1980s, I ran into her again on a flight to Albuquerque. She was now the mother of two little girls, and giving out flight attendant's pins and pilot's wings to children on board—as airlines often do to welcome families—

and offering either one to both boys and girls. She had discovered there were boys who liked her job of taking care of passengers, and girls who wanted to pilot the plane.

What had changed her mind? Two things, she said. Because her airline finally had been forced to democratize its hiring, she worked with male flight attendants and realized they could do the job because "people are people." Second, she had read that Whitney Young, the late civil rights leader, confessed to boarding a plane in Africa and feeling an involuntary moment of fear when he saw that the pilot was black. He realized how much self-hatred had been bred into him by a racist culture. "I also mistrusted myself and other women," she said with tears in her eyes. "I learned that from my mother—but I'm not going to pass it on to my daughters." When I last saw her, she was standing at the front of the plane, giving out pilot's wings to two little girls.

Some women were novels in themselves. Tommie Hutto-Blake was a flight attendant I saw in 1972 in a Manhattan church basement at the first meeting of Stewardesses for Women's Rights; then again at the National Women's Conference in Houston in 1977; then as an activist at a 1994 political event in Dallas; then in 2008 when she was campaigning for Hillary Clinton; then on a flight of American Airlines just before she retired after thirty-eight years as a flight attendant, thirty-five of them as a union activist, and took on political activism full time. That last time, she was a revered passenger. I was led back to where she was sitting by two younger women flight attendants, and one was a union vice president who was just finishing law school. It was a long way from lighting cigars and doing Air Strips.

In the 1970s, I had read a newspaper report of an African American stewardess who showed up for work with an Afro at a time when the few black flight attendants were expected to look as "white" as possible. She compounded the offense by carrying a copy of Eldridge Cleaver's **Soul on Ice.** The pilot of the flight refused to take off until she was put off the plane. When I was back on the same airline, I asked a stewardess if there had been a protest. She said yes, but as far as she knew, the pilot got away with it. Like a captain of a ship at sea, he could do anything he wanted.

More than twenty years later, I was in a big-city radio station for a news interview, and a female station manager showed me around. She was a rarity in an industry where 85 percent of managers were males, so I asked how she had come to this position. She explained that after a divorce, she had gone back to school, started in radio at the bottom, loved its ability to create community, and discovered she had a gift for managing people.

"Do you happen to remember," she asked me as we finished our tour, "a news story about an airline pilot who put a black flight attendant off the plane for reading Eldridge Cleaver?"

I said I definitely did. I'd always wondered what became of him.

"Well, that pilot was my husband," she said calmly. "So I divorced him. That one true act was my beginning."

Over the years, those stories in the sky would teach me more than I could have imagined: from deregulation, fare wars, and nonunion airlines, to post-Iraq fuel costs, hijacking fears, and bankruptcies that somehow required pay cuts for everybody except executives with golden parachutes. I experienced the kindness of flight attendants who brought me back a dessert or a meal from first class, or let me lie down in the middle of an aisle when I had a back spasm, or took the armrests out of three-across seats so I could sleep coast to coast, or illegally moved me up to first class when there was an empty seat, or sent me off with a split of champagne to thank me for supporting their job struggles. They still are not part of the job ladder into the executive airline ranks, and they still are far more likely to take pay cuts than the almost totally male machinists and pilots even though about a quarter of flight attendants are now men. But ever since they won the right to work beyond marriage and beyond thirty, I've seen more and more whose stories had begun on flights decades before. A modern airliner is very different from a timeless village in India, but it dawned on me one day that all my air travel has much in common with long-ago village walking. If you do anything people care about, people will take care of you.

With my mother, Ruth Nuneviller Steinem,
at Oberlin College, 1972.

IV.

One Big Campus

Hᴏᴡ ᴅᴏ I ʟᴏᴠᴇ ᴄᴀᴍᴘᴜsᴇs? Lᴇᴛ ᴍᴇ ᴄᴏᴜɴᴛ ᴛʜᴇ ways. I love the coffee shops and reading rooms where one can sit and talk or browse forever. I love the buildings with no addresses that only the initiated can find, and the idiosyncratic clothes that would never make it in the outside world. I love the flash parties that start in some odd spot and can't be moved, and the flash seminars that any discussion can turn into. I love the bulletin boards that are an education in themselves, the friendships between people who would never otherwise have met, and the time for inventiveness that produces, say, an exercise bike that powers a computer. Most of all, I love graduations. They are individual and communal, an end and a beginning, more permanent than weddings, more inclusive than religions, and possibly the most moving ceremonies on earth.

I'm often asked how many campuses I've visited.

The truth is I have no idea. I've gone to several each month of my lifetime on the road, and I've gone back to many more than once. All I know for sure is that university and college campuses, with some high schools and prep schools added, have been the single largest slice of my traveling pie—and they still are.

When I started traveling to campuses, protest against the draft and the war in Vietnam was empowering students as a political force—and there were many more movements to come. They have brought about change, from what gets taught to who gets tenure; from how the university invests its money to where athletic uniforms are made; from students taking a role in campus decision-making to Take Back the Night marches against sexualized violence on campus; from marginalizing some by class, race, sexuality, and physical ability to including diverse people and new courses of study.

In my own college life, I got through four years as a government major without learning that women were not just "given" the vote, that the real number of slave rebellions was suppressed because rebelling was contagious, or that the model for the U.S. Constitution was not ancient Greece but the Iroquois Confederacy. Then, academic courses on Europe far outnumbered those on Africa, even though it is the birthplace of us all and is bigger than Europe, China, India, and the United States combined. When I'm on campus now and look at course listings, the relative importance reflected in them is much better but still way off.

There has always been this question of what is being taught. As Gerda Lerner, a pioneer of women's history in general and African American women's history in particular, summed it up, "We have long known that rape has been a way of terrorizing us and keeping us in subjection. Now we also know that we have participated, although unwittingly, in the rape of our minds."[1]

No wonder studies show that women's intellectual self-esteem tends to go down as years of education go up. We have been studying our own absence. I say this as a reminder that campuses not only help create social justice movements, they need them.

Now, campuses look more like the country in terms of race and ethnicity—though we're not there yet, and bias can survive college degrees. I see women outnumbering their male counterparts on some campuses, but degrees are often a way out of the pink-collar ghetto and into a white-collar one. Women still average much less in earnings over a lifetime than men do and have to pay back the same college debt.

I see campuses representing more age diversity. More than a third of college students are over twenty-five, and this age group is growing faster than students of conventional age, a change that was pioneered by veterans and the GI Bill of Rights, then by older women returning to campus. I remember watching a thirty-year-old pregnant woman arguing about the health care system with an eighteen-year-old male student, and thinking: **This has to be good for education.**

In campus terms, you might say I've gone from mimeographing to tweeting; from curfews to hooking up; from no-credit women's studies courses in summer school to the National Women's Studies Association; from African American history as demanded by black students to such history as the expectation of all students; from gay and lesbian groups forbidden to meet on campus to transgender and transsexual students who challenge all gender binaries; from blue book exams to handwriting as a disappearing art; and from limited seminars to limitless Web hangouts.

For instance, during early visits to campuses, I saw students painting a big red X on sidewalks wherever a woman had been sexually assaulted—and ending up getting arrested for vandalism instead of being praised. Now I see their daughters and granddaughters using Title IX—the federal civil rights law that prohibits discrimination in education, including sports—to threaten campuses with the loss of federal funding if sexual assault creates an environment hostile to women's education. For decades, places of higher education obscured the rates of sexual assault, in order to protect a campus reputation and encourage parents to send their daughters. Now I see a few campuses that are honest about and have policies to deal with sexual assault—which happens to an average of one in five women on campus, and a few men, too.[2] It shows this is beginning to be taken seriously, which is a reason for parents to trust those campuses.

As feminism has changed academia by enlarging what is taught, academia has sometimes changed feminism. Scholarly language may be so theoretical that it obscures the source of feminism in women's lived experience. One of the saddest things I hear as I travel is "I don't know enough to be a feminist." Or even "I'm not smart enough to be a feminist." It breaks my heart.

But despite all these differences, with the passage of time, I've found there is a pattern to campus visits. It goes like this:

I arrive at the airport—or train station or bus station—where I'm met by one or more of the hardy band of activists who invited me. In the car on the way to the campus—or hotel or classroom or press conference—I learn they are worried. In the South or Midwest, they may warn that this is the most "conservative" place I've ever been. If we are on the East or West Coast, they're more likely to say it's the most "apathetic." Or perhaps it's "activist," but on environmental and economic problems, without understanding that pressuring women to have too many children is the biggest cause of environmental distress, and economic courses should start with reproduction, not just production. They have reserved a hall for tonight and have publicized the event, but they're worried that hardly anyone will come. After all, they've been told that feminism is too radical or not radical enough, antimale or male-imitative, impossible because men are from Mars and women are from Venus, or unnecessary because we're now in a postfeminist, postracist age. The nature and specifics of the negative depend on the part of the country and the year, but the common thread is: self-doubt.

I tell them they've done their best—now it's up to the universe. Then I ask about current events or controversies on campus so I will know what to use as examples in my speech. After all, my job is to make their work easier after I leave than it was before I came. It's already easy for me. I don't have to worry about getting good grades, negotiating faculty politics, achieving tenure, publishing in scholarly journals, becoming department chair, or crossing other hurdles that those in academia have to cross. I can bring up problems and possibilities that students want brought up. I can also carry ideas from one campus to the next, in the bee-and-flower model of organizing. I'm here to make them look reasonable. After all, I'm leaving in the morning.

At first, my student hosts may cite faraway subjects—say, global warming or foreign policy—as if only the big, distant, and well publicized could be serious. But since revolutions, like houses, are built from the bottom up, I ask what changes they want to see on campus and in their daily lives.

In this way, I find out that, say, the business school is getting a new building while the college of education is still in Quonset huts; or that the state legislature has raised tuition and cut scholarships but is now paying $50,000 a year per prisoner to Wackenhut, which operates prisons for profit; or that military recruiters are offering impoverished female and male students big signing bonuses but giving little forewarning of combat or sexual assault statistics; or that faculty of color somehow never become department chairs; or that the mostly female nonprofessional staff is being paid bubkes and forbidden to unionize; or that fraternities are defending brothers against sexual assault charges by threatening to bring libel suits against the women who report them; or that a newly "out" lesbian basketball coach has to take a monitoring faculty member along on team travels; or that a law school professor is famous for asking only female students about cases with a sexual component; or that a male medical school professor hires prostituted women on whom to demonstrate gynecological exams; or that the football team spends a lot on Astroturf but not on preventing brain injury—and many other indicators of a need for change.

In short, serious politics are happening right here on campus.

After visiting a class or two, maybe having dinner with student leaders and faculty—where I find out still more about what's happening on campus—we go to the lecture hall. There we discover that it's already full, and people are waiting outside: Perhaps someone is hooking up a public address system for the overflow, or people are being put into rooms with closed-circuit television, and paper is being handed out so they can send in their comments for the postlecture discussion. In the same way that individual women are often underestimated, a movement of women is also underestimated, but the truth is that, if people realize someone is willing to talk about these deep and daily concerns, they show up.

Now the organizers are apologetic for thinking too small. Public opinion polls have long proved there is majority support for pretty much every issue that the women's movement has brought up, but those of us, women or men, who identify with feminism are still made to feel isolated, wrong, out of step. At first, feminists were assumed to be only discontented suburban housewives; then a small bunch of women's libbers, "bra burners,"[3] and radicals; then women on welfare; then briefcase-carrying imitations of male executives; then unfulfilled women who forgot to have children; then women voters responsible for a gender gap that really could decide elections. That last was too dangerous, so suddenly we were told we were in a "postfeminist" age, so we would relax, stop, quit. Indeed, the common purpose in all these disparate and contradictory descriptions is to slow and stop a challenge to the current hierarchy.

But controversy is a teacher. The accusation that feminism is bad for the family leads to understanding that it's bad for the patriarchal variety, but good for democratic families that are the basis of democracy. The idea that women are "our own worst enemies" forces us to admit that we don't have the power to be, even if we wanted to. When occasionally a lecture hall has to be emptied and searched after an anti-abortion group has sent in a bomb threat, I've noticed that when we return, the audience has grown bigger out of support.

So far, I've also noticed that, if an audience is half women and half men, women worry about the reaction of the men around them. But in one that is two-thirds women and one-third men, women respond as they would on their own, and men hear women speaking honestly. When people of color are in the majority instead of the minority, audiences are often the best education that white listeners can have.

Sometimes, hostility shows up, and that is educational in itself. Without campuses in the Bible Belt, I wouldn't know that the belief that women's subordinate role is ordained by God is still with us, or that it can take courage for a student from a strict Christian family—or a Jewish or Muslim equivalent—to go to any college that doesn't teach the New Testament, the Old Testament, or the Koran as the literal truth. A student from Bob Jones University who sought counseling there after being sexually assaulted was asked to "repent," as if she had attracted the assault. In Texas, I saw people outside an auditorium where I was about to speak. Because their signs called me a humanist, I assumed they were welcoming—until a former fundamentalist explained to me that because humanism is bad and secular, Christians were demonstrating against my speech.

In some audiences, feminism is blamed for, say, divorce or plummeting birthrates or lower salaries—instead of blaming unequal marriage or lack of child care or employers who profiteer—but this is an education, too. People who arrive assuming that no one could possibly disagree with equal pay may learn otherwise from someone who rises to say that the free market takes care of that; unequal pay just means that women aren't worth as much as employees. Anyone who believes we're living in a postfeminist age will learn that violence against females—from female infanticide and child marriage to honor killings and sex trafficking—has now produced a world with fewer females than males, a first in recorded history. On the other hand, hearing men say they want to humanize the "masculine" role that is literally killing them, and that they want to raise their own children, keeps all those present from measuring progress by what was, and raises a new standard: what could be.

Altogether I've seen enough change to have faith that more will come.

I.

• It's 1971, and I'm just beginning to talk about the women's movement—with Dorothy, not yet on my own—when I get an invitation to give the address at the **Harvard Law Review** banquet. This annual event is reserved for top students, and guest speakers tend to be political leaders or prestigious legal scholars—definitely all men. Once I discover this isn't a practical joke, it's an easy no. I tell them the woman they should ask is Ruth Bader Ginsburg, a brilliant lawyer who was one of the first female students at Harvard Law School, and who has just created the first Women's Rights Project at the American Civil Liberties Union.

Then I get a call from Brenda Feigen, a friend who also was one of the early women at Harvard Law and who now runs the Women's Rights Project with Ruth. She says I have to do it—Ruth will never be asked because she left Harvard to go to Columbia Law School—and besides, if I say no, they may go back to men-as-usual. Brenda promises to help with research and to ask current women law students to do the same. I remind her that my fear of public speaking is just as serious as her fear of flying, but she says I can write every word, and it will be more like reading than speaking. This and other arguments finally make me say yes to my worst nightmare.

This is how I find myself on the Harvard campus with Brenda, interviewing women who make up just 7 percent of its law students. I learn that the segregated tradition of "Ladies Day," the only time when women are called on in class, has only just ended, and that the faculty are still 100 percent white and male. So sure of themselves are the powers-that-be that the sign over the men's room in the library stacks just says FACULTY. I write this all down and become even more nervous. These students are depending on me.

Ultimately, I find myself standing at a podium in Boston's Sheraton Plaza Hotel. The Harvard Club of Boston, where the banquet is usually held, makes women enter through a side door. I look down at the long 1930s dress I've found in a thrift shop and see its velvet skirt vibrating slightly due to my shaking knees. I'm not sure how much this nervousness is audible in my voice—Brenda is pretending I'm fine; this is a piece of cake—but twenty-seven years later, Ira Lupu, then a third-year Harvard law student in the audience, will write his remembrance: "Her delivery was rhetorically unimpressive; she seemed nervous, and spoke quietly and without sharp effect or physical punctuation."[4]

He didn't know the half of it.

My speech is called "Why Harvard Law School Needs Women More Than Women Need It." I manage to get through the main part, arguing that only equality creates respect for the law, and that only democratic families create democracy. Yet I know that the audience knows that women law students have provided ammunition—interviewing them has already created resentful rumblings among the faculty—and I launch into their testimony at the end:

With this humanist vision in mind, you can imagine how a female human being suffers at Harvard Law School. She spends much of her time feeling lonely, since male classmates often regard her as a freak. She spends the rest of it feeling mad as hell. Much more seriously, the catalog betrays no interest in her half of the human race. There is a course on racism and American law but none on sexism. There is a course on international whaling law but none on women's rights internationally. An eminent professor of administrative law said as late as last night that he didn't know what the Equal Employment Opportunity Commission was. The same man replied to a request that at least one female full-time professor be hired by answering that women faculty brought problems because of "sexual vibrations" . . . and an eminent securities law expert used descriptions of "stupid" widows and wives to explain sample cases of stock loss. . . . Professors may joke about the "reasonable man" test, explaining that there is no such thing as a reasonable woman. They may describe rape as "a very small assault"; gape at bosoms and legs in the front row; encourage the hissing and booing from male colleagues that often follow a female colleague's classroom remarks on women's rights; and

use "stupid woman" stories or sex jokes
that humiliate women to illustrate some
legal point. . . . From now on, no man
can call himself liberal or radical, or even
a conservative advocate of fair play, if his
work depends in any way on the unpaid
or underpaid labor of women at home
or in the office. Politics don't begin in
Washington. Politics begin with those who
are oppressed right here.

I'm so relieved to be finished that I can't tell
whether the applause is approving, disapproving, or just polite. But then something happens that, I will later learn, is unprecedented.
A portly man in a tuxedo rises from his table,
his face flushed with anger, and protests not the
content of what I have said but the very idea
that I dare to judge Harvard Law School at all.
I don't know who he is, but I definitely know
he's outraged. When he finally sits down, there
is silence in the ballroom—then talk gradually
resumes, like an ocean covering a volcano.

Later Brenda tells me this was Vernon Countryman, a Harvard Law professor of debtor-
creditor relations. I'm unsure whether to be
scared or proud of his response, yet something
tells me it's more the latter. He has embodied
what women at Harvard Law School are dealing with.

Only decades later will that law student in the audience confirm my feeling in the moment. "I remember being shocked that a Harvard Law professor could publicly appear so incoherent and out of control," Ira Lupu wrote. "His remarks seemed designed to put Steinem in her place as a young woman untutored in the facts and values of the Harvard Law School, rather than to rebut her comments in any rigorous way. The banquet ended with the quietly held yet widespread sense that Countryman had underlined Steinem's theme of male boorishness and disrespect for women in a way that her words alone could not do."[5]

Finally, Lupu solved the mystery of why I was invited in the first place. His belated essay explains that his then wife, Jana Sax, had felt "profound alienation from the principles and methods reflected in her spouse's legal education." She suggested me as a speaker, and the president of the **Harvard Law Review** said yes. We each played a role: a wife, women law students, Brenda, me, even the angry professor.

In this way, Harvard Law School gives me a big gift: I worry less about hostile responses. Ultimately, they educate an audience. As the great Flo Kennedy will suggest later when we begin to speak together, "Just pause, let the audience absorb the hostility, then say, 'I didn't pay him to say that.'"

• It's 1972, and Margaret Sloan and I are traveling to Texas campuses. One is East Texas State University, where future farmers study agriculture, and another is Southern Methodist University in Dallas, where future leaders study whatever they please. Yet as different as they are, a pair of women students approach us afterward with the same passionate message in each place: **If you think this is bad, you should come to Texas Women's University.** Each pair is also one white woman and one black woman, unusual in itself.

Back home in New York, we keep hearing from more TWU students. It's a campaign to get us there, without a speakers' program to pay expenses—at least, without one willing to invite us. Who can resist?

Denton turns out to be a small town known for its rodeos and hot summers. Students take us around the campus of low buildings, plus one tower that is topped by the president's office—like a warden's aerie overlooking a prison, as the students point out. The good news about this state-supported women's university is that its low cost invites women who might never otherwise be able to go to college, including black and Latina students. The not-so-good news is that TWU is known for two specialties. One is domestic science, which was originally a way of elevating women's work in the home but has become a field that students feel is training them for marriage or domestic service jobs. The other is nursing, the most organized of the professions that are mostly female, but it is still paid less than such similar but mostly male professions as pharmacy. The worst news is that the many sexual assaults on campus have been met with fences, curfews, and male guards that restrict the victims, but not the victimizers. In fact, students suspect that a couple of the guards **are** the rapists.

Margaret and I find ourselves in TWU's main auditorium. It is packed with students and exploding with new feminism, combined with civil rights and black power, plus the newly founded La Raza Unida, a national party created by Mexican American leaders in Texas. Already, La Raza has confounded expectations by becoming the first national political party to support reproductive freedom, including abortion.

Many of these students have experienced the double discrimination of sex and race—not only in the mainstream but also by race in the women's movement, and by sex in the black power movement. They applaud when Margaret says, "I still have scars on my head and dust between my toes from marching across that bridge in Selma. Once I was left for dead. But when the organizing began, they asked me to make coffee." They laugh with relief when she says, "I want to make sure that when the revolution comes, I'm not cooking grits for it." As she sums up, "I'm not black on Monday, Tuesday, and Wednesday, and a woman on Thursday, Friday, and Saturday."

Since many have also been raised with traditional southern ideas of womanhood, they also cheer when I talk about women feeling like a half-person without a man standing next to them, whether on Saturday night or throughout life. This would surprise men, too, I explain, if they realized how little it matters **which** man is standing there. More laughter, and cries of "Tell it!" They're glad to hear what a black woman once said to her white southern sisters: "A pedestal is as much a prison as any small space."

Though some in the audience yell out objections to Margaret's sprinkling of four-letter words—after all, she is a poet from the South Side of Chicago—she gets applause when she says that if critics don't like the way she talks, they can leave. When someone asks me if I believe in God and I say no—I believe in people—I get a hushed silence. So I go on: If, in monotheism, God is man, man is God. Why does God look suspiciously like the ruling class? Why is Jesus, a Jewish guy from the Middle East, blond and blue-eyed? There is a relieved response of laughter, and even a few shouts of "Tell it!"

At the end, the student organizers give us the highest praise: the result has been worth the year they spent persuading us to come. We have made them look reasonable by comparison.

Home in New York, we read newspaper clippings from Denton that sum up our subject matter as "sexism, racism, job discrimination, children, welfare, abortion, homosexuality, bisexuality," in a discussion described as "emotional, controversial, thought provoking, relevant." There are also quotes from audience members who call this lecture and discussion "embarrassing" and "the worst thing I've ever heard." It seems that people went away either angry or inspired. For Margaret, it's a proof of need that helps her decide to cofound the National Black Feminist Organization—together with Eleanor Holmes Norton from the EEOC, Jane Galvin Lewis of the Women's Action Alliance, artist Faith Ringgold, author Michele Wallace, and many others.

After Margaret moves to Oakland, she keeps organizing and working in women's centers there. When I visit her, we reminisce about the two dozen campuses we visited together in less than one year—but our conversation always comes back to TWU.

Thirty-five years pass before I'm back on that campus again. This time I'm campaigning for Hillary Clinton in her 2008 primary race for the presidency, and speaking together with Jehmu Greene, a young African American woman who, like me, has decided, after much soul-searching, to campaign for Clinton—because of her longer experience in battling the ultra-right wing—and to support Obama in the future. Now this campus is offering a master's degree in women's studies, though many others still don't offer even a women's studies major. Rarer still, TWU will soon offer a Ph.D. It also encourages men as well as women to enter its nursing program. Most unusual, a student cannot graduate without taking a course in multicultural women's studies. No wonder Oprah Winfrey has spoken here—twice. Except for a library still famous for its cookbook collection, the campus bears little resemblance to the past.

After our brief talks and a lively discussion about getting out the vote, one woman comes up to tell me that she was on campus when Margaret and I were here decades ago. She calls our visit "shock therapy" that began a year of organizing. The TWU human rights movement forced the administration to deal with student grievances, took on sexism and racism together, and is now working with undocumented immigrants in North Texas.

I have to tell her that Margaret, who moved with her daughter to California about a year after we were at TWU, died after a long illness at only fifty-seven. Her daughter held a memorial in California, and together, we organized one in New York. It's hard to believe that Margaret isn't here on this campus where she was once so alive.

"You know the hospital shows on television?" this woman asks. "When someone's heart stops and has to be restarted with electric paddles? That's what you and Margaret did for us. Please tell her daughter our hearts have been going ever since."

• We learn most where we know the least. For me, this means Gallaudet University in Washington, D.C., the only institution of higher learning in the world that is designed for students who are deaf. It's a revelation.

I arrive there in 1983 to spend a day meeting students, then giving a lecture in the evening. Aside from the fact that I need an interpreter, this campus seems like any other. Students ask me how we started **Ms.** magazine, since they're thinking of starting a magazine on campus. I ask them about the courses they love. There is a controversy about the presidency. Students want a role in choosing the next one, so they at last will have a leader who is also deaf and understands their world. We talk about tactics for making that happen, from petitions to tuition strikes. I see that it's harder to take risks when there is no other campus like the one you're on, yet they're determined. Like more than 80 percent of the students here, those I meet come from hearing families, and they value this short time of being with people who share their experience and culture.

I know enough to look at the person speaking to me, not at the interpreter who is making sign language audible for my benefit. I have the feeling of understanding and being understood.

But the more time I spend with the Gallaudet students, the more I enter into a world where liveliness of expression is a universal art form. Because their words are kinetic and their faces expressive, I feel as if I'm fully present in conversation in a rare way. I know how much I would be missing without a signer as the bridge, but an effort is being made to include me. Young women tell me how misinterpreted they feel in, say, a room full of hearing men, given the stereotype of deaf women as doubly helpless, no matter how strong they really are. I learn how much less likely a deaf woman is, statistically speaking, to be employed or married or in a long-term relationship—even less than her male counterparts—given this double standard. Yet both the men and women are so fast, subtle, and nuanced in talking to me and to each other that I feel as if my audible words are like bricks, and their visual ones are sea shells and feathers.

Ever since Judy Heumann and other disability activists made the point of inclusion in Houston in 1977, feminist speakers have been better about asking that a meeting provide signing and be wheelchair accessible, although it doesn't always happen. At Gallaudet, however, there is not just one signer where the audience can see him or her and I cannot, but one on each side of the stage, and also on each of a dozen or so special platforms around the audience. This means I can see a chorus of motion while I'm speaking. There is also the signing of lyrics and poetry. It's like watching a ballet—a democratic ballet that everyone could learn if we tried.

By the time I leave the signing world for the world of the hearing, I'm not quite the same person. I've seen an expressive, visual world that isn't like the one I've been walking around in. Coming home, I feel let down. Where are all those expressive people?

Five years later, I read that the student movement there, with the wonderfully direct name **Deaf President Now**, has succeeded. In 1988 Gallaudet University finally hires its first deaf president and even appoints a first deaf chair of its board of trustees. This is a long overdue victory on a campus where Abraham Lincoln authorized the first degrees. I also see that on other campuses, activists are framing deafness and disability as a civil rights issue, not as a medical problem that needs fixing. They are developing a whole new field called disability studies. Like black studies and women's studies, these programs begun by a social justice movement are about changing the system to fit people, not the other way around. Since disability may be a state that people both enter and leave—from skiing accidents to combat injuries, from giving birth to aging and crutches—ramps instead of steps turn out to be important to most people at some time in their lives. A few are even citing the 360 million deaf people in the world—or the million in this country—and studying sign language as a language requirement.

Will we get to the point that learning sign language is a part of literacy? That knowing both an audible and a physical language is routine? Thanks to those Gallaudet students, I can imagine it.

• On campuses that offer courses in hospitality training or hotel management, visitors often stay in a hotel that is the practice lab for students. I'm having coffee in the lobby of one in the Midwest when a tall, rangy, fair-haired young man in cowboy boots asks if he can sit down. Because he seems so shy—and because he says he has long admired both me and a particular professional baseball player—I'm surprised. Never before have I been so paired.

As we talk about his hopes of starting a country inn, I have the odd and overwhelming feeling that I'm talking to another woman. He is a cowboy, very taciturn and masculine, yet I can't shake the feeling. When I finally get up the courage to say so, he says, "Of course, that's because I was raised as a girl."

Then he tells me this story. I tell you from memory. It isn't the kind of story that you can forget.

I grew up in a family that lived outside of town, in a big old house in the desert. There were three generations of us. I knew my grandfather was also my father, and he was also my mother's father, but I didn't know there was anything wrong with that. What I did know and hated was that, whenever we stopped for gas and didn't have enough money, my mother or some other relative would send me into the gas station to do a blowjob for the guy who worked there. I don't remember when this started, I was maybe four or five, but I had learned to do this sexual service for my grandfather. He used to say that I should have been his granddaughter. Maybe he felt strange about doing this with a boy—my mother began dressing me in girl's clothes and calling me a girl's name. When I went to school, I wore boy clothes, but I didn't have friends. I learned right away that ours was the family other families told their kids not to play with.

As soon as I was old enough to run away,

I lied about my age, and joined the Navy. I felt safer than I ever had at home. Getting out was the first thing that saved me. By the time I came back home and rented a room in town, there was a women's center where groups talked about a lot of things, including sexual abuse in childhood. I had no idea this had happened to anyone else. The therapist there explained that once women started talking to each other, they discovered that this happened a lot, especially but not only to girls. When survivors needed help but couldn't afford therapy, this therapist helped them form a group—and I joined; it was six women and me. I discovered it wasn't my fault. But when people in the town knew we were telling family secrets, even the women's center had to turn the therapist out. Still, she kept on meeting with us on our own.

But what really saved me was what you felt. I had dressed and lived as a girl until I was about eight, so I never felt I was a man like my grandfather. As my therapist put it, I never identified with the aggressor. If I had, I might have become an abuser myself. It's terrible to be a victim, and to believe sex is the only thing you're worth—without help, girls grow up to keep believing that. But some boys start abusing other people because that's a way of being a man.

That means guilt, being afraid you'll get arrested if you tell the truth, cutting off all empathy—everything that makes it harder to get out. I wouldn't say I was lucky—but it would have been worse if I thought I had to control and abuse other people.

He is telling me his story to say thank you. Because the women's movement was born of women talking to each other, childhood sexual abuse was revealed to be a fact, not a Freudian fantasy—and children began to be believed.

We finish our coffee. He is a rare person—a man who knows what it is to be a woman— and also someone who has ended abuse in one generation. I thank him for surviving—and teaching. There are many kinds of lessons on a campus.

• It's 1995, and I am at the Dominican College, near San Francisco. Because an outdoor amphitheater on its campus holds a thousand people, it is about to be the site of a fund-raiser for Planned Parenthood. No one has uttered a peep of protest. Planned Parenthood clinics have provided health care for so many for so long that it has become one of the most trusted organizations in America. Even some anti-abortion protesters seem to have figured out that demonstrating against clinics only turns public opinion against them, especially since just 3 percent of Planned Parenthood services are related to abortion.

But this is the calm before the storm. Archbishop John Quinn of San Francisco writes a letter to the college's president condemning me as a "leading advocate for virtually unrestricted abortion in the United States." Though the college gets not a penny from the Catholic Church, it was founded by Dominican nuns long ago. They are no longer around to speak for themselves, but the archbishop says their legacy is being betrayed.

Everything just keeps going, both the accusations and the event. Some contributors do indeed withhold their funds from this college, which is hurtful. But when the trustees hold firm to their support for free speech on campus, new contributions make up for the loss of the old. If anything, the archbishop has only brought more media coverage of an era of declining church membership, aging priests, shutdowns of a dozen historic churches, the revelations of sexual abuse by priests, and many other troubles that caused him to be summoned to the Vatican for a tactical consultation.

On the day itself, I'm impressed to see a small protest plane circling over the amphitheater, pulling an anti-abortion banner. Someone yells out, "Look, the right-to-lifers have an air force!" There is laughter. The event goes right on. Even though I know this lonely little plane is a commercial one that can be hired for birthdays, weddings, and advertising, the symbolism of its constant circling makes me sad.

Talking later to Dolores Huerta, my friend of thirty years—a lifetime organizer of farm workers and efforts to elect progressive women—I tell her that I can't shake the sadness of this symbolic distance between an airplane representing the church and the real lives of women on the ground.

She reminds me of the organizer's mantra: **Roots can exist without flowers, but no flower can exist without roots.** Religion may be a flower, but people are its roots.

Three months later, Archbishop John Quinn retires at the age of sixty-six, nine years ahead of schedule. San Francisco newspapers report that he was too distant from the people.

• In rural Oklahoma, where oil wells grow in fields next to cattle and winter wheat, I'm talking with a university auditorium full of students in a postlecture discussion. Most people are trying to figure out how to make their daily lives more fair—whether it's who gets tenure or who gets the kids ready for school—but I notice that an all-white group of twenty or so people in Jesus T-shirts are not taking part.

Finally, a young T-shirted man stands up to protest my support for legal abortion, which is odd because we haven't been talking about abortion at all. He says abortion isn't even in the Constitution, so how can it be protected by it? A female college student who looks about twelve rises to say that women aren't included in the Constitution either, but now that we're citizens, we have reproductive freedom as part of a constitutional right to privacy. If the Founding Fathers had included Founding Mothers, that freedom would have been in the Bill of Rights to begin with.

The crowd applauds. I can see we've reached the magical point when people start to answer each other's questions. I can just listen and learn. An older man who seems to be the leader of the Jesus T-shirt group says that the Bible forbids abortion in its commandment "Thou shall not kill." But being in the Bible Belt, people really know their Bible, and an older woman cites Exodus 21:22–23, a passage that says a man who causes a pregnant woman to miscarry must pay a fine but is not charged with murder, not unless the woman herself dies. Thus the Bible is making clear that a dependent life is not the same as an independent life.

This quiets the T-shirt wearers, but probably not for long; I can see them conferring. Meanwhile another student rises to object to parental and judicial consent laws that treat a young woman as if she were the property of her parents or the state. "If you're old enough to get pregnant," she says, "you're old enough to get unpregnant." A man chimes in, pointing out that if a woman serving in the military is raped by another soldier or even by the enemy, she can't get an abortion in an army hospital or anywhere with government funds. She's not even guaranteed a leave to find one on her own. There is a rumble of disapproval and learning.

A nurse arises to explain the metal bracelet she is wearing. It looks like the prisoner of war bracelets that bear the birth date of a loved one, but she explains that hers bears the birth and death dates of Rosie Jimenez, the first woman— but not the last—to die from an illegal abortion because the Hyde Amendment forbids not only the use of military tax dollars but health care or any tax dollars for abortion. Rosie was on welfare, only a few months away from graduating with teaching credentials so she could support herself and her five-year-old daughter. But she got pregnant, crossed the Mexican border to get an illegal abortion, the only kind she could afford, returned to Texas, and spent seven painful and fevered days in a hospital being treated for septic shock—at hundreds of times the taxpayers' expense of an abortion. She died, leaving behind her daughter and a $700 scholarship check that was proof of Rosie's promising future. This happened only two months after the Hyde Amendment went into effect. Hundreds and perhaps thousands of women have lost their health or lives since.

With an eye on the T-shirt group, I explain that reproductive freedom means what it says and also protects the right to have a child. A woman can't be forced into an abortion, just as she can't be forced out of childbirth by sterilization or anything else: the women's movement is as devoted to the latter as the former—including the economic ability to support a child. It just seems lopsided because the opponents of safe and legal abortion have focused there.

I hope the quiet T-shirt group might be realizing that this protects their choice, too—that government with the power to forbid birth control or abortion could also enforce one or the other—but no such luck. Suddenly they stand up in unison, chant "Abortion! Murder! Abortion! Murder!" and walk out en masse.

In the silence that follows, I can feel people trying to figure out what went wrong. I too wonder what I could have said or done. I express my regret at their walkout, which seems to break the spell.

A young white man in jeans—slender, shy, perhaps in his late twenties—raises his hand and begins a story that seems unrelated. He has invented a new kind of bit for oil rigs. He just sold the patent and received an unexpected amount of money. He would like to donate $90,000, about half of his windfall, to the cause of reproductive freedom as a basic human right—like freedom of speech.

There is silence, then laughter, and then cheers. Never in my four decades of traveling and fund-raising will anything like this happen again. If people pledge money, it's usually after an appeal and in requested sums. Also they tend to give according to what others are giving. To me and to everyone in that room, this young man has shown how to give without being asked and according to ability—more than ability, since he is sharing a rare windfall. He has given us all the gift of spontaneity—and hope.

We stay in touch. He comes to New York and stops to say hello. When I'm on another trip, a young woman introduces herself to me as his sister. When he and I cross paths in Denver, we have breakfast. Every few years, the road seems to bring us together. That day in Oklahoma became a landmark in all our lives.

II.

FOR ME, TALKING AND ORGANIZING AFTER A CAMpus or any other lecture is the big reward—because then I am learning. We often continue in a restaurant or campus hangout or just sit on the nearest available floor. With a shared lecture to respond to—plus my request to overcome the hierarchical setting and pretend we're all sitting in a circle, even if there are five hundred or five thousand of us—people get up and say things they might not say to friends or family. It's as if the audience creates its own magnetic field that draws out stories and ideas.

I also read aloud from notes handed to me by the audience—about, say, cuts of hard-won new courses that aren't yet in the core curriculum, but plenty of money allocated for a new football stadium—because I can do this without punishment. Often a kind of alchemy takes place. When someone on one side of the hall asks a question, and someone on the other side answers it, I know this magic has happened. The group has acquired a life of its own.

There are rock-bottom subjects for men as well as women. If there is one that men want to talk about most, it's how much they missed having nurturing fathers, or any man in their lives who cared. Once they delve into that, the question is how to become that father or man themselves. This childhood wish is one of the greatest allies that feminism could have. Men also talk about seeing their mothers treated with violence or humiliation by fathers or stepfathers. I've watched the biggest, baddest-looking college athletes with tears rolling down their faces because they were remembering how they felt while witnessing their mothers being beaten.

Whatever the makeup of the audience, I've learned to have faith in the smart, funny, revelatory responses and the surprises of a discussion that usually goes on longer than the lecture itself. I wish I could bring you a thousand YouTube videos of people standing up and asking what they need to know, or sharing what they've learned, or telling their stories, or asking for help, or saving me from some impasse I can't solve.

A sample:

• At a law school in Canada, we are deep in a discussion of the law as a universal instrument that feminists should not expect to be flexible. I am arguing that this is what judges are for—otherwise, justice could be meted out by a computer. The mostly male law students are arguing that any exception is dangerous and creates a "slippery slope." Make one exception, and the number will grow until the law will be overturned de facto.

I am not a lawyer. I am stuck. Those young men may or may not represent the common-sense majority in the audience, but they have triumphed.

Then a tall young woman in jeans rises from the back of the room. "Well," she says calmly, "I have a boa constrictor." This quiets the audience right down.

"Once a month," she continues, "I go to a dissection lab on campus to get frozen mice to feed my boa constrictor. But this month, there was a new professor in charge, and he said to me: 'I can't give you frozen mice. If I give you frozen mice, everyone will want frozen mice.'"

There is such an explosion of laughter that

even the argumentative young men can't resist.
She has made her point: not everyone wants
the same thing. A just law can be flexible. To be
just, a law **has** to be flexible. She has saved the
day.

• At a community college in California, an
auditorium full of returning women students
is into a long and serious discussion about how
difficult it is to get their male partners to share
equally in the housework and child care. It's not
just because the men are resistant; it's because
the women themselves feel guilty, or don't want
to seem like nags, or don't know how to divide
work and child care because they've never seen
it at home.

One woman rises to speak: "Close your eyes
and pretend you are living with a woman—how
would you divide the housework?"

There is a long pause. "Now, don't lower your
standards." There are cheers of approval.

• On another campus, some women tell me
about men who leave their underwear on the
floor and don't feel compelled to pick it up—
or even notice. By now, the shouts and laughter have become quite rowdy, and I've begun
to worry about a silent young Japanese woman
near the front. Perhaps we are offending her.

As if summoned by my thought, she stands
and turns to face all five hundred or so women.

"When my husband leaves his underwear on the floor," she says quietly, "I find it quite useful to **nail** it to the floor."

Amid laughter and cheers, this shy young woman seems surprised to find herself laughing, too. She tells the group this is the first time she has ever said anything in public.

• In a discussion of the advantages of having younger men as husbands and lovers—because they're more likely to treat women as equals—one woman rises to say, "Of course they understand better. We were their mothers!" Once again I worry about a much older and ladylike woman in a front row who looks disapproving. When I ask if we are offending her, she rises, turns to the audience, and says, "When you are having an affair with a younger man"—I notice she doesn't say **if,** but **when**—"try never to get on top. You look like a bulldog." This remark coming from an unlikely woman—but one who had clearly been there—brought down the house.

IF THERE IS ONE thing that these campus visits have affirmed for me, it's that the miraculous but impersonal Internet is not enough. As in the abolitionist and suffragist era, when there were only six hundred or so colleges with a hundred students each—and itinerant organizers like the Grimké sisters, Frederick

Douglass, and Sojourner Truth traveled to speak in town halls, granges, churches, and campgrounds—nothing can replace being in the same space. That's exactly why we need to keep creating the temporary worlds of meetings, small and large, on campuses and everywhere else. In them, we discover we're not alone, we learn from one another, and so we keep going toward shared goals. Individual organizers in the civil rights movement had a network of black churches, not just phones and mimeograph machines, and veterans speaking against the war in Vietnam had coffeehouses and rock concerts. Now that there are at least four thousand campuses with more than fifteen million students—not yet diverse enough, but more diverse than ever before—they are the mainstay for wandering organizers like me.

I recommend trying this kind of grassroots organizing for a week or a year, a month or a lifetime—working for whatever change you want to see in the world. Then one day you will be talking to a stranger who has no idea you played any part in the victory she or he is celebrating.

You'll learn that, say, students and staff and faculty created child care that changed who could go to a college; or that the best-qualified candidate got elected instead of the best-financed one; or that high school students here worked summers to pay the school fees of their counterparts in Africa; or that a governor learned about wrongful convictions, including of women who killed their batterers in self-defense, and commuted the sentences of everyone on death row; or that male executives insisted on parental leave and equal time with their kids; or that an entire state rose up against turning its prisons and public schools into corporate profit centers; or that domestic violence became grounds for firing police and police brutality plummeted; or that a school system ordered texts that covered all the continents and populations equally; or that American history courses actually began when people first populated this land they called Turtle Island; or that gun ownership went down and public transportation went up; or that reproductive freedom became the Fifth Freedom—and other hopes that only you and your future self can imagine.

Then, as if in answer to a riddle posed years before, you will realize that this growth came from seeds you planted or watered or carried from place to place— and you'll be rewarded in the way that we as communal beings need most: you'll know you made a difference.

WITH BELLA ABZUG, TRYING TO SAY THAT POLITICALLY
"WE'RE ALL IN THE SAME BOAT."

PHOTOGRAPH BY JOHN PEDIN, NEW YORK *DAILY NEWS*

V.

When the Political
Is Personal

My mother's stories of suffering during the Depression—and how Franklin and Eleanor Roosevelt helped us out of it—taught me that politics are a part of daily life. She described making soup from leftover potato skins, then listening to Roosevelt's speeches on the radio to nourish her spirit. Or cutting up a blanket to make a warm coat for my older sister and protecting her from ridicule by saying that if people loved a new kind of First Lady, they could love a new kind of coat. She even told me that my grandfather had died not of pneumonia, as everybody said, but of a broken heart after losing everything he worked for. Had he lived to see President Roosevelt create jobs and dignity where they were needed most—by building bridges, planting forests, even painting murals in post offices—she was sure he would be with us still.

It made perfect sense to me that my mother's stories began in a personal place, and came to a political point. So did her belief that Franklin and Eleanor understood our lives at the bottom, even though they were born at the top. "Always look at what people do," as my mother said, "not at who they are." She also was sure the Roosevelts wanted us to become independent, not dependent. Since, like most children, I said things like "It's not fair" and "You are not the boss of me," this idea made me love them even more.

Not all my mother's stories had a happy ending. When I saw a mysterious newspaper photo of police dragging dark-skinned people through city streets, she explained there were race riots in nearby Detroit—because the Depression had never ended for people called Negroes. I imagined people making soup from potato peelings and coats from blankets, yet somehow I couldn't imagine my family being attacked by police. She also sat with me as we listened to a radio drama about a mother and child trying to survive in a place called a concentration camp. I knew my mother didn't want to frighten me, only to teach me something serious, and this made me feel important and grown-up. In later years, I wondered if she meant such small doses of hard realities to immunize me against the depression that, in her, could be triggered by as little as a sad movie or a hurt animal.

Yet I never asked why my happy-go-lucky father had zero interest in politics. Both were kind and loving, just very different.

I was eleven when President Roosevelt died. By then, my mother and I were living in the small town in Massachusetts where we had moved after she and my father separated. I can still see the exact look of the cracks in the sidewalk where I was riding my bike when my mother came out to tell me. It was hard to believe that Franklin and Eleanor would no longer be part of our lives. It was harder still when I realized that not everyone was sorry. Some in that town blamed the president for getting us into World War II, and others thought his idea of a United Nations would just let foreigners tell us what to do. A newspaper cartoon said, "Goodbye to President Rosenfeld." My mother explained that no, Roosevelt wasn't Jewish; it was just that prejudiced people linked together things they didn't like.

Our only companion in mourning was an elderly man across the street who wore a tie with FDR woven into it, something he showed to us as if to coconspirators. My mother was brave enough to put a black-draped photo of the president in our front window, but not brave enough to explain it to the neighbors. I was beginning to suspect that conflict follows politics as night follows day, yet the mere thought of conflict was enough to depress my already depressed mother. I myself cried when I got angry, then became unable to explain why I was angry in the first place. Later I would discover this was endemic among female

human beings. Anger is supposed to be "unfemi-
nine," so we suppress it—until it overflows.

I could see that not speaking up made my mother
feel worse. This was my first hint of the truism that
depression is anger turned inward; thus women are
twice as likely to be depressed. My mother paid a
high price for caring so much, yet being able to do
so little about it. In this way, she led me toward an
activist place where she herself could never go.

MY OWN POLITICAL LIFE didn't begin until my
last year in high school. I was living with my sister in Washington, D.C., where she was a buyer in
a department store and shared a house with three
other young working women. They assumed I must
be homesick, and it seemed disloyal to tell the truth.
Because I was responsible only for myself, I was in
heaven.

In my new high school, everyone seemed headed
for college. Some had even taken the college boards
before **just for practice**, something I'd never heard
of. They came from families with bank accounts
instead of pay envelopes, dinner parties instead of
TV dinners, and vacations in countries my Toledo
friends' families had fled in poverty.

Many of my new classmates came from high-level
military families, and regarded presidential candidate Dwight D. Eisenhower as war hero and father-
figure combined. To me Adlai Stevenson, a reluctant
candidate drafted by Democrats, sounded more like

Roosevelt, but I wasn't about to argue. I had a handsome new boyfriend who was headed for West Point, the son and grandson of generals. Only by accident did I discover that a makeshift Stevenson for President office was just a streetcar ride away.

The minute I walked into that big room full of ringing phones and rushing people, I felt it was the most exciting place I'd ever been. Staff members were presiding over cluttered desks, volunteers were talking intensely while stuffing envelopes, and teenagers were stacking lawn signs for nearby Maryland and Virginia, where people could actually vote for president, unlike residents of D.C. who were supposed to be neutral. Most amazing, all this was open to anyone off the street.

Soon I had a place working alongside other young women volunteers, getting purple ink on our hands while tending a big drumlike mimeograph machine churning out **Students for Stevenson.** It was a newsletter designed to attract volunteers, since no one under twenty-one could vote.

I could see there was a clear hierarchy. Male staffers made decisions, and women carried them out, even women old enough to be their mothers. Paid staff were white men, and the few black women and men were volunteers or messengers. Still, this was much more like the real world than my new high school. I spent my first days there trying to figure out why the halls full of students looked so odd. Suddenly I realized that everyone was white. I asked a teacher if this reflected the neighborhood, and he said of course not, it reflected segregation. Washington was two separate cities, he said, and the black majority wanted separate schools, too. Besides, the city had come a long way since slaves built the White House.

This was news to me. My Toledo high school was segregated socially, too—not only by race but by whose family had a television set, spoke Polish or Hungarian at home, or had a father who was a foreman instead of working the line—but at least we all went to the same classes, ate in the same cafeteria, and cheered the same football team.

Altogether, this Stevenson for President office was the most open and welcoming place I'd ever been. But one Saturday when I and the other young women arrived, we found ourselves stashed away on an upper floor. We were devastated. A staffer explained that Stevenson himself might drop in and must not be seen with any female unless she was old enough to be his mother. After all, he was that terrible thing—divorced—something no president had ever been. Though everyone seemed to know that Eisenhower had imported the beautiful young English woman who was his driver during the war—and even arranged for her U.S. citizenship—he would have his wife, Mamie, as a proper First Lady. Appearances were all that mattered.

We didn't object to being hidden away; we felt like Typhoid Marys who might endanger the cause we cared about. When we went out for ten-cent hamburgers at the local White Castle, we talked about staying out of sight. What we didn't talk about were the male staffers who rated our looks, brushed against us in close quarters, and became hazards to be navigated. Our presence was the problem; their behavior was inevitable. Avoiding them while keeping their egos intact was just part of our job.

The truth is that we would have put up with almost anything to stay in this exciting place with its air of fighting for outsiders—even though we didn't yet know we were outsiders, too. Or to put it another way, we didn't believe we could ever be insiders. I didn't know that political change could make me feel safer in the street, or allow me an identity of my own instead of marrying it, or send my Toledo classmates to college instead of to factories, or get my current classmates out of their white ghetto. I didn't realize that changes made through politics might have helped my mother remain the pioneer journalist she had been years before I was born.

My only thought was **Where else could I find such openness, excitement, and hope?** I was hooked.

And I've stayed hooked on campaigns to this day. Despite all their faults, campaigns are based on the fact that every vote counts, and therefore every person counts. As freestanding societies, they are more open than academia, more idealistic than corporations, more unifying than religions, and more accessible than government itself. Campaign season is the only time of public debate about what we want for the future. It can change consciousness even more than who gets elected. In short, campaigns may be the closest thing we have to democracy itself.

—

LIVING IN INDIA, where people lined up for hours and even days to cast their ballots, confirmed my oddball love of campaigns. So did returning home to find a growing and brave civil rights movement of people willing to risk their lives to register and vote.

But as a freelance writer, it was hard to combine what I loved with what I did. If I tried for an assignment covering a major political leader, I would be asked to write about his wife instead. If I worked hard, I could get assignments I was proud of—for instance, a profile of Truman Capote, or a long article about the contraceptive pill—but the world of politics allowed few women into it, even as journalists.

Then, in 1968, I joined a group of writers—led by Clay Felker, my editor at **Esquire**—who were starting **New York** magazine. I was the only "girl reporter," but finally I would be able to write about politics. This was the home of the New Journalism as practiced by Tom Wolfe, and also of Jimmy Breslin, an in-the-streets chronicler of New York life. Since Wolfe wrote satirically from outside about subjects he probably disliked, and Breslin wrote from inside about the lives of people he probably loved, they helped establish the right of nonfiction writers to be both personal and political—as long as we got our facts straight.[1]

When I joined the press corps on campaign planes, I noticed that each one seemed to reflect the candidate's character. Eugene McCarthy isolated himself, talked philosophy, and told reporters that only the well educated supported him—as if that were a good thing. This set the tone for his staff, who also seemed cool and disengaged. On the other hand, Richard Nixon gave the same speech at every stop, disappeared behind closed doors with local political leaders, and once on every campaign trip walked back in the plane to greet each reporter with a carefully memorized personal fact, almost always out of date. Reporters on his plane seemed to overcompensate for not really liking him by being less critical, and there was none of the usual air of excitement about talking to the candidate.

When Bobby Kennedy's campaign plane was scheduled for a stop at an Indian reservation, his staff objected because there were too few votes to be worth his time. He accused them of not caring and stopped anyway. His was probably the only plane with a folksinger playing guitar in the aisle. Because so many reporters loved Bobby, they overcompensated—but by being critical. Later I would wonder if journalists' guilt about their personal feelings meant that readers couldn't know who Bobby Kennedy was until after he was dead, or who Richard Nixon was until after he was in the White House.

As a VOLUNTEER, campaigning has meant many different things for me. I've stuffed envelopes and leafleted and picketed and phone-banked and fundraised. I've lobbied and researched and written

speeches and, once, served on a platform committee, though only because Bella Abzug couldn't. I've
shortened my life by trying to accomplish anything
at political conventions, then shortened it even more
by staying up all night to draft group statements and
press releases for movement protests against exclu-
sions at those conventions. I've campaigned for more
candidates than I can remember. In 1996 alone, I look
back at a schedule that lists twenty-nine candidates,
not counting a president. I've spoken in backyards
to a dozen neighbors, at huge concerts of rock and
grunge bands, at teas in quiet living rooms, on flat-
bed trucks with bullhorns, and on foot while door-
to-door canvassing. Once the women's movement
was really under way, we sometimes found ourselves
speaking at marches in Washington of more than a
million people. I recommend all these tasks, high
and low. It's one of the great things about campaigns
that experience trumps everything, and people just
try to do what needs to be done. A domestic worker
lobbying to be included in the minimum wage may
be a major speaker, and a Ph.D. may be making get-
out-the-vote phone calls.

When I look back, I see three stages, though I
didn't know they were stages at the time.

First, I was volunteering inside campaigns and
doing whatever I was asked to do—for instance,
phone-banking until I thought the receiver would
have to be surgically removed from my ear. I called
big-city contributors from on-the-road places so I
could say, "You don't know what it's like out here."

Sometimes I also did such unusual tasks as urging George McGovern to wear longer, TV-appropriate socks when he was a presidential candidate, going out to get Chinese food for Kennedy volunteers, or helping to run a discothèque as a fund-raiser for Lyndon Johnson's campaign against Goldwater. My proudest moment was writing a televised speech for Shirley Chisholm in her 1972 run for the U.S. presidency. She was on the ballot in only fourteen states, but she was the first major-party black presidential candidate and the first woman to run for the Democratic presidential nomination. Single-handedly, she took the "white males only" sign off the White House door. Because she was "whited out"—as Flo Kennedy put it—of a televised debate before the New York primary, Chisholm and her campaign manager, Ludwig Gelobter, brought a legal action for equal time. She was given a half-hour at the last minute. Ludwig asked me to write overnight a speech that knit together Shirley's farsighted positions. Staying up to do it, then watching her deliver it on television, was a high I won't forget.

Second, I helped to found—and then campaigned with—women's movement groups, for instance, the National Women's Political Caucus (NWPC), which supported pro-equality women for elected and appointed office, and then Voters for Choice, a political action committee that helped male and female candidates from either party who supported reproductive freedom. **Ms.** magazine rated presidential candidates on everything from pay equity and child care to the Machismo Factor—by which we meant support for the military and the death penalty. This did nothing to keep Richard Nixon out of the White House, but some Australian women who visited the **Ms.** office told us they used our rating system to help bring in the Labor Party. Also, the NWPC compiled the names of diverse women qualified for appointment to high office. More than forty years later, Mitt Romney would claim personal credit for having "binders full of women" as governor of Massachusetts, advancing it as one of his credentials for the presidency. In fact, those binders had been prepared and pressed on him by the Massachusetts Women's Political Caucus, as the group had done for decades.

Only in my sixties did I arrive at my third and favorite form of campaigning, independent of any organization. With a few friends who were also activists and organizers, I rode cross-country in a van, found places to stay in swing states where local activists told us we were needed, and held meetings at school gyms, libraries, shopping centers, bowling alleys, rock concerts, backyard barbecues, campus rallies, subway stops, union halls, immigration lines, movie theaters, and bagel shops—all the places where voters are but candidates rarely go. Because I wasn't a surrogate for any candidate, I didn't have to say only what the candidate would say, or risk getting him or her into trouble by saying more. Because we all were free agents who paid our own way by raising small sums from friends, we could be trusted messengers, people who benefited in no way except as citizens and could say why we were supporting a candidate.

By the time of Obama's election campaign for the White House in 2008, we had extended these independent road trips to distant places. In the swing state of Colorado, which was crucial to Obama's victory and also had some threatening ballot initiatives, we rented a house in Denver and, using it as a hub, traveled each day to different living rooms and community centers full of Independent or Republican women, the groups most likely to be neglected by the Democratic Party. They felt abandoned by the Republican War Against Women, yet were turned off by accusatory Democratic women saying, **"How can you be a Republican?"** Instead, we talked about the reasons to support political leaders who support us, never mind party labels. It was the kind of campaigning only a movement could do.

In the end, Colorado defeated the biased ballot initiatives, including one that would have conferred legal personhood on a fertilized egg, and also gave its support to Obama. On the night of the election, he won this 80 percent white state with about 60 percent of the votes from women of all races, and more than 70 percent of the votes from all single women. Even more so than in the rest of the country, John McCain would have won if only men had voted. We danced with crowds in the streets of downtown

Denver to celebrate a victory for Barack Obama, a man with a great mind and a good heart, as the first African American president of the United States.

On very good days, I knew our little group was part of the great tradition of abolitionists and suffragists who traveled by horse-drawn carriage and train to meetings in parlors, town halls, churches, schoolhouses, granges, and barns. They couldn't rely only on letters, newspapers, and books to spread the word, just as we must not rely only on television, email, Skype, and Twitter. Then and now, we take to the road to hold communal meetings where listeners can speak, speakers can listen, facts can be debated, and empathy can create trust and understanding.

In each of these stages of campaigning, I've been inspired, angry, hopeless, hopeful, sleepless, surprised, betrayed, exhausted, educated, energized, despairing, and impatient—but never sorry. I wasn't tempted to join a campaign staff. That is important but a one-way street. Volunteering as a citizen—or with an issue group or a movement—allows ideas to flow both ways. Nor was I tempted to become a candidate myself. That would have meant taking on conflict as a daily diet. I've noticed that great political leaders are energized by conflict. I'm energized by listening to people's stories and trying to figure out shared solutions. That's the work of an organizer.

Sometimes when I'm in the midst of all this, I can hear my mother saying, "Democracy is just something you must do every day, like brushing your teeth."

I.

As a freelancer, I finally did get one assignment in our nation's capital—to write about the style of the Kennedy White House. It paid less than I would spend traveling back and forth from New York, but I was as fascinated as anybody with the Kennedys. Also I would be reading otherwise tedious research in the West Wing office of Ted Sorensen, JFK's speechwriter, someone I knew from campaigning. Just being in that political energy field was reward enough. Since Sorensen felt humor was his weak point, there was a small chance I could contribute a word or two to a speech he was finishing on a deadline.

A man of sober Nebraska stock, Ted purchased his own stamps, just in case a letter might not be deemed job-related. He was definitely not part of the glamorous Kennedy social life. Indeed, he disapproved of Kennedy's affairs, especially since he sometimes had to serve as a cover. He also thought smoking made a woman look immoral, and since I thought a cigarette made me look like a writer—though I couldn't inhale without getting sick—I smoked and felt judged by him. Far more important was his mastery of parallel construction, with sentences as elegant and inspiring as "Ask not what your country can do for you, ask what you can do for your country." If I hung out in his office for a day or two, I hoped I might learn, contribute, or both.

That's why, on a November day, I was sorting clippings while Ted hurried to finish a speech for Kennedy's trip to Dallas. He ran the final copy out onto the White House lawn, where a helicopter waited to take the president to **Air Force One.** I watched as Kennedy, that familiar man I'd never met, walked into the wind from the whirling blades.

It was the last time Ted or I would ever see him.

In New York the next day, I could tell, from the faces of people in the street, who knew about the shooting and who did not. Ted called to say the bullet had shattered the president's skull. There was no hope.

I thought, **When the past dies, we mourn for the dead. When the future dies, we mourn for ourselves.**

ONCE VICE PRESIDENT LYNDON JOHNSON was president, Bobby Kennedy stepped down as attorney general to give LBJ the right to name his own. Then this younger Kennedy declared his candidacy for U.S. Senate from New York State. It seemed to be a painful effort to fill his brother's shoes. Bobby Kennedy hated even public speaking. I once heard him give a brief talk, and I related to his uncomfortable voyage from one sentence to the next.

Hoping to publish a freelance article, I followed Bobby Kennedy around for a day of campaigning in New York City. He was a very unusual candidate. When avoiding a reporter's question, for instance, he didn't just give a skillful nonanswer, as most politicians do. "As you can see," he would say, "I'm trying to avoid that question." He seemed interested in engaging only with people who asked questions to which they really didn't know the answers.

Jack Newfield of **The Village Voice** told me the secret of interviewing Bobby: Bring along someone who doesn't know the subject—or better yet, who disagrees. Then Bobby will see a purpose in explaining, and you'll get lots of quotes.

In Manhattan, two famous writers, journalist Gay Talese and novelist Saul Bellow, joined Kennedy's Senate campaign for the day. I knew Talese and had recently met Bellow when I interviewed him and followed him around his beloved Chicago. The three of us shared a taxi to Kennedy events. Sitting between them on the backseat, I was in the midst of passing along Jack Newfield's useful advice when Talese leaned across me—as if I were neither talking nor present—and said to Bellow, **You know how every year there's a pretty girl who comes to New York and pretends to be a writer? Well, Gloria is this year's pretty girl.** Then they began to discuss the awful traffic.

My initial response was to be embarrassed. Would Bellow regret having given an interview to someone now being called an unworthy writer?

But once I was out of the taxi and away from their self-assured presence, I got angry. How could Talese behave as if I weren't even there? Why didn't I object? Yell? Get out and slam the door?

———

FOUR YEARS LATER I was volunteering for Eugene McCarthy's primary bid for the Democratic nomination—not imagining I would ever write about it—when I climbed up to a barren, third-floor campaign headquarters in Manhattan. I sat in a circle of rickety chairs with other writers and editors who were helping with press releases and position papers for a candidate we hadn't met. McCarthy had been the third choice of the anti–Vietnam War peace movement, but he was the only one who said yes to challenging President Johnson in New Hampshire, the first primary of the 1968 campaign. Senator Robert Kennedy and then Senator George McGovern had been asked first, but both had refused. For anyone opposed to the Vietnam War, this reserved, sardonic senator from Minnesota was the only game in town.

All this helped to explain why we were such a disparate group, including a Republican woman who hoped that strengthening the antiwar cause would help a dovish Nelson Rockefeller beat the hawklike Nixon in the Republican primaries, and one other apostate Democrat I knew from our effort to organize writers and editors to withhold the percentage of our tax money going to Vietnam. Though we had imagined dire consequences, it turned out to be like punching a pillow: our unpaid taxes were just collected from our bank accounts, an odd form of voting.

Because McCarthy was coming to town for a benefit, four of us volunteer writers were assigned to interview him and write a Sunday newspaper supplement for his New Hampshire campaign. We met him at his suite at the St. Regis Hotel, all prepared with questions on his key issues. As it turned out, we might as well have stayed home. Whatever we asked, McCarthy just turned to an aide and instructed him to find this or that quote from the past. He was aloof and cool. Unlike Bobby Kennedy, he didn't seem to care whether we knew the answer or not—only that he had once given it. This awkward session became more so when he cautioned us not to write about Vietnam. Why? Because New Hampshire was "a hawk state."

We recovered enough to protest that his opposition to the Vietnam War was the source of his appeal, especially to kids all over the country who were volunteering to work in New Hampshire, even cutting their long hippie hair and adopting the motto "Clean for Gene." Finally, he agreed that we could include Vietnam, but only if we put it right next to his support for veterans' benefits. By the end, he reminded me of the executive at Household Finance who used to listen to my father's plea for a loan, lean back, put his fingertips together in a steeple, and say, "No."

FOLLOWING MCCARTHY'S SURPRISING SHOWING in New Hampshire, Bobby Kennedy announced that he would run for president after all. Also LBJ, a sitting president embarrassed by this little-known senator from Minnesota, stunned the country by announcing that he wouldn't run again. Now that Bobby Kennedy was the only other major outside contender, the McCarthy campaign set out to portray him as an opportunist for not having braved "the snows of New Hampshire." His absence from that primary nullified all virtue, just as McCarthy's presence in New Hampshire nullified all faults.

In the upstairs McCarthy headquarters where I was still volunteering, it was no longer enough to be for McCarthy as a candidate; one also had to be against Kennedy as a man. Bitter social divisions broke out among people who otherwise agreed on issues. Friends no longer spoke to friends, common goals were forgotten, and gossip about who had switched to whom politically was suddenly as juicy as who was having an affair with whom—but less tolerant.

Four decades later, I would be reminded of this painful tension when the followers of Hillary Clinton and Barack Obama fell into a similar division. Though those two presidential candidates were far more the same on issues than were McCarthy and Kennedy—and though they actually liked each other, unlike McCarthy, who had contempt for Bobby Kennedy and considered him a bad Catholic—Obama became the face of the future, just as McCarthy had done after New Hampshire, and Hillary Clinton supposedly became a part of the past for sharing a political name, just as Bobby Kennedy had done.

Of course, this parallel was imperfect. Bobby Kennedy was not the "past" to the big majority of black and Hispanic voters who supported him as a symbol of hope, and McCarthy's constituency for the "future" was overwhelmingly white and not poor. Also, neither McCarthy nor Kennedy embodied a huge and historic breakthrough, as did both Hillary Clinton and Barack Obama. Their politics were also too organic to imagine either one metamorphosing, as Eugene McCarthy would later do, into supporting Ronald Reagan against Jimmy Carter, a stunner for aging idealists who had been "Clean for Gene." But in each era, deep feelings about social justice at home and an unpopular war abroad produced candidates who were not so different in content, yet different enough in form and style to generate conflict among intimate allies. McCarthy/Obama came to symbolize hope because they were new and unknown, while Kennedy/Clinton seemed like pragmatists just because they had been near power. In fact, all four were both.

I FLED THIS UNCIVIL civil war and went to California, where Cesar Chavez and his United Farm Workers had asked me to help get the word out about the consumer boycott that they hoped would pressure growers into giving farmworkers the same rights as other workers. And it was Cesar and his main organizer, Dolores Huerta, who reminded me of what I'd learned in India: the clearest view is always from the bottom. Kennedy's compassion, his peculiar ability

to identify with the excluded, was far more important than whether he had declared before or after
a New Hampshire primary. Only Bobby Kennedy
had supported the farm workers' strike, even though
the growers were key Democratic contributors.
Only Bobby Kennedy had credentials and a track
record acceptable to the Latino and African American nation-within-a-nation.

At home in New York a month later, I turned
on the television to see Bobby Kennedy delivering
the news of Martin Luther King, Jr.'s, murder to a
largely black crowd in Indianapolis. Security forces
and his own campaign staff had urged him not to
be the one to tell this volatile crowd, but he went on
stage anyway. He stood quietly at the microphone
until the crowd understood something was wrong—
and quieted, too. Then he announced the death of
Martin Luther King. Over cries and shouts, he just
kept on talking in a low voice—about King's legacy
as a man dedicated to "love and justice," about the
white man who shot him and had been caught, and
about the country's choice now between revenge and
healing.

Finally he said, "For those of you who are black
and are tempted to be filled with hatred and mistrust . . . I had a member of my family killed . . . by
a white man."

There was silence. Then applause that went on
and on.

—

LESS THAN TWO MONTHS later, just after a victory in the California and South Dakota primaries probably would have given Bobby Kennedy the Democratic nomination, a self-described Arab nationalist assassinated him as he left a victory speech in Los Angeles. From a hotel room on the road, I had been watching Kennedy's speech and the familiar faces of friends like Dolores Huerta and Rafer Johnson, who were celebrating with him. Then there were shots, his body on the concrete floor . . . I just kept watching. Seeing the same lethal scenes over and over again had become a form of national mourning.

WITH MCCARTHY ONCE AGAIN the only antiwar candidate, Clay Felker suggested that I join the press corps on his campaign plane and write a piece for **New York** magazine titled "Trying to Love Eugene."[2] Truthfully, that's what I and many others were trying to do.

Flying to four states in five days, I saw a traveling political culture that would prepare me for many campaigns to come. First, the candidate's staff was divided into professional pragmatists and true believers, with each group worrying about the other's influence on the candidate. Second, there were locals at every stop who were good or not so good at getting the right crowds to disparate events in venues that were a little too small, so reporters would write, "Speaking to an overflow crowd . . ." Third, there were journalists themselves, a traveling press corps who hid their emotions under the armor of objectivity, and jockeyed for a seat next to the candidate with the goal of getting some unique tidbit before filing time.

As the lowest person on this journalistic totem pole—a position I hoped was unrelated to the fact that I was also the only woman—I had just one turn at the seat next to McCarthy. Since his political appeal was based on opposing LBJ's war, I asked what I'd been wondering: **Was he glad now that he hadn't become LBJ's vice president?** "Yes," he said ambiguously, "vice presidents don't have much influence on policy." If he had been chosen as he once sought to be, could he still be a peace candidate? There was a long pause. In an earlier interview, I'd asked another question when he failed to answer a first one. Now I'd figured out that the key to getting an answer was to outwait him. "I would have had to stay silent," he said. Nothing about protesting the war, much less resigning.

Only my question about the recent firing of some of his youthful aides elicited emotion. He was angry at press criticism of a firing that he saw as routine and justified. As McCarthy put it, "Some of them are like ski bums in summer. They ought to go home and get jobs. They just like to hang around."

I was surprised at his description of young men whose belief in him had turned a political campaign into a movement. After that interview, I began to pay more attention to the few young staffers on the plane who had survived. Unlike the enthusiasts who had been the ground troops in New Hampshire, they had adopted McCarthy's cool, his cynicism, and his disdain for emotion.

If I'd followed my instincts, I would have stopped volunteering for McCarthy the moment I met him. As soon as Bobby Kennedy declared, I would have worked for him instead of just escaping to California. Fear of conflict with those who supported McCarthy so fiercely had kept me from trusting what I knew.

SINCE DEMOCRATS OWNED THE Vietnam War, might a Republican president be able to end it sooner? Addressing this question was my **New York** assignment on a next long journal-keeping trip on the campaign plane of Richard Nixon. It had taken three murders—Martin Luther King, Jr., and two Kennedys—to leave the country with this choice between Nixon and Hubert Humphrey. Neither one spoke for the national majority that was now against the war in Vietnam. This choice marked the low point in my campaigning life until then.

After an eight-day cross-continental campaign trip, our planeload of journalists and campaign staff ended up in Tampa, where Florida governor Claude Kirk had filled an auditorium with patriotic banners and bleachers full of chanting Nixon supporters. Even sitting in the elevated press section overlooking the floor, we could barely see each other above the balloons and banners and choreographed enthusiasm. Resuming a game that the press corps had invented to stay attentive while Nixon gave The Speech, Max Frankel of **The New York Times** tossed us a note: "$1 reward still available for the first black face." It was a tough dollar to win.

Behind us, a choir began to sing "The Battle Hymn of the Republic." Its lyrics by abolitionist Julia Ward Howe celebrated an end to war and "the grapes of wrath" if one listened carefully—which no one did. The familiar music didn't quite sink in for a moment, but when it did, some of the armor of objectivity began to crack in the male reporters around me. "They shouldn't sing Bobby's favorite hymn," said a reporter softly. "It doesn't belong to them."

Suddenly I felt tears welling up. It was as if we were surrounded by resentful, neighbor-fearing people—or rather by good people whose neighbor-fearing instincts were being played upon—and these ungenerous ones were going to win, and not just this election but the power to impose themselves, here and in many other countries, for a long dark time to come. I had got through funerals, the brutal streets of Chicago in 1968, and much personal sadness dry-eyed, but this ridiculous rally in Tampa was too much. It wasn't the victory of one man or even the death of another. It was the resentment of those who feared the new majority that the civil rights and antiwar movements and rebellious women were creating. As I wrote then: **We might be rather old before the conservers left and compassionate men came back.**

—

As I would learn in the years to follow, I hadn't guessed the half of it. Then, even Nixon supported the Equal Rights Amendment and allowed his Justice Department to support civil rights, much as Goldwater and later the first President Bush did. But by the time of Bush II, none of those earlier candidates could have made it past Republican primaries inundated with busloads of voters from about thirty thousand fundamentalist churches plus other white ultraconservatives, many of whom had been Democrats before that party got "too inclusive" of black, brown, and female human beings. Nor could any remaining liberal or centrist Republicans run on a right-wing national platform shaped by the likes of Senator Jesse Helms, the famously racist and formerly Democratic senator from North Carolina, who long opposed sanctions against apartheid South Africa. He had been among the first to abandon the Democratic Party and become a Republican, out of anger at the Civil Rights Act of 1964. Certainly, President Eisenhower, who had warned against the military-industrial complex, would have had no place in the party anymore.

Slowly, control of the Republican platform and most primaries was taken over by economic and religious interests that opposed efforts to increase equality by race, sex, class, or sexuality.[3] They would become more entrenched in opposition to the Clinton era, and more still in the Obama one. A right-wing and supposedly populist group called the Tea Party—supported by such rich hyperconservatives as the Koch brothers—would make the Republican Party so extreme that much of its platform wouldn't have been supported in public opinion polls by most Republicans. This in turn encouraged some Democrats to become more money-hungry and cautious in the name of winning.

I would watch as Republican women especially— who once could say that their party was the first to support the Equal Rights Amendment and was as good or better on equality than the Democrats— swelled the ranks of independents, or quit politics, or were turned off by Democratic women who condemned them for ever having been Republicans.

When I was campaigning on the road and meeting with Republican or independent women, what I tried to say was: **You didn't leave your party. Your party left you. Forget about party labels. Just vote on the issues and for candidates who support equality.**

II.

IF I WAS ALREADY HOOKED ON POLITICS AND CAMpaigning before Bella Abzug's 1970 campaign for Congress, I was mainlining after it. Bella was the first woman I campaigned for. Smart, brave, and larger than life, a one-woman movement, she dared to run for Congress from Manhattan at a time when many feminists were still demonstrating against Congress.

We had first met in the mid-1960s at an anti–Vietnam War demonstration outside the Pentagon, and I had been put off by her brashness. I'd never seen a female human so free of any need to be lady-like. Then, when we were both volunteering in the 1965 New York mayoralty campaign of John Lindsay, I saw her warmth, kindness, and political skill. Gradually, it dawned on me that my first response had been my problem, not hers.

As I got to know Bella, I learned that as a young lawyer she had taken a civil rights case so unpopular that she had been forced to sleep in bus stations in Mississippi. No hotel would give her shelter, and black families, while grateful for her intervention on behalf of Willie McGee, a black man accused of raping a white woman, would have been endangered. An all-white jury had sentenced him to death after deliberating two and a half minutes, and Bella pursued an appeal that delayed the death penalty. Yet after eight years in jail, he would be executed, still protesting his innocence.

She was also a pioneer activist against nuclear testing, and a leader in the global women's peace movement. Ironically, Bella was once rejected as a spokeswoman for Women Strike for Peace. Despite being happily married and the mother of two daughters, her image wasn't "motherly" enough.

Altogether she was a great example of expanding beyond the usual candidate supply lines, and into social justice movements. She didn't just respond to public opinion; she changed it. She didn't put her finger to the wind; she became the wind.

She also had an ego as big as her heart, and believed, as did her husband, Martin Abzug, that she should be president. Yet she had a sense of humor about herself. When I was organizing fund-raisers for her in the same liberal suburbs that had supported Gene McCarthy, I had to tell her that her candidacy wasn't being well received there. "Of course not," she said. "I'm everything they moved to the suburbs to escape." As the daughter of an immigrant Jewish butcher from the Bronx, she explained, she was a class step down, but McCarthy, a very un-Jewish silver-haired poet from Minnesota, was a class step up. She said this as cheerfully as she talked about beating boys at street marbles, or going to college on the subway with a liverwurst sandwich prepared by her mother for lunch, or loving the name of her father's store, the Live and Let Live Butcher Shop.

It was great to work with Bella. For one thing, I no longer had to give my suggestions to the man sitting next to me in order to have them taken seriously. For another, I wasn't banished from strategy meetings by someone saying, "No broads." Even walking in the street with her was an education. Truck drivers leaned out of their cabs to yell, "Give 'em hell, Bella!" Women stopped to say she made them feel proud. Neighbors asked if she could help them with a harassing landlord or a new child care center.

In a very New York way, she reminded me of the Gandhians walking through villages.

In that first congressional race, her opponent was Barry Farber, a conservative radio talk show host whose main asset was his ability to talk endlessly about anything.[4] She beat him by going to supermarkets and subway stops, and listening as well as talking. She was elected to Congress in 1970, as a war raged in Vietnam, and Richard Nixon was in the White House. It was hard to imagine any two people more different than Bella and Nixon. Indeed, after the Watergate scandal broke, she would become one of the first members of Congress to call for his impeachment.

A YEAR AFTER HER ELECTION, Bella, Shirley Chisholm, and their sister congresswoman, Patsy Mink from Hawaii, decided to hurry history along. Though this new wave of feminism had many groups working on issues, there was no nationwide organization to advance them all by getting more pro-equality women into elected and appointed office. It was clear that neither the Republican nor the Democratic Party would do this on its own. Indeed, both parties doubted there were women who could win elections or be "qualified" for appointments.

When Bella, Shirley, and Patsy called a dozen or so of us into a congressional meeting room to talk about founding a new national organization, I felt as if we were already breaking barriers just by being there. It was the first of many such meetings. Our job was to research a few hundred names for a founding meeting that would include women from new feminist groups as well as such established ones as the YWCA, the National Council of Negro Women, and the National Council of Jewish Women. All this needed to be done yesterday if we were to form a national group that could have an impact on the upcoming 1972 elections.

Washington can be so hot that the British Embassy once gave its workers extra pay for working in a tropical climate. It was that kind of July in 1971, when 320 diverse women began arriving for three days of big meetings and nights of caucuses. I'm not sure any of us ever left the hotel to see the light of day. We were saved from chaos by the creative chairing of Aileen Hernandez, a labor organizer who had been the first African American and first woman on the Equal Employment Opportunity Commission, and also the first African American president of NOW. We voted to call ourselves the National Women's Political Caucus (NWPC); to have a structure that included state, city, and local caucuses; to be multipartisan; and to adopt a statement of purpose that opposed sexism, racism, institutional violence, and poverty through the election and appointment of pro-equality women to political office.

I was elected to a temporary twenty-four-member policy council along with Bella, Betty Friedan, Shirley Chisholm, Fannie Lou Hamer, Dorothy Height,

Beulah Sanders from the National Welfare Rights Organization, Native American leader LaDonna Harris, and many more. Our job was to initiate state and city caucuses and to meet with those already forming by contagion just from reading news reports of the NWPC. I traveled to a dozen states, from familiar California to unfamiliar Tennessee. All this happened so fast that once, I was plucked off a train from New York to Philadelphia at the wrong stop by a group that thought it should be the NWPC affiliate, not the one meeting me at the next stop. Fortunately, the two groups later merged.

At home, I went to the founding of the Manhattan Women's Political Caucus, where at least six hundred women showed up for a daylong meeting chaired by Eleanor Holmes Norton, then the head of New York City's commission on human rights. At least a third of those attending were black, Latina, Asian, and more. It was the only meeting I'd ever seen in Manhattan that looked like Manhattan.

Once chapters were established and a structure was in place, NWPC's goal was to increase the number and diversity of women delegates to both the Republican and Democratic National Conventions of 1972, and to get the Equal Rights Amendment, reproductive freedom, and other basic issues of equality written into both parties' platforms. It was a task worthy of years. By the time all the state chapters of the NWPC were up and running, the first convention was less than two months away.

At that Democratic Convention held in July in

Miami, political women were in the national spotlight for the first time since suffrage. All of us were some mixture of excited and scared. Conventions then were still working meetings at which critical decisions were made, not just televised political showcases. We needed places where hundreds of women delegates could gather each morning to make such tactical decisions as whether to challenge the seating of unrepresentative delegations, plus fighting for minority platform planks, answering media queries, and other daily dilemmas on which our fates might rest. In addition to Bella, Shirley, and other leaders, the NWPC had elected one spokeswoman for each party's convention so the press and other outsiders would know who to go to.

That job sounded like the last thing I wanted to do, so I had asked not to be nominated and stayed away from an earlier NWPC meeting where those elections were to happen. Unfortunately, as I learned, a reluctant spokeswoman was considered more likely to represent the group, while an eager one might seek the spotlight. Betty Friedan was at the meeting and among those campaigning to be elected, but I was elected in absentia. As I was to learn, avoiding conflict causes conflict to seek you out.

And conflict there was. I'd seen Friedan only in group meetings. Contrary to myth, all feminists don't know each other, and we were differnt ages and from different parts of a diverse movement. I understood that running for spokeswoman and losing would be painful for anyone, but especially for Friedan. Having written **The Feminine Mystique,** a sanity-saving book for millions of college-educated homemakers in the suburbs who were feeling, **There must be more to life than this,** she had been crowned "the Mother Superior to Women's Lib" by **The New York Times.** Earlier that summer, when she hadn't been reelected to an NWPC position, she had threatened to sue and sent a lawyer to examine the ballots; but no irregularities were found.

She also took it personally when Bella Abzug said she didn't want to replace "a white, male, middle-class elite with a white, female, middle-class elite." I agreed with Bella and thought it was okay to say since that description fit us, too. We were explaining we wanted to transform the system, not imitate it. Still, Betty yelled at Bella for being anti-elite, and yelled at me for inviting my speaking partner, Flo Kennedy, to the founding meeting of the NWPC. She feared that Flo would "mau-mau" the meeting, though actually Flo set a unifying tone. Also, Friedan had made clear in the media for several years that she thought Bella, Kate Millett, I, and others were damaging the movement by supporting the issues of lesbians, welfare mothers, and others she regarded as outside the mainstream. As Betty wrote in **The New York Times,** "The disrupters of the women's movement were the ones continually trying to push lesbianism or hatred of men, even though many weren't lesbians themselves and didn't act privately as if they

hated men." Together with Flo Kennedy, Kate Millett, Robin Morgan, and others, I was named one of
the disrupters.[5]

Betty's antipathy to Bella, me, and others would
persist for years to come. For instance, all of us
who started **Ms.** magazine were fine with the financial sacrifice and fund-raising that required, but we
were shocked to find ourselves accused by Friedan
of "profiteering off the movement." Most painful to
me, Friedan refused to shake my mother's hand when
Millie Jeffrey, a leader of labor union women, tried
to introduce them. Bella and I each handled this hostility in our own way. Bella once literally damaged
her vocal cords by shouting back at Betty, and as a
result Friedan attacked her less. I never responded in
person or print, on the grounds that it would only
feed the stereotype that women couldn't get along,
so Friedan wasn't afraid of me and attacked more.
Truthfully and in retrospect, I was avoiding conflict.
I was being my mother's daughter. I needed a teacher
in surviving conflict, and Friedan was definitely it.

When the Democratic convention was about to
meet in Miami, I was worried about private tensions
turning public, not only with Bella and me, but with
such rising stars as Sissy Farenthold, a Texas legislator who was among Friedan's rivals for the leadership of the NWPC. This tension was symbolized
by the distance between the posh oceanfront hotel
where many Democratic officials, media people, and
Friedan were staying, and the tacky motel where
NWPC headquarters were located and where most

of us slept. As Nora Ephron would report, "Every day, Friedan would call N.W.P.C. headquarters at the dingy Betsy Ross Hotel downtown and threaten to call a press conference to expose the caucus; every day . . . movement leaders would watch with a kind of horrified fascination to see what Betty Friedan would do next."

But women's new presence and activism in and around that convention created enough good news to make up for all the worry. More than a third of the delegates were women—up from 13 percent four years earlier—surpassing even Eleanor Roosevelt's record of 15 percent in 1936; not her (or our) goal of 50/50, but a record. There was a strong women's plank in the platform, where four years ago there had been none. Our only serious failure was our inability to get a plank supporting reproductive freedom included—because Senator George McGovern, the probable nominee, feared running on it. Still, it was the first time this human right had been raised as an issue and voted on by a major party.

We also saw our NWPC co-founder Shirley Chisholm receive a roll call vote of 151 delegates for her symbolic run for political equality and against the Vietnam War, which she had opposed in her first speech in Congress.[6] Shirley's mere presence in the race brought the NWPC goals to national attention, and although her total campaign budget was probably what other presidential campaigns spent on take-out food, she had just kept going. Indeed, she might have received more delegate votes if McGovern hadn't passed the victory point before the roll call was completed.

Even Theodore White, a chronicler of presidential campaigns who was rarely interested in the non-powerful, reported that the NWPC had put women on the political map. About our impoverished headquarters at what he called the "derelict" Betsy Ross Hotel, he wrote: "One might be amused by the high-octave span of women's voices gathered together, or the rooms with the unmade beds, half-unpacked suitcases, yogurt cartons, chests covered with blue jeans and bras—but only briefly. The Betsy Ross Hotel was a power center. Mimeograph and Xerox machines spewed out leaflets . . . the switchboard jammed; fuses blew; and each night, after dark, couriers boarded buses to travel north on Collins Avenue and persuade night clerks of the forty or more major hotels to stuff mailboxes or let them slip leaflets under delegates' doors. . . . When the convention broke up, women power 1972 was real."

That was the beginning of campaigning from inside a movement rather than on a candidate's turf. Up until then I had supported campaigns by writing about them or volunteering in them. Now I was learning that the best way to help was to strengthen the movements that embody principles, so those movements could themselves generate support for the candidates who voted for those principles. More than any volunteer or staff member inside a candidate's race—or any journalist or activist making points from outside—a movement can pioneer new issues and motivate voters. As Bella always knew, you didn't just ask for support, you created support—from what Bella named "the gender gap." Women of all groups were measurably more likely than their male counterparts to vote for equality, health, and education, and against violence as a way of solving conflict. It wasn't about biology, but experience.

IN 1984 I SAW WHAT I wasn't sure I ever would: a woman as the vice-presidential candidate on a major party ticket, not just a symbol but someone who had a chance of winning. Geraldine Ferraro was no older or more conflict-loving than I, yet she had survived political opposition and media attacks by campaigning from the bottom up. In fact, she would travel more miles around the country than her presidential running mate, Walter Mondale, and twice as many as their opponents, Ronald Reagan and George Bush, combined.

I noticed that she was supported by everyday citizens who gathered in halls large and small. Even at the Democratic Convention in San Francisco, she traded an elite, high-level reception for a populist event organized by the NWPC, and stood on a huge stage surrounded by women elected leaders—a category that couldn't have filled a small room a few years before. Parents put their little girls on their shoulders to see the future, and more than a few women were in tears. They weren't witnessing one woman's win, but what they, too, could become.

And Ferraro would need their support. At every stop, Catholic officials condemned her for supporting family planning and legal abortion. I noticed they hadn't attacked Senator Ted Kennedy, also a pro-choice Catholic, in the same way—as if tacitly admitting that it was strong, rebellious women who were the problem. Also reporters kept asking Ferraro if a woman could be "tough enough" to "push the button," meaning declare a war, though they didn't ask male candidates if they could be wise enough not to. Forests of newsprint were spent on her hair, though not on Reagan's obviously dyed and sprayed pompadour. Barbara Bush told reporters that Ferraro was something that couldn't be said on television but "rhymes with rich." Most of all, Ferraro was accused of profiting from questionable real estate dealings by her husband, a charge that seemed partly attached to their Italian names. Such accusations subsided only after she spent hours answering questions until even reporters ran out of things to ask.

At a campaign rally in Pennsylvania, I'd climbed onto a makeshift stage to stand at the side with other reporters, all of us awaiting Ferraro's arrival. I was amazed to get cheers from this big and diverse audience. When Ferraro mounted the stage, she also got cheers—but fewer and not as loud. How could this be? She was making history, and I was not. I said so to an experienced reporter. He looked at me as if I'd said there was oxygen in the air. "Americans don't like politicians much," he explained patiently. "And if they do trust Ferraro, they credit the women's movement—and you're part of that."

This really drove home for me that in the future, any of us who were recognizable as part of a social justice movement had to use ourselves to support the candidates we believed in. However controversial our movements might be, at least voters know that they stand for principles. Being backed by one was a signal that politicians are not all alike.

In the beginning of my campaigning movement style, I thought, **It's as if fate has sent me a good experience so I'll keep showing up.** And there kept on being more and more terrific women to show up for in the years that followed. Indeed, 1992 came to be called the Year of the Woman, though as Senator Barbara Mikulski pointed out, "We're not a fad, a fancy, or a year." Later, she would prove her point by being elected five times and serving thirty years.

That quantum 1992 leap in the number of women in Congress was born out of the aftermath of the Clarence Thomas confirmation hearings. Watching the dignified Anita Hill face an all-white and all-male Senate Judiciary Committee—and then seeing Thomas confirmed for the Supreme Court—had inspired more women to be elected to Congress in that single year than had been elected in any previous decade—though they still made up only a little over 10 percent of a body that should have been more like 50/50. This record wouldn't be surpassed until 2013, with 20 women in the Senate and 81 in the House.

But the most widespread and lasting impact of the Senate Judiciary hearings was not the Year of the Woman—and perhaps not even the ascension to the Supreme Court of a very right-wing and young Clarence Thomas, likely to be there for a long time; it was the new national understanding of sexualized intimidation as a means of keeping females in a subordinate place. The whole country learned that sexual harassment was illegal. Millions of women learned they were not alone in their experience of it. The use of sex to humiliate and dominate would never seem normal again.

III.

AS LONG AS I'VE BEEN CAMPAIGNING, I'VE HEARD two questions: "When will we have a woman president?" and "When will we have a black president?"

Ironically, the 2008 primary campaign between Hillary Clinton and Barack Obama, which gave us the chance for both, was the best contest in terms of candidates and the worst in terms of conflict.

I knew Hillary Clinton mostly in the way we all do, as a public figure in good times and bad, one who became part of our lives and even our dreams. I once introduced her to a thousand women in a hotel ballroom at a breakfast in New York City. Standing behind her as she spoke, I could see the White House binder on the lectern with her speech carefully laid out—and also that she wasn't reading from it. Instead, she was responding to people who had spoken before her, addressing activists and leaders she saw in the audience, and putting their work in a national and global context—all in such clear and graceful sentences that no one would have guessed she hadn't written them in advance. It was an on-the-spot tour de force, perhaps the best I've ever heard.

But what clinched it for me was listening to her speak after a performance of Eve Ensler's play **Necessary Targets,** based on interviews with women in one of the camps set up to treat women who had endured unspeakable suffering, humiliation, and torture in the ethnic wars within the former Yugoslavia. To speak to an audience that had just heard these heartbreaking horrors seemed impossible for anyone, and Hillary had the added burden of representing the Clinton administration, which had been criticized for slowness in stopping this genocide.

Nonetheless, she rose in the silence, with no possibility of preparing, and began to speak quietly—about suffering, about the importance of serving as witnesses to suffering. Most crucial of all, she admitted this country's slowness in intervening. By the time she sat down, she had brought the audience together and given us all a shared meeting place: the simple truth.

So when she left the White House and decided to

run for the U.S. Senate from her new home in New York State—something no First Lady, not even Eleanor Roosevelt, had dared to do—I was blindsided by the hostility toward her from some women. They called her cold, calculating, ambitious, and even "unfeminist" for using political experience gained as a wife. These were not the right-wing extremists who had accused the Clintons of everything from perpetrating real estate scams in Arkansas to murdering a White House aide with whom Hillary supposedly had an affair. On the contrary, they mostly agreed with her on the issues, yet some were so opposed to her that they came to be called Hillary Haters. It took me weeks of listening on the road to begin to understand why.

In living rooms from Dallas to Chicago, I noticed that the Hillary Haters often turned out to be the women most like her: white, well educated, and married to or linked with powerful men. They were by no means all such women, but their numbers were still surprising. Also they hadn't objected to sons, brothers, and sons-in-law using family connections and political names to further careers—say, the Bushes or the Rockefellers or the Kennedys—yet they objected to Hillary doing the same. The more they talked, the more it was clear that their own husbands hadn't shared power with them. If Hillary had a husband who regarded her as an equal—who had always said this country got "two presidents for the price of one"—it only dramatized their own lack of power and respect. After one long night and a lot of wine, one woman told me that Hillary's marriage made her aware of just how unequal hers was.

In San Francisco and Seattle, I listened to self-identified Hillary Haters condemn her for staying with her husband, despite his well-publicized affairs. It turned out that many of them had suffered a faithless husband, too, but lacked the ability or the will to leave. They wanted Hillary to punish a powerful man in public on their behalf. I reminded them that presidents from Roosevelt to Kennedy had affairs, but the haters identified with those First Ladies and assumed they couldn't leave. It was Hillary's very strength and independence that made them blame her. When I tried describing the public condemnation Hillary would have suffered had she abandoned her duties in the White House for such a personal reason, this changed the minds of some—but not many.

Finally, I resorted to explaining my own reasons for thinking the Clintons just might be, in Shakespeare's phrase, "the marriage of true minds." I had seen them together for a long afternoon during a White House ceremony for recipients of the Medal of Freedom. One medalist was my friend Wilma Mankiller, chief of the Cherokee Nation. She and I were both struck by the obvious connection between the Clintons as they walked from one group of awardees and their families to the next, talking to guests and each other. In a roomful of interesting people, they seemed just as interested in listening and talking to each other. What they were sharing,

I don't know, but what was clear was their intimacy and pleasure in each other's company. Of how many long-married couples could that be said?

Yet when I brought this up, some Hillary Haters became even angrier. Many were longtime wives and others were new wives replacing older ones, but the fact that Bill valued Hillary as an equal partner—and vice versa—seemed to make them more aware that their own marriages were different. It dawned on me that if a sexual connection is the only bond between a husband and wife, an affair can make her feel replaceable—and perhaps cause her to be replaced. This was not only emotionally painful but devastating when it also meant losing social identity and economic security as well. I began to understand that Hillary represented the very public, in-your-face opposite of the precarious and unequal lives that some women were living. In a classic sense, they were trying to kill the messenger.

Their projections made me realize that I was projecting, too. I couldn't understand why Hillary wanted to go back to Washington, and so campaigned for the Senate in the first place. After eight years in the White House with political piranhas circling, and every move accompanied by hostile lawsuits and media attacks—from ultra-right-wing groups spending unlimited money on anti-Clinton conspiracy theories—why ask for six more years in the Senate with a target painted on her back? It seemed quixotic and self-punishing, especially now that she had such great alternatives as creating her

own foundation, and supporting female empower-
ment globally.

Finally, I had to admit that the latter would have
been my choice, not hers. If she was willing to face
a degree of combat that I couldn't even imagine, I
should celebrate.

As my own part of her Senate campaign, I began to
invite Hillary Haters to the living room events where
Hillary herself was fund-raising. To my surprise, all
but a few turned around once they had spent time
in her presence. This woman they had imagined as
smart, cold, and calculating turned out to be smart,
warm, and responsive. Instead of someone who
excused a husband's behavior, she was potentially, as
one said, "a great girlfriend" who had their backs.

They also saw her expertise. For instance, George
Soros, the Hungarian-born financier and philan-
thropist, introduced her in his Manhattan living
room by saying, "Hillary knows more about Eastern
Europe than any other American."

After she was elected to the U.S. Senate on her
own merits, she worked constructively, even with
old enemies there, and was solidly reelected to a second term. I began to hear the first serious talk of
Hillary Clinton as a presidential candidate. By the
time the election of 2008 was in the wind, she had
a higher popularity rating than any other potential
candidate, Republican or Democrat.

Meanwhile, I knew from campaigning in Illinois
with Voters for Choice that a young two-term state
legislator named Barack Obama had helped defeat

a bill designed to weaken **Roe v. Wade** there. But when I went to the 2004 Democratic Convention in Boston, I was as surprised as the rest of the country to watch his inspirational blockbuster of a speech. His rise was much more like a movement event than politics as usual.

After his election to the U.S. Senate, Obama appeared at a living room fund-raiser in Manhattan to celebrate, and to help pay off his campaign debt. I watched as supporters urged him to disobey traditional rules for a freshman senator and refuse to follow the quiet example of the newly elected. He was reluctant, citing his need to learn and the power of the Bush presidency. I urged him, too. After all, everybody knew that George W. Bush would never have become president without his family, and everybody also knew that Obama had become senator against all odds.

By the following year, progressive forces looking for a new candidate—not just in the Senate but for the presidency—were approaching him with offers to, as Obama said, "drink the Kool-Aid." Though he resisted at first, the draft effort gradually became a movement with a life of its own. Though such African American leaders as Congresswoman Shirley Chisholm and Reverend Jesse Jackson had run, Obama became the first with a serious chance of being a major-party candidate. Together, he and Hillary could turn this election into the first in history with candidates who looked like the country. It wasn't campaign season yet, but wherever I went, from campuses to living rooms, questions about the possibility of a new kind of president were being raised.

Though Obama was younger, with less national, international, and Senate experience than Hillary, I still thought it was too soon for the country to accept a woman commander in chief. Moreover, Obama's Kennedyesque appeal created a rare and precious chance to break the racial barrier. But to me, their shared content was way more important than different forms. She was a civil rights advocate. He was a feminist. They were a modern-day echo of the abolitionist and suffragist era, when black men, black women, and white women—the groups white male supremacists had worked so hard and cruelly to keep apart—turned this country on its head by working together for universal adult suffrage.

Whenever I was on the road before the primaries, I saw a revival of this unconscious coalition in audiences that were interested in politics as never before. There was enthusiasm for these two new faces that stood for a shared worldview. In audiences from very blue states to very red ones, support was more like a Rorschach test than a division by race and sex. For instance, 94 percent of black Democrats had a favorable view of Hillary Clinton, compared to an 88 percent favorable view of Obama. After all, he was new on the national stage and the Clintons had earned a reputation for racial inclusiveness that caused African American novelist Toni Morrison to famously call Bill Clinton "the first black president." Both white and black women were more likely than their male counterparts to support Hillary Clinton—and in my observation, also more likely to believe that she couldn't win. Male and female black voters were more likely than white voters to support Obama and also to believe he couldn't win. Each group was made pessimistic by the depth of the bias they had experienced.

Some mostly white audiences seemed to hope this country could expiate past sins by electing Obama. As one white music teacher rose in an audience to say, "Racism puts me in prison, too—a prison of guilt." Many parents of little girls, black and white, were taking them to Clinton rallies so they would know that they, too, could be president. Older women especially saw Hillary Clinton as their last and best chance to see a woman in the White House. And not just any woman:[7] as one said, "This isn't just about biology. We don't want a Margaret Thatcher, who cut off milk for schoolchildren." They wanted Hillary Clinton because she supported the majority interests of women. On the other hand, many young black single mothers said they supported Obama because their sons needed a positive black male role model. A divorced white father told me that Obama's life story had inspired him to drive hundreds of miles to see his son every week. "I don't want to be the father Obama almost never saw," he explained. "I want to be the father he wished he had." In Austin, Texas, an eighty-year-old black woman said she was supporting Hillary because "I've seen too many women who earned it, and too many young men who came along and took it."

But the press, instead of reporting on these shared and often boundary-crossing views as an asset for the Democratic Party—after all, Democratic voters would have to unify around one of these candidates eventually—responded with disappointment and even condescension. They seemed to want news-worthy division. Soon frustrated reporters were creating conflict by turning any millimeter of dif-ference between Hillary Clinton and Barack Obama into a mile. Since there was almost none in content, they emphasized ones of form. Clinton was entirely summed up by sex, and Obama was entirely summed up by race. Journalists sounded like sports fans who arrived for a football game and were outraged to find all the players on the same team.

It dawned on me that in the abolitionist and suf-fragist past, a universal suffragist movement of black men and white and black women also had been consciously divided by giving the vote to black men only—and then limiting even that with violence, impossible literacy tests, and poll taxes. Now, this echo of divide-and-conquer in the past was polar-izing the constituencies of two barrier-breaking "firsts," never mind that the candidates were almost identical in content. As in history, a potentially pow-erful majority was being divided by an entrenched powerful few.

Maybe attributing a divide-and-conquer motive was unfair in a country that treats everything like a horse race, but there had to be some reason why the press did not consider what I witnessed on the road—delight in two "firsts" with similar purpose—worth reporting.

Soon, a person or a group's choice of one candidate was assumed to be a condemnation of the other. I could feel fissures opening up between people who had been allies on issues for years. The long knives of reporters—plus a few shortsighted partisans in both campaigns—deepened those fissures until they bled.

To make a case for linking racism and sexism instead of ranking them—and for unifying around one of these two firsts in the national election—I wrote a **New York Times** op-ed titled "Coalition vs. Competition."[8] I called either/or media questions "dumb and destructive," since the two candidates were so much the same on issues. Also, it was way too soon to know who could survive the primaries, so I ended this way: "We could double our chances by working for one of these candidates, not against the other. For now, I've figured out how to answer reporters when they ask if I'm supporting Hillary Clinton or Barack Obama. I just say yes."

As the New York primary approached, I certainly wasn't against either candidate, but I still had to decide who to vote for. So I sat down with a yellow pad and made a list of pros and cons for each. On the issues, there were differences of emphasis, but both wanted a country in which individual futures were not limited by sex or race, class or sexuality. Both advocated a foreign policy that was less about oil and support for dictators and more about support for democracies and the environment. Hillary had voted in the Senate for the first U.S. military action in Iraq—and some Obama supporters were making much of that—but Obama himself was honest enough to say that had he been in the Senate at that time and given the same false information about Iraq's "weapons of mass destruction," he didn't know how he would have voted. The only obvious difference was experience. As a partner, Hillary Clinton had spent twelve years in state government, eight in the White House, plus eight more on her own in the U.S. Senate—all of them fighting the right-wing extremists who controlled what once was the Republican Party; the next president would face the same opposition. Obama had crucial multicultural experience growing up, time spent as an organizer in Chicago that meant a lot to me, seven years in a state legislature, three years in the U.S. Senate, but much less experience fighting and being attacked by the political ultra-right wing. Both the good and the bad news was that he was a peacemaker and skilled in the art of finding a middle path. This primary race was a rare case in which the female candidate was more experienced in big-time political conflict than the male candidate. She was more familiar with extremists for whom there was no middle ground.

I knew that outside the women's movement, I would be better liked if I chose Obama. Women are always better liked if we sacrifice ourselves for something bigger—and **something bigger** always means including men, even though **something bigger** for men doesn't usually mean including women. In choosing Hillary, I would be seen as selfish for supporting a woman "like" me. But that was a warning, too. Needing approval is a female cultural disease, and often a sign of doing the wrong thing.

There was one more note on my yellow pad. Because I still believed it was too soon for Hillary or any woman to be accepted as commander in chief, I wrote: **If I were Obama, I would not feel personally betrayed by lack of support from someone like me, a new ally. If I were Hillary Clinton, I might feel betrayed by a longtime supporter who left me for a new face.** In other words: Obama didn't need me to win. Hillary Clinton might need me to lose.

ONCE AGAIN THE ROAD educated me—by showing me what voters were subjected to. I began to think that the wait for a female president might be even longer than I imagined. At airport gift shops, a nutcracker made to look like Hillary Clinton was sold as an election novelty. Her legs were handles, and her crotch was the place for cracking nuts. When I asked a sales clerk in the Washington, D.C., airport if there were complaints, she said yes, there had been a few, but it was selling well. When I asked her if there were similar nutcrackers of the male candidates, she said, "Certainly not!"

On campuses, I saw young men wearing T-shirts that said TOO BAD O.J. DIDN'T MARRY HILLARY. All the wearers I saw were white. When I asked students what they thought about this slogan, they agreed it was uncool. They assured me most guys just put on their T-shirts and Facebook pages BROS BEFORE HOS.

I watched as MSNBC political analyst Tucker Carlson said of Hillary Clinton, "I have often said when she comes on television, I involuntarily cross my legs." I thought: **No wonder that nutcracker is selling well.** Also on MSNBC, Chris Matthews announced, "Let's not forget—and I'll be brutal— the reason she's a U.S. senator, the reason she's a candidate for president, the reason she may be a frontrunner, is her husband messed around. That's how she got to be senator from New York. We keep forgetting it. She didn't win there on her merit."[9]

A woman reporter for **The Washington Post** wrote about a Hillary suit jacket that disclosed a bit of cleavage and called it "a provocation." No such charge had been leveled at male presidential candidates, from John F. Kennedy to Obama, when they were photographed on the beach in bathing suits. About Hillary, Rush Limbaugh asked: "Will this country want to actually watch a woman get older on a daily basis?" According to another Fox News analyst, "If that's the face of experience, I think it's going to scare away a lot of those independent voters." At CNN, women correspondents told me they had been cautioned not to wear pantsuits on camera—they might look too much like Hillary.

All this reductionist commentary might have been fair game, had it been directed at all the primary candidates: say, Senator Joe Biden's obvious hair transplants; or Senator John Edwards's resemblance to a Ken doll; or Governor Mitt Romney's capped teeth and dyed hair; or Senator John McCain's special shoes to make him taller; or Governor Bill Richardson's resemblance to an unmade bed; or Senator Obama's ears, about which he himself made jokes. But it wasn't.

No wonder such misogyny was almost never named by the media. It **was** the media.

In making my list about the pluses and minuses of Hillary Clinton and Barack Obama, I discovered I was angry. I was angry because it was okay for two generations of Bush sons to inherit power from a political patriarchy even if they spent no time in the White House, but not okay for one Clinton wife to claim experience and inherit power from a husband whose full political partner she had been for twenty years. I was angry because young men in politics were treated like rising stars, but young women were treated like—well, young women. I was angry about all the women candidates who put their political skills on hold to raise children—and all the male candidates who didn't. I was angry about the human talent that was lost just because it was born into a female body, and the mediocrity that was rewarded because it was born into a male one. And I was angry because the media took racism seriously—or pretended to—but with sexism, they rarely bothered even to pretend. Resentment of women still seemed safe, whether it took the form of demonizing black single mothers or making routine jokes about powerful women being ball-busters.

In other cases of unadmitted bias, I had used the time-honored movement tactic of reversing the race or sex or ethnicity or sexuality involved, then seeing if the response would be the same. Fueled by months of repressed anger, I asked: **What might have happened if even an empathetic man like Obama had been exactly the same person—but born female?**

I called the result "A Short History of Change." **The New York Times** op-ed page changed it to "Women Are Never Front-Runners." Published on the morning of the New Hampshire primary, it asked why the sex barrier was not taken as seriously as the racial one.

> The reasons are as pervasive as the air we breathe: because sexism is still confused with nature as racism once was; because anything that affects males is seen as more serious than anything that affects "only" the female half of the human race; because children are still raised mostly by women (to put it mildly) so men especially tend to feel they are regressing to childhood when dealing with a powerful woman; because racism stereotyped black men as more "masculine" for so long that some white men find their presence to be masculinity-affirming (as long as there aren't too many of them); and

because there is still no "right" way to be a woman in public power without being considered a you-know-what.

I'm not advocating a competition for who has it toughest. The caste systems of sex and race are interdependent and can only be uprooted together. . . .

It's time to take equal pride in breaking all the barriers.

I added that I was supporting Hillary Clinton based only on her greater experience. About Obama, I wrote, "If he's the nominee, I'll volunteer. . . . To clean up the mess left by President Bush, we may need two terms of President Clinton and two of President Obama."

The first response was overwhelmingly positive. Because Hillary Clinton unexpectedly won that New Hampshire primary, my column was even given some of the credit. **The New York Times** published a letter from a voter there to that effect. It was as if I'd written what many people were thinking. Most just seemed glad that I'd spoken up about the humiliation of a good woman.

But then a few calls came in from interviewers assuming that by supporting Hillary I was ranking sex over race—despite my lifetime of arguing that sexism and racism were linked, not ranked, and despite writing in that same op-ed that the caste systems of sex and race could only be uprooted together, I was seen as asking people to take sexism more seriously than racism.

When I went on a television show, an Obama supporter, a black woman academic, accused me by saying that "white women have been complicit in the oppression of black men and black women." She talked many times more than I did, mentioned lynching, and said, "To take this kind of position in **The New York Times** struck me as the very worst of what feminism can offer." I was left saying things like "I refuse to be divided on this" and pointing out that whether Hillary or Obama won the primary, she and I would be united in the general election. Afterward I felt as if I had been hit by a Mack truck.

From then on, every morning brought new attacks. I came to dread the particular ring of my cell phone. Though I had been called many things, from a baby killer to a destroyer of the family, those had come from people with whom I really disagreed. These attacks came from people whose opinion I valued and who were accusing me of holding a position I didn't hold.

Online, I discovered part of the reason. The **Times** had used an ambiguous pull-quote to characterize the whole op-ed: "Gender is probably the most restricting force in American life, whether the question is who must be in the kitchen or who could be in the White House." I meant that in terms of pervasiveness, kitchen to White House, not that it was more—or less—important. However, I realized with a sinking heart that I should have known, in this context, that **most** is a four-letter word. Only conflict is news, and in agreeing to edits on the phone I had failed to make every sentence bulletproof. Definitely my fault. That quote was going around the world on the Web, and was seen by many more people than read the op-ed. I withdrew the whole thing from syndication by **The New York Times,** but it didn't matter. The attacks grew increasingly virulent.

ANYBODY CAN BE WITH YOU when you're right, but only friends are with you when you mess up. Many called to comfort me. At least one prominent African American woman leader said she had been asked by the Obama campaign to launch a major attack against me, and had refused. She told them I had earned the right to say what I thought.

If hard things ultimately have a purpose, then they aren't so hard anymore. Therefore, I listed what I had learned:

1. It's easy to forget that people can **think** you think what you **don't** think.

2. Don't write when you're angry and under deadline, with time to test it only on friends who know what you mean, not on strangers who don't.

3. A writer's greatest reward is naming something unnamed that many people are

feeling. A writer's greatest punishment is being misunderstood. The same words can do both.

I also thought suddenly of the wisdom of my speaking partner, the late generous, outrageous, matchless Flo Kennedy. She found value in conflict, no matter what. "The purpose of ass-kicking is not that your ass gets kicked at the right time or for the right reason," she often explained. "It's to keep your ass **sensitive**."

Remembering her words made me laugh out loud.

ONCE OBAMA WON, a few wise people in his and Hillary's campaigns—who had been in touch all along—knew there had to be a healing.

With my friend and colleague Judy Gold, who was in charge of women's issues for Obama's campaign, I planned what we knew would be the first of many healing meetings. There were heartbroken older women who now knew they would never live to see a woman in the White House. There were younger ones who had grown up being told they could be anything, then been shocked by Hillary's treatment and defeat. African American women and men who had supported Hillary also worried that some would punish them for working across racial lines. Oprah Winfrey and other women in public life who had supported Obama paid a price, too. Some criticized them for not supporting Hillary Clinton, since women were their main supporters and constituency. This was also true for Karen Mulhauser, a white woman and an important and longtime feminist leader, who supported Obama. I had written and spoken in support of their right to choose Obama, and now they, too, helped to heal the wounds of Hillary Clinton's defeat.

As my last campaign effort, I made hundreds of buttons that said:

HILLARY SUPPORTS OBAMA
SO DO I

Then I got on the plane to Washington, went to join the crowd at her historic and generous concession speech—in which she pledged her wholehearted support to Obama—and distributed the buttons to the audience. They were in great demand.

IV.

ALL MY YEARS OF CAMPAIGNING HAVE GIVEN ME ONE clear message: Voting isn't the most we can do, but it is the least. To have a democracy, you have to want one. Still, I realize this fully only by looking back.

At the beginning of the 1980s, I went to Missouri to campaign for Harriett Woods in her U.S. Senate race. She was a great candidate, and I empathized with the difficult time she'd had as a woman journalist. Her path into politics was so improbable that no one could have made it up. As a mother of two young children, she complained about a noisy manhole cover that awakened them every time a car rolled over it in her otherwise quiet street. When she got nowhere with the city council, she circulated a neighborhood petition to close the street to cars. It worked. This success led her to run for the city council. She won, served eight years, got appointed to the state highway commission, ran a successful race for the state legislature, and was reelected there, too. She also became the producer of a much-loved local television show. All this made her a viable state-wide candidate.

Still, this was not enough for the state Democratic Party. When it came time to choose a primary candidate in a U.S. Senate race, it backed a well-to-do banker who had never run for anything, just written checks. To be fair, Woods might have seemed like a lost cause in Missouri, where no woman had ever won a statewide office. She also wasn't rich like the banker. But she turned out to have something more important than her party's blessing: community support and volunteers. She beat the rich guy two to one.

Suddenly, Harriett Woods was in a race with Republican Senator John Danforth. He was not only the incumbent but a former attorney general of Missouri, an ordained Episcopal priest, and the rich grandson of the founder of Ralston Purina. It was as if she were running against the entire patriarchy.

When I went to campaign for her, I could see that

all the new feminist electoral groups were working their hearts out. So were the volunteers in her state-wide network. Though Missouri was often counted as an antichoice state, Woods refused to budge from her support for reproductive freedom.

In the end, she won in rural Republican areas anyway, including one so conservative that it was known as Little Dixie. But in the final week, she had run out of money and couldn't answer the last-minute storm of virulent attacks. She lost by less than 2 percent of the vote. This heartbreaking hairbreadth defeat drew special attention, as did the fact that she had been the only female U.S. Senate candidate in the whole country, from either party. It was so clear that she could have won with money to answer attacks that her race inspired the founding of EMILY's List, a political action committee that supports pro-choice Democratic women candidates. As proof that even failure can be turned to good purpose, this PAC went on to attract three million members and become one of the biggest in the nation, as well as the single biggest resource for women in politics.

But Danforth did win. He took with him to Washington an African American lawyer named Clarence Thomas, who had been working for Monsanto, the agrochemical giant that gave us Agent Orange, genetically engineered seeds, and more. Indeed, Danforth got him that job, too. As Danforth explained, he was very attracted to Thomas, not only because he was a rare African American conservative, but also because he, too, had studied to be a priest—in his case, a Catholic priest.

All this happened decades ago. Woods died in 2007 from leukemia at the age of seventy-nine, yet the impact of her loss by a few hundred votes goes on.

If you don't believe me, flash-forward to the morning after the 2000 Bush-versus-Gore presidential election, with national results hanging by the thread of a few thousand disputed votes in Florida.

I just happened to be speaking at Palm Beach County Community College that morning, a long-arranged event unrelated to any election, and its campus just happened to be in a poor area. I'd been asked to talk about social justice movements generally, but I could see that nobody wanted to talk about anything but the election cliffhanger that was upon us.

A young African American woman rose to say she'd registered to vote by phone, then been challenged at her polling place because "Caucasian" had been printed next to her name. She never did get to vote. An older African American man said he had been denied the right to vote because he was told he had a felony conviction, yet he'd never been accused of a crime, much less convicted of one. Someone shouted out, "Yes, you have—it's called Voting While Black!" Amid the laughter, another man stood to explain that names of people with felonies had been merged with the voter rolls without checking whether more than one person shared the same name. Then an older white woman said the bus from her retirement home had been sent to the wrong polling place. Others testified that polling places were fewer and lines were longer in poor and more Democratic areas. People had given up because they were hourly workers who lost pay if they weren't at their jobs. Then a white man of fifty or so said he'd seen the illustration of the ballot only on the way out—and realized he had accidentally voted for an extreme right-wing candidate when he thought he was voting for Al Gore. That caused a dozen more people to groan or shout out that this had also happened to them.

One by one, people in this random audience told their confusing and disenfranchising experiences. Out of the approximately seven hundred people in the auditorium, at least a hundred had been unable either to vote for their chosen candidate or to vote at all. I wondered: **If there are this many in one auditorium, how many in all of Palm Beach County? Or in the state?**

Finally, a white man of thirty or so rose to face me. In the name of his military service to his country, he said, and also of his young daughter, whom he wanted to grow up in a democracy, he asked: "Will you stay and help us organize a protest tomorrow—and the next day and the next—whatever it takes?"

I could feel a deep pull to say yes. Yet I thought my presence might be used to call this a rebellion instigated by an outsider. Instead, I promised to take the name, address, and polling place of everyone who hadn't been able to vote at all, or to vote for their chosen candidate, and give them to lawyers for Gore as well as nonpartisan watchdogs outside the state.

I went home, called election lawyers, and delivered the lists as promised. When Bush's lead was down to a mere 537 votes out of about six million cast, the reexamination of ballots was stopped. Florida's secretary of state, Katherine Harris, also the co-chair of Bush's Florida campaign, declared Bush the winner.

Calls for a recount were deafening, and supported by the Florida Supreme Court. However, the U.S. Supreme Court ruled 5 to 4 that there was no uniform recount standard to meet the equal protection clause, and no time to create one. Therefore, the recount was stopped. It was a decision that would be compared with **Dred Scott**—the nineteenth-century Supreme Court ruling that no black person, slave or free, could ever become a citizen of the United States—for its impact and clear bias.

Remember: "For want of a nail, the horseshoe was lost, for want of a horseshoe, the horse was lost, for want of a horse, the battle was lost, for want of a battle, the war was lost." This parable should be the mantra of everyone who thinks her or his vote doesn't count.

• If Harriett Woods hadn't been defeated by less than 2 percent of the votes in Missouri, Danforth wouldn't have been a U.S. senator.

• If Danforth hadn't been senator, Clarence Thomas wouldn't have gone with him to Washington as a staff member.

• If Thomas hadn't been visible in Washington as a rare African American who opposed his community's majority views, he wouldn't have been appointed by the first President Bush to head—and to disempower—the Equal Employment Opportunity Commission, and then to sit on the D.C. Court of Appeals.

• If Thomas hadn't been given such credentials, he couldn't have been nominated by the same President Bush to succeed the great civil rights advocate Justice Thurgood Marshall on the Supreme Court.

• If Thomas hadn't been on the Supreme Court, he couldn't have supplied the one-vote margin that halted the Florida court-ordered recount.

• If there had been a recount, Al Gore, not George W. Bush, would have been president—as was concluded by a postelection examination of all uncounted ballots commissioned by twelve major news organizations.[10]

• If George W. Bush had not been president, the United States would have been less likely to lose the world's sympathy after 9/11 by launching the longest war in U.S. history, with more bombs dropped on Afghanistan during fourteen years than in all of World War II, plus billions in tax dollars given to twenty thousand private contractors, and thousands killed and wounded on both sides.

• If Al Gore, not George W. Bush, had been president, global warming would have been taken seriously. Also, the United States would not have falsified evidence to justify invading oil-rich Iraq, thus starting an eight-year war, and, together with Afghanistan, convincing some in Islamic countries that the United States is waging war against Islam.

• Without George W. Bush, there would not be the biggest transfer of wealth into private hands in the history of this nation; a pay ratio in which the average CEO earns 475 times more than the average worker (in Canada, it's 20 times); an executive order giving an estimated $40 billion in tax dollars to Catholic, evangelical, and other religious groups, without congressional approval, often with the appearance of turning churches into a vote delivery system.

• Without Clarence Thomas to supply the one-vote majority, the Supreme Court might not

have ruled that corporations are people, with a
right to unlimited political spending in order to
continue all the above. . . .

Well, you get the idea.[11] The list goes on.

We must not only vote but fight to vote. The voting booth really is the one place on earth where the
least powerful equal the most powerful.

I still dream about that veteran and his daughter.
I so wish I had said yes. I have no idea whether we
in the room could have made a difference. In truth,
we don't know which of our acts in the present will
shape the future. But we have to behave as if everything we do matters. Because it might.

As my mother would say, "Democracy is a seed
that can only be planted where you are."

A Coda

PART OF TRAVELING OVER YEARS MEANS COMING
back to the same place and knowing it for the first
time. I had learned my best political lesson in college—I just didn't know it yet.

I took a course in geology because I thought it was
the easiest way of fulfilling a science requirement.
One day the professor took us out into the Connect-
icut River Valley to show us the "meander curves" of
an old-age river.

I was paying no attention because I had walked

up a dirt path and found a big turtle, a giant mud turtle about two feet across, on the muddy embankment of an asphalt road. I was sure it was going to crawl onto the road and be crushed by a car.

So with a lot of difficulty, I picked up this huge snapping turtle and slowly carried it down the road to the river.

Just as I had slipped it into the water and was watching it swim away, my geology professor came up behind me.

"You know," he said quietly, "that turtle has probably spent a month crawling up the dirt path to lay its eggs in the mud on the side of the road—you have just put it back in the river."

I felt terrible. I couldn't believe what I had done, but it was too late.

It took me many more years to realize this parable had taught me the first rule of organizing.

Always ask the turtle.

With Loretta Swit, racing to raise money, Freestate Raceway, Laurel, Maryland, 1982.

VI.

Surrealism in Everyday Life

A JOURNEY—WHETHER IT'S TO THE CORNER grocery or through life—is supposed to have a beginning, middle, and end, right? Well, the road is not like that at all. It's the very illogic and the juxtaposed differences of the road—combined with our search for meaning—that make travel so addictive.

Fortunately, I already had a phrase for this road craziness. As Susanne Langer, the philosopher of mind and art, explained, "The notion of giving something a name is the vastest generative idea that was ever conceived." It was the good luck and bad luck of writing for **That Was the Week That Was (TW3)**, a pioneer of political satire on television, that caused me to create a category called Surrealism in Everyday Life.

I.

IN 1963, A TIME OF CONTROVERSY OVER CIVIL RIGHTS and Vietnam, **political** scared network executives, and **satire** still evoked George S. Kaufman's show business adage "Satire is what closes on Saturday night." Though **TW3** would eventually become the parent of the much sillier **Laugh-In**, then of such true heirs as **Saturday Night Live, The Daily Show with Jon Stewart**, and **The Colbert Report**, the continuity acceptance department, otherwise known as the censors, was in a snit of nervousness. Because the show really was live, if anyone departed from the script, the only remedy was to bleep a word or pull the plug completely. Censors also once tried to convince us that the Fairness Doctrine of the Federal Communications Commission required writing a prowar joke for every antiwar joke. Fortunately, they couldn't think of a prowar joke either.

But limits lead to invention. My favorite skit got past "the suits," as we mercilessly called all network executives, by hiring a juggler to toss huge butcher knives into the air and keep them circling overhead while the audience barely breathed. After what seemed an eternity, a stagehand appeared with a vaudeville-type placard: THE NUCLEAR ARMS RACE.

Thanks to Surrealism in Everyday Life, I could comment on such events as the high-rise bordellos being subsidized by the government of Holland. All I had to do was comb through the newspapers of the world every Saturday morning—while also watching **Soul Train,** thus learning new disco moves at the same time—and search for the sort of events about which one says, "You can't make this stuff up!"

I was the **only** "girl writer," probably because the power to make people laugh is also a power, so women have been kept out of comedy. Polls show that what women fear most from men is violence, and what men fear most from women is ridicule. Later, when Tina Fey was head writer and star of **Saturday Night Live,** she could still say, "Only in comedy does an obedient white girl from the suburbs count as diversity."

TW3 was fun. It was pioneering. It couldn't last. But what did last was Surrealism in Everyday Life as a category in my mind. Never again would I be able to confront the unimaginable without imagining an award for it.

When I began to travel as an organizer and was plunged into irrational juxtapositions on the road, I finally understood why laughter is a mark of wanderers, from the holy fools of Old Russia to the roadies of rock music. It's the surprise, the unexpected, the out of control. It turns out that laughter is the only free emotion—the only one that can't be compelled. We can be made to fear. We can even be made to believe we're in love because, if we're kept dependent and isolated for long enough, we bond in order to survive. But laughter explodes like an **aha!** It comes when the punch line changes everything that has gone before, when two opposites collide and make a third, when we suddenly see a new reality. Einstein said he had to be very careful while shaving, because when he had an idea, he laughed—and he cut himself. Laughter is an orgasm of the mind.

On the road, moments of surrealism may come and go in a second: **I'm looking out the scenic window of a train speeding through miles of empty moonlit desert—when acres of neatly arranged abandoned refrigerators flash by.** They may also last for hours: **I'm returning tired to a sterile hotel lobby, and am invited into a reunion of the last living members of a Negro baseball league, whose stories take me into another world.** Since learning causes our brains to grow new synapses, I like to believe that the road is sharpening my mind and lengthening my life with surprise.

II.

IT'S 1997, TOWARD THE END OF MY THIRD DECADE traveling as an organizer, and I'm speaking at a campus near Boston. The postlecture discussion has lasted until midnight, the last plane to New York is long gone, and I must get home so I can leave on another trip in the morning. Fortunately, kindhearted students come to my rescue with a local car service, and even steal a pillow from a dorm so I can sleep all the way home.

But once on the road, I'm still wide awake with postlecture adrenaline. Also the driver, a cheerful white guy in his fifties, wants to talk. As we make our way through a blinding rainstorm, he explains that we're safe because he used to be a cross-country trucker driving in all kinds of weather. He pulled down $200,000 a year, and owned his own rig, but quit because he was a stranger to his wife and grand-kids. Now that he owns this local car service, he has a family again—but still, he misses, really misses, his old cross-country life.

"What do you miss?" I ask, imagining he'll say speed, going it alone, adrenaline, danger—everything I remember from the classic movie **They Drive by Night.**

"I miss the community," he says. Since this isn't at all what I expected, I ask him to explain. He says civilians just don't understand, and asks if I want to see for myself.

We turn off the turnpike onto a service road. Near three gas pumps, I see several parked trucks, their huge shapes outlined by multicolored safety lights that shine through the black rain like Christmas. Behind them is a windowless shack that's dark except for a couple of neon beer signs.

Opening the door is like throwing a switch. We're plunged into bright lights, laughter, music, the smell of fresh bread, and an energy level more like noon than two a.m. At the counter, we are served coffee in mugs as heavy as dumbbells plus slabs of a pie that must have been big enough for ten-and-twenty blackbirds. My driver and the waitress exchange news about who's still working, who's still married, who jackknifed a semi on black ice, and who was driving a rig that got blown over in a tornado. At least, I think that's what they're saying. Words like **anteater,** which is a kind of rig, and **bear,** which means a law enforcement officer, need translation.

A bearded driver in cowboy boots sits down next to me. He orders lemon meringue pie, a side of chocolate ice cream, a pot of tea, and a can of motor oil. The waitress slides each item down the Formica counter to exactly the right spot in front of him, all with the skill of a great pool player. I compliment her. From there we get to talking about women truck drivers. She says there are a few more these days. Fleet owners have begun to hire them because they listen to their trainers and have better safety records. Still, women get ribbed and talked dirty to on CB radio. She respects them for hanging in there, and even driving eighteen-wheelers. What started as husband-and-wife teams, the pioneers of job sharing—one sleeping in the back of the cab while the other drove—has now become a crack in the glass ceiling of jobs with good pay.

Over by the booths, one older white guy and two young black men are feeding coins into an old-fashioned jukebox and arguing about the relative merits of rappers versus classics like Stevie Wonder and Sam Cooke. They seem to agree that Brook Benton's "Rainy Night in Georgia" is the truckers' anthem, and play it three times straight.

"Just wait," my driver says. "The next place has **real** truckers' music."

Back on the shining highway, he explains that truck stops aren't chains of sameness like McDonald's; they're more like idiosyncratic relatives. Each one offers down-home food, talk, music, and timelessness, plus trucker necessities, from motor oil to mosquito spray, all sold over the counter.

When we turn off again and head into another warm, tacky, welcoming world, the jukebox features such songs as "Girl on the Billboard," "A Tombstone Every Mile," and "18 Wheels and a Dozen Roses," the last being the ode of a trucker coming home to his wife. Truckers are such constant listeners that they dictate pop music hits. Also, Nashville produces specialty truckers' songs as a profitable category. Who knew?

At our third stop, I sit next to a truck-driving wife. She started teaming up with her husband as a defensive measure. "Pimps work the truck stops," she explains. "They drop off girls to work the cabs as they pull up, then take them to the next stop. I know because I had a niece who got caught up with drugs, and her pimp beat her to death for trying to get out. I used to hate the girls. Now I hate the pimps." She says truckers tend to be family men— executives are probably more likely to be johns—

and she's proud that husband-and-wife teams have a better safety record than men driving alone.

At a fourth stop, there is a twenty-four-hour poker game. At a fifth, there is what seems to be a permanent floating argument about cross-country trucking and whether it can flex enough political muscle to make better safety laws.[1] In this way, we hit every major truck stop between Boston and New York.

I've spent most of my life on the road, yet I'd never seen this world that wakes when others sleep. My driver tells me it's global. He's met immigrant truckers looking for work who have driven English lorries, and everywhere from Eritrea's mountainous roads to the crowded streets of India, where trucks are painted with flowers and gods and goddesses, an art form that drivers carried photos of, right along with photos of their families.

Back in our shared cocoon in the rain, we're quiet. The rhythm of our windshield wipers merges in my head with Brook Benton's sensuous baritone:

It's a rainy night in Georgia
and it looks like
it's rainin'
all over the world.

I see Manhattan lights reflecting into the night sky, but I've lost all sense of time. This could go on forever. I realize I've been swimming in the shallows, and am only now discovering the deeps where the great whales meet.

III.

• I'm having lunch at West Hollywood's Café Figaro with Florynce Kennedy. She is explaining to me that she quit being a lawyer because "the law is a one-ass-at-a-time proposition, and what you have to do is stop the wringer." This is inspired by the sight of seven waitresses and no waiters, an index of suspicion. Flo says tips are probably being used as a legal excuse to pay less than the minimum wage.[2] We quiz the manager. He assures us the pay is terrific, all seven waitresses adore their jobs, and more women are waiting in line.

Back home in New York a week later, I find a letter waiting from those waitresses: "We don't think any other occupational group can appreciate what you do for women as much as we. It's not enough that we work hard for ridiculously low wages, we're expected to softly come on to male customers so that they'll spend more and return again. Our wonderful male manager advances the theory that it's really to our benefit—we'll get bigger tips. God, what an intellectual cripple. Don't ever let up! The Subversive Seven."

Now it's decades later, in 2014. I'm reading about beloved comedian and actor Bill Cosby, who has been accused by no fewer than thirty-nine women of drugging and sexually assaulting them at some time in the past. Each one feared she would not be believed, but when one came forward, they all began to. One is Linda Joy Traitz, who at nineteen was a waitress at Café Figaro, where Cosby dropped in occasionally because he was its part owner. He offered her a ride home, then, in his car, she says that she was confronted by a briefcase full of drugs and booze, plus his sexual assault.

I wish Flo were here to learn her instincts were right. Eighteen years older than I, with a life that stretched from seeing her parents threatened by the Ku Klux Klan to becoming a civil rights and show business lawyer, she was nearly always right. Traveling with her was better than any college education.

I once saw her buy a purple pantsuit for a young white salesgirl in a small-town dress shop, something the salesgirl wanted but could never have afforded. When I went back after Flo's death, that now middle-aged woman told me Flo's generosity had opened up a new view of life.

• In 1980 I board a crowded plane for Detroit and find myself seated among a group of Hasidic Jews. The men are wearing wide-brimmed black fedoras over their yarmulkes, the women are in dark-haired wigs and long-sleeved dresses, and the children are as neat and well behaved as miniature grown-ups. I notice some hurried rearranging of seats. The goal seems to be that no woman sits next to a man not her husband—or next to me. My seatmate turns out to be the oldest man, stooped and gentle, reading his prayer book. Knowing that no Hasidic man is allowed to touch a woman outside his family, not even to shake hands, I do my best to be respectful and keep my arm off our shared armrest. Still, I'm surprised that separating me from the women seemed to be a higher priority than isolating me from the men. I hear the word **feminist** in English amid the Yiddish from two young men sitting in front of us, and they peer back at me between the seats.

When we arrive at the Detroit airport, I go into a ladies' room—and there are the wives and daughters. The youngest wife checks the stalls into which the older ones have disappeared, looks me straight in the eye, and smiles. "Hello, Gloria," she says firmly. "My name is Miriam." That smile is worth the whole trip.

• It's 1996, and I'm in Kansas, home state of U.S. senator Robert Dole, who has just run for president of the United States. I turn on the television in my motel. Dole is on camera, smiling, talking about his ED—erectile dysfunction—in a paid commercial for Viagra. As Liz Smith, the smart and funny Manhattan gossip columnist, always says, "You can't make this stuff up."

• Just as the millennium is about to end, I'm in a car with two women students on our way to a political meeting in Arizona. We've stopped at a construction roadblock in the searing desert heat, and a big man is walking toward us carrying a pickax. Suddenly, we're hyperaware that no other car is in sight. Leaning into my window, he says he noticed our **Ms.** T-shirts—he's a **Ms.** reader. This seems so improbable that I'm sure it's a joke or a con. Then he cites an article of a year ago about **los feminicidios,** the hundreds of young women whose raped, tortured, and mutilated bodies have been found in the Mexican desert across from El Paso. Speculation about the motive has ranged from sex trafficking to the sale of organs, from raping and murdering young women as part of a gang initiation to a twisted taking of revenge against women for being wage earners. These murders have been going on for decades, but since they are sexualized and the victims are "only" workers in the **maquiladoras**—factories just across the Mexican border where products are assembled cheaply for sale in the United States—news coverage has been sensational and arrests have been zero.

I notice tears in this man's eyes. He is saying that ten years ago his sixteen-year-old sister became one of **las feminicidios** and today is the anniversary of her death. He wants to thank us for paying attention, for remembering. He is grateful to anyone who makes these deaths visible. He himself will remain in mourning until her murderer is caught.

We shake his callused hands. He says there is something mystical about our appearance on this day. We are feeling it, too. As he walks back to his roadwork, we sit silent for a long time. Over the years, I will forget the larger purpose of this trip, but I will never forget this man and his sister.

• In 2000 I'm driving with a friend from Texas into rural Oklahoma. I can tell where the first state ends and the second begins because roads get better, cattle roam freely instead of being tethered in the boiling sun, and roadside businesses are more likely to be gas stations with convenience stores than topless bars and entertainment arcades. This seems like a good thing—until the Bible Belt gets tighter, and I see paired billboards along the road. One promises everlasting life through Jesus Christ. The other promises to reverse vasectomies.

• During a discussion after a university lecture in the early fall of 2003, a student stands up in the audience and says that President George W. Bush will board a plane carrying a large plastic turkey and fly to Iraq for a Thanksgiving photo op with our troops. Since we've been discussing the phony pretext of weapons of mass destruction with which Bush justified the invasion of Iraq in the first place, the phony turkey gets a big laugh.

After Thanksgiving the press breaks a top secret: Bush boarded **Air Force One** carrying a big hand-painted plastic turkey, flew to Iraq in the middle of the war, posed for photos with our troops and the turkey, and flew back to Washington—all at taxpayers' expense.

Who was that student? How did he know?

• While traveling in Georgia, I see lawn signs for the reelection campaign of Max Cleland, a much-admired U.S. senator and a war hero who lost both legs and one arm to a grenade in Vietnam.

I'm in Atlanta again in 2002 and see TV ads that call him unpatriotic, and compare him to Osama bin Laden and Saddam Hussein. The excuse is only his vote against two of many anti-terrorism measures. This is a Joe McCarthy–type Big Lie. Veterans in both parties protest the ad, and eventually it is removed. Still, its very extremity has created doubt in a where-there's-smoke-there's-fire way. Cleland is defeated.

A year later, I see this successful tactic rolled out nationally against U.S. senator John Kerry, also a Vietnam War hero, who is running for president. Television ads feature veterans who deny his heroism as a Swift boat captain. Though the charges are later disproved, they contribute to Kerry's defeat. **Swiftboating** enters the English language as a verb that means attacking strength instead of weakness. In feminist and other social justice contexts, this has long been called **trashing,** attacking leaders for daring to write, speak, or lead at all.[3] Taking away the good is even more lethal than pointing out the bad.

• In the presidential election of 2008, a banner year for Surrealism in Everyday Life, right-wing talk show host Rush Limbaugh opposes the Democratic candidacy of Hillary Clinton. He accuses her of wearing pantsuits to conceal "bad" legs. Instead, he supports Sarah Palin as the Republican vice-presidential candidate because she wears skirts to reveal "good" legs. Actually, Republicans have nominated Palin at the last minute to pick up some votes from disappointed Hillary Clinton supporters. This makes no sense. Palin opposes reproductive freedom and most other majority needs of women, enjoys shooting animals from helicopters, and has always earned more support from white male voters than from diverse female voters. Her selection is the biggest political mistake since the first President Bush appointed Clarence Thomas to the Supreme Court, expecting to get more votes from African Americans. Surrealism is the triumph of form over content.

• For serial surrealism, nothing beats right-wing and religious efforts to confer legal personhood on fertilized eggs. This would nationalize women's bodies throughout their childbearing years. Not surprisingly, the Human Life Amendment to the U.S. Constitution has failed, but many state and local tactics are succeeding, from bombing clinics and murdering doctors in the name of "pro-life," to denying birth control as a part of health insurance, and closing clinics with impossible building regulations imposed by antichoice state legislatures. Over time, I've also noticed that local pickets of clinics often personify this surrealism.

To enter the Blue Mountain Clinic in Missoula, Montana, I have to pass picketers who are crowded at the edge of the legal buffer zone. They are shouting, "Abortion is murder!" and "Baby killer!" Inside, staff members show me around the clinic, which has been providing a full range of health services since the early 1970s. In 1993 its building was firebombed and completely destroyed by anti-abortion terrorists, even though, as with most such clinics, providing safe abortions is a tiny fraction of its health care mission. I understand that repairing the damage has taken two years and a lot of work. Now Blue Mountain is operating behind a slender buffer zone and a tall protective fence.

A staff member tells me that one of the female picketers has come in when the men were not around, had an abortion, and gone back to picket the next day. This sounds surrealistic to me—but not to the staff member. She explains that women in such anti-abortion groups are more likely to be deprived of birth control and so to need an abortion. They then feel guilty—and picket even more. This restriction on birth control may also explain why studies have long shown that Catholic women in general are more likely to have an abortion than are their Protestant counterparts.[4]

When I visit clinics, I've learned to ask the staff if they have ever seen a picketer come in, have an abortion, and go back to picketing again. From Atlanta to Wichita, the answer is yes. Yet because staff members see the woman's suffering and guard her right to privacy, they don't blow the whistle.

Meanwhile in Wichita, Kansas, Dr. George Tiller, one of the few doctors who performs late-term abortions—only about 1 percent of all procedures but crucial when, for instance, a fetus develops without a brain—is shot in both arms by a female picketer. He recovers and continues serving women who come to him from many states.

I finally meet Dr. Tiller in 2008 at a New York gathering of Physicians for Reproductive Choice and Health. I ask him if he has ever helped a woman who was protesting at his clinic. He says: "Of course, I'm there to help them, not to add to their troubles. They probably already feel guilty."

In 2009 Dr. Tiller is shot in the head at close range by a male activist hiding inside the Lutheran church where the Tiller family worships each Sunday. This is done in the name of being "pro-life."

• I'm sitting next to a very old and elegant woman on a plane from Dallas to New York. Assuming that she needs company, I start a conversation. She turns out to be a ninety-eight-year-old former Ziegfeld girl who is on her way to dance in an AIDS benefit on Broadway with her hundred-and-one-year-old friend from chorus girl days—something they've been doing since the tragedy of AIDS first appeared. Humbled by this response and looking for advice on my own future now that I'm past seventy, I ask her how she has remained herself all these years. She looks at me as if at a slow pupil. "You're always the person you were when you were born," she says impatiently. "You just keep finding new ways to express it."

IV.

AN ORGANIZER'S JOB IS SURREALISTIC BY DEFINI-tion. I often find myself in front of an expensive painting or amid a sea of designer clothes or in an elegantly furnished room that could pay for dozens of the projects I'm raising money for. This is a crucial part of the job of an organizer. You leave a dark base-ment and try to explain to people in the sunshine what it's like to live down there. I've learned this is best done by bringing these different groups of peo-ple together. Those with extra money discover how much more satisfying it is to see talent and fairness grow than to see objects accumulate. Those without money learn the valuable lesson that money doesn't cure all woes. Instead, it may actually insulate and isolate.

I think this contrast between excess and need is the source of anger and joy for most organizers: anger that it exists in the first place, and joy that the contrast can be diminished. Raising money is the price of our greatest gift: we love what we do.

Fund-raising is often described as the second-oldest profession, after prostitution—though that last should be called the world's oldest oppression. Karl Marx pawned the silverware and jewelry of his wife, Jenny, the daughter of a baron, and depended on handouts from the well-to-do Friedrich Engels. Harriet Tubman worked odd jobs and passed the hat in churches to support her underground railroad, which freed more than three hundred enslaved people. Isadora Duncan enlisted her lover, an heir to the Singer sewing machine fortune, to finance her dancing and her trips to a newly Communist Russia. Gandhi learned about fund-raising and accounting in South Africa and brought both skills to the independence movement in India. Emma Goldman, who started out with five dollars and a sewing machine, raised money from such well-to-do supporters as the art collector Peggy Guggenheim. Eva and Anne Morgan, one a niece and the other a daughter of J. P. Morgan, the most powerful financier in U.S. history, used their family's money to finance women workers who were protesting before and after the Triangle Shirtwaist fire, even putting up a Fifth Avenue mansion as security for bail when those protesters were arrested. The suffrage movement might not have succeeded without the support of Alva Belmont and Mrs. Frank Leslie, two of the few women who gained control of fortunes through widowhood. Wealth next to poverty is surrealistic. Fund-raising is pointing that out.

• It's the end of the 1980s, a time of corporate profits going up and the Berlin Wall coming down. I'm on a private plane to Palm Springs. I know only one of the ten people on board, the man I'm with. He's one of only two rich men I've dated in my life. The first inherited his wealth and so was terminally insecure, though he headed his father's book publishing business.

Since in my East Toledo neighborhood reading books was a sign of rebellion, I didn't realize that, for him, books meant conforming. The man on the plane is more secure because he made his own money, yet he has acquired limousine and private plane habits that have begun to isolate him. On the plus side, however, we both love dancing and laughing and have no time to argue about all the things we disagree on.

Together with four presidents of major corporations plus their wives or long-term girlfriends, we're headed for a long Thanksgiving weekend. This is business for the man I'm with and, I hope, fund-raising from his colleagues for me. The executives on the plane respectively reign over a snack food empire, a pharmaceutical company, a cable channel, and a major credit card company. They just might support health and antiviolence projects for women and girls, who are as much as 80 percent of their consumers, yet receive only about 6 percent of corporate charitable dollars.

We land at a private airport near Palm Springs and are driven in air-conditioned limos through a scorching hot desert. We arrive at a compound with high stucco walls and double electronic gates. After a security check, we're in the midst of emerald lawns, manicured gardens, and pools of water lilies, all drenched by twirling water sprays. In the desert, water is gold. This is Fort Knox.

Each couple is taken to a bungalow with its own garden. Men are changing for a fast game of golf, women for tennis. Since I learned neither growing up in East Toledo—a bowling and canasta kind of place—I stay in the air-conditioned bungalow to work on a seriously overdue article. I discover a pantry full of unhealthy snack foods made by one of the host corporations, and begin to eat my way through it.

Thus begins a time of sports and camaraderie for my companions, and writing, air-conditioning, and eating junk food for me. Evenings consist of banquets of flown-in food and wine, and amusing anecdotes that sound as if they've been told before.

For Thanksgiving Day, we've been invited to an afternoon buffet at the nearby desert home of Frank Sinatra and his fourth wife. Our connection is tenuous. It seems the late father of one of the women in our party knew this famous singer. When we arrive, three older men in pastel golf sweaters are watching a football game on television, one with a holstered gun in his belt. Servants bring us rounds of drinks, but our hosts are nowhere to be seen. We're served Thanksgiving dinner from a massive buffet that has all the intimacy of a hotel.

Finally, Barbara Sinatra, a onetime Las Vegas showgirl and a former wife of one of the Marx brothers, arrives to greet us. She is a calm and queenly presence. My hope of fund-raising rises when she mentions chairing a Palm Springs hospital benefit for abused women and children, but it goes down when she chastises me and the women's movement for not taking up this new-to-her issue.

I swallow my pride. I don't have time to explain that the women's movement named domestic violence in the first place, sought its prosecution by police and by new laws, created the first shelters, and has been working for thirty years to explain, for instance, that the moment of leaving is the time when a woman is most likely to be murdered, thus answering questions like "Why doesn't she just leave?" Instead, I just describe effective survivor-run programs that are in need of support.

Still, I can feel her interest straying. For one thing, those programs aren't linked to the charity ball she is chairing, and for another, Frank Sinatra is finally arriving with a drink in his hand. He looks very much like, well, Frank Sinatra. I watch as this queenly woman turns into a geisha serving him turkey.

After dessert, our group is ushered into a separate building that houses the largest collection of toy trains I've ever seen. Tracks stretch out on tables that are themselves miniature landscapes, with roads, trees, lakes, and tiny buildings. Passenger cars are lighted from within and have tiny people silhouetted in the windows. Sinatra puts on a conductor's hat, presses buttons, and speeds trains through tunnels and over bridges. He looks happy and in his own world. I try not to think about how much all this cost.

The next day, back in our lush compound, I return to writing and junk food. Before we leave Palm Springs, there is one activity that I love: riding horses in the desert. However, I discover that the junk food has taken its toll. While I am riding, my jeans split up the back. I retreat to the bungalow for needle and thread.

On the plane going home, men talk about mergers and acquisitions, and women talk about weight loss. I know that one wife once had a high-level job in Washington, and another recently climbed Mount Everest, yet neither brings this up. Since we're all in a small space, I try one last time to describe projects that individuals and corporations might well please women consumers by supporting—but I get polite disinterest. I am an isolated island around which an ocean of talk flows. I fantasize about parachuting out of the plane.

We land at a private airport in New Jersey. Each couple gets in a separate limousine, though one could have held us all. In three days of talk about how to make money, I haven't been able to insert one idea about what to do with it. I'm angry—at myself. They are playing the game as it exists. I'm trying to change it—and I've failed. There is little more painful than surrealism when you yourself are the only contrast.

• I've passed by Laurel, Maryland, on trips to and from Washington, D.C., for years, but I haven't a clue what goes on there. Then one day in 1982 when I'm enjoying being at my desk at **Ms.** magazine after a long stretch of road trips, I get a call from Connie Bowman, a brand-new marketing director at the Freestate Raceway in Laurel. Since harness racing is a national and global attraction for the subcultures of racing and betting—and since both subcultures are overwhelmingly male—Bowman wants to attract more women. Her idea is to invite me and Loretta Swit, star of one of the most-watched series in TV history, to race each other in an event to be called **M*A*S*H** vs. **Ms.** In return, each of us will get a percentage of the gate to give away.

This captures my attention. **Ms.** magazine has discovered that very few advertisers will support a women's magazine that doesn't devote its editorial pages to praising the products it advertises: fashion, beauty, home decoration, and the like. To make up for the lack of ads in **Ms.**—and to meet requests for subscriptions from battered women's shelters, prisons, welfare programs, and just readers who can't afford them—we have to raise contributions.

This is why I find myself on a warm summer evening, dressed in white pants and green and gold racing silks, standing in front of a huge, blindingly lit stadium filled with thousands of shouting strangers cheering for their favorite horses plus the novelty bet of Loretta or me. Loretta is wearing white pants plus blue and red silks, and we are both peering out from under white crash helmets emblazoned "M*A*S*H vs. Ms." Beyond us is a huge oval racetrack so preternaturally lit up by klieg lights that I'm told astronauts can see it from space. Both of us are about to put our lives in the hands of horses and jockeys we don't know. This feels more surrealistic than it sounded on the phone.

Officials walk us to our respective rigs. Mine is pulled by a beautiful chestnut mare and guided by a skinny, older black driver. He is unusual in this traditionally white world of southern horse racing. Loretta has a younger white driver and a dark-coated gelding. We each seat ourselves next to the driver on a plank no bigger than an ironing board that is attached to a super-light rig. The whole thing is more like a coat hanger than the Ben-Hur chariot I envisioned. As we trot out to the track where other teams are assembled, we already seem to be going very fast. After the starting signal, that speed is much faster. I realize I'm sitting only inches above a track that is whizzing underneath me in a blur. Nothing but the ironing board is between me and being trampled by the horses behind us.

Then suddenly horse, driver, and I are in a capsule by ourselves. A blur of light and wind surrounds us. We are isolated for what could be minutes or hours, as one with this powerful horse. I think: Racing a car may be about ego, but racing a horse is about trust.

As we begin to slow down, the blur sharpens back into trees, stadium, fence, people. My driver turns to me, smiles, and says, **We won!**

We parade in front of the huge, noisy stadium. An amplified male voice booms out, "**Ms.** beat **M*A*S*H!**" He doesn't say that a mare beat a gelding, or that an old black driver beat a young white one, but I hear Loretta saying to a reporter with delight: **The outs beat the ins!**

Like Alice in Wonderland, I feel as if I've fallen into another universe. I was horse crazy as a child. Now I remember why I loved these smart, sleek creatures that deign to let us travel with them.

Our share of the gate turns out to be disappointing—under $5,000 each. We even forgot to bet on ourselves. Each of us could have raised more money in less time and with way less danger. However, now whenever I pass the Laurel sign on the way to and from Washington, I have a sense memory of speed and blur, a proud driver, a beautiful mare, a moment of altered reality.

V.

IT'S 1967, AND I'M SITTING IN A DINER IN RURAL Virginia, preparing for an interview nearby. Public schools have been ordered to integrate racially, and most white parents have put their kids into newly created, all-white "private" schools that are actually funded with tax dollars by a racist state legislature. My interview is with a sixth-grade white girl who is a prodigy of organizing. She is buzzing around the halls, welcoming black students into this newly desegregated public school. She has her parents' permission, but this was her idea. If I write about her story, I think she might inspire more students to take the lead, but so far I can't even get past editors. Newspapers say it's apolitical "soft news" and women's magazines say it's political "hard news."[5]

Next to me at the counter are three young white guys who are also talking about school integration or, in their words, "race mixing." They seem oblivious to the older black waitress who is serving us, and her face is inscrutable. These guys start arguing about Vietnam, and whether black GIs will follow orders from white officers.

"I hope not," says a solitary older white man sitting down at the counter. "We're on the wrong side in this war."

Silence. I wonder if combat will start right here. The older man has interrupted the younger ones, at a minimum, and at a maximum, he's talking treason. But like Scheherazade, who evaded death by telling irresistible stories, the loner moves his coffee mug toward us and begins to talk:

In World War II, I was in Indochina—that's what Vietnam was called then—and I didn't just meet Ho Chi Minh, I knew him. We were fighting the Japanese, and so was he. We were allies. Plus he was our hero because his guerrilla fighters rescued American pilots shot down in the jungle by the Japanese. Ho spent so much time with Americans that sometimes his own men only recognized him by the pack of Camels in his shirt pocket. Also, he loved President Roosevelt for pissing off Churchill by saying that colonialism had to end after the war. Ho even knew our Declaration of Independence by heart—it was his model for sending the French colonists home.

But after FDR died, everything changed. Truman sold Ho Chi Minh down the river by supporting the French—otherwise France wouldn't join NATO. But didn't we also fight a revolution to get rid of the British? Didn't we fight a civil war to keep our country from

being split into north and south? Well, that's what Ho Chi Minh is doing now—and we're on the wrong side.

There is silence. I can't tell whether the three young guys think this is truth or treason, but they slap money on the counter and drift away. I go over to talk to this man I now think of as the Prophet of the Diner. He's the first American I've ever heard say what I was told as a student in India long ago: that Ho Chi Minh just wanted independence for his country and would make it a buffer against China— the very opposite of the American belief that Ho's victory would have a "domino effect" of pushing other Asian countries toward China.

At the risk of sounding around the bend, I explain to the Prophet that I've read Ho Chi Minh's poetry and he doesn't sound power-mad to me. It's part of the reason I keep a sign on my bulletin board:

ALIENATION IS WHEN YOUR COUNTRY IS AT WAR
AND YOU WANT THE OTHER SIDE TO WIN.

He laughs and says he himself went to the State Department to remind them that Ho Chi Minh was once an ally—and could be again. Other vets have done the same thing, including a former OSS doctor who treated Ho Chi Minh for malaria. Some have offered to be go-betweens and help bring the United States and Ho together to talk. But as far as the Prophet knows, everyone has been turned down.

When he learns that I'm a writer from New York, he says I should write about Ho Chi Minh, who once lived in and loved New York. It's a personal note that might humanize him. I promise to try, but I don't have much hope in the middle of a war.

I do some reading. Sure enough, Ho Chi Minh was once a cabin boy on a French freighter. Historians believe he left this job to stay for a while in Manhattan, Brooklyn, maybe also Boston. That was between 1912 and 1918, a time when Trotsky and many other revolutionaries came here. Though America was the home of racism and capitalism, it also had waged the biggest successful anticolonial revolution. Ho was said to have worked as a pastry chef, maybe a photographer as he later did in Paris, but most of all, he kept writing and agitating for his country's independence.

By the end of World War I, Ho had become a recognized leader of independence for his country. That made him a criminal in the eyes of the French, who condemned him to death in absentia. He had so many aliases that when he finally became the leader of North Vietnam, the French recognized him in a photo only by his ears. Yet in 1919 he put on a rented suit and a bowler hat, went to the Versailles Peace Conference, and gave President Woodrow Wilson a petition for the independence of Indochina, based on our own Declaration of Independence. There was no reply. After World War II, he delivered yet another petition to President Truman. Still no reply.

For the first issue of **New York** magazine I write an article called "Ho Chi Minh in New York." Clay Felker, its founding editor, accepts it on shock value alone. After all, Ho Chi Minh is the enemy leader in an ongoing war that is dividing our own country.

In an effort to check facts, I send Ho Chi Minh a telegram. This is surrealism itself. The Western Union operator asks, "Do you have a street address in Hanoi, honey?" Finally, she agrees that "Presidential Palace" is probably enough, "what with the war and all." I think we both envision this telegram in our FBI files.

I get no answer, but thanks to a kindhearted woman in the French consulate, I confirm that the French freighter on which Ho worked did indeed dock in New York. Despite his different revolutionary aliases, I find a reference to two years he spent living in New York around the time of World War I. I also talk to journalist David Schoenbrun, who interviewed Ho during World War II and heard him speak with knowledge and affection about New York City. Other American journalists who met him later in Hanoi say that he often ended their interviews by asking nostalgically, "Tell me, how is New York?"

I even find his photo in what is said to be Harlem, though the black neighborhood then would have been the Sugar Hill district above 145th Street. There, Marcus Garvey spoke about black pride and anticolonialism, and leaders from Asia, Africa, and Haiti came to listen. So many independence movements were active in the early 1900s that New York tabloids printed fearful articles about the "Yellow Peril" of Asia joining the "Black Peril" of Africa to encircle the globe. The young Ho Chi Minh of those days is described in Jean Lacouture's classic biography as slender and beardless, wearing a dark suit, a high-collared shirt, and "a small hat perched on top of his head, looking delicate and unsure of himself, a bit lost, a bit battered, like Chaplin at his most affecting." When I walk past old New York buildings he might have seen, I try to imagine him looking at them, too.

Due to the last-minute chaos and printing problems of the first issue of **New York**, my article is cut by two-thirds. It becomes so concentrated that readers will have to pour water on it.[6] Still, I hope the Prophet of the Diner sees it.

Now as I write this almost four decades later, Ho Chi Minh, who owned nothing in his life but a typewriter, remains the only leader ever to defeat the United States in a war. We dropped more bombs on Vietnam than on all of Europe during World War II. About sixty thousand U.S. troops died; twice as many Vietnamese soldiers died; and nearly two million civilians in North and South Vietnam lost their lives. Both here and in a now-independent, unified, and prosperous Vietnam, where tourists travel, there are still broken families, traumatized veterans, chemicals in the soil—and much more. In South Korea when I visited in this new millennium, newspaper headlines were protesting Agent Orange, stored underground by the United States on its way to deforesting North Vietnam. Now it was leaking and poisoning the water table.

According to the wisdom of Indian Country on my own continent, it takes four generations to heal one act of violence. What if Americans had heard the Prophet in the Diner?

VI.

IN 1978 FATHER HARVEY EGAN, PASTOR OF ST. JOAN of Arc Catholic Church in Minneapolis, invites me to join him on a Sunday morning and give the homily or sermon to his congregation. This isn't as surrealistic as it sounds. He has invited other lay-people, from union organizers to peace activists, and at least one woman, Maggie Kuhn, founder of the Gray Panthers. He also welcomes gays and lesbians into his congregation, supports peace movements from here to Latin America, and generally behaves in a way that he and many other Catholics believe Jesus had in mind. Though it's just a coincidence that his church bears the name of a woman who was burned at the stake for being a heretic who wore men's clothes (not for being a witch, as Hollywood told us), I think Father Egan enjoys inviting someone who's been regarded as a jeans-wearing heretic, too. He himself prays to God the Mother to make up for centuries of Catholic priests and popes who pray only to God the Father.

Needless to say, Father Egan is not a favorite of the Catholic hierarchy, but he has the biggest Catholic congregation in the state. People want to come home to the church of their childhood without having to leave their adult selves behind. "There are two churches," as Cesar Chavez, leader of the farmworkers, always said, "one of buildings and one of people." Father Egan's church is definitely the people. They love him; it's his landlord who is the problem.

I'm worried about getting him into even more trouble, since I'm more of a pagan than a monotheist, but pagan just means nature, and Father Egan, too, believes that God is present in all living things. Since most American Catholics live, vote, and act more like the rest of the country than like the Vatican, I figure Father Egan knows what he's doing. I decide to say yes.

When I arrive on our appointed Sunday, it is clear Minnesota right-wing groups have been working overtime. Cars are circling St. Joan of Arc with huge blow-ups of fetuses mounted on their roofs, and loudspeakers are blasting, "Gloria Steinem is a murderer, Gloria Steinem is a baby killer."[7] There are police to keep demonstrators at the distance required by law, but it is not a peaceful scene. It's also familiar after being picketed over the years. Repetition can take the surrealism out of anything.

Once inside, Father Egan tells me not to worry, the positive response has been overwhelming. There is a waiting list, even after he doubled the capacity of this large church by holding two masses. The news that I'll have to speak twice makes me more nervous than the presence of protesters.

As I wait alone in this cavernous space, stage fright hits in a very big way. A pulpit in a Catholic church is nowhere I ever expected to be. My heart thumps, my mouth gets dry, my mind goes blank, and I wish I were anywhere but here. Father Egan finishes introducing me, lifts his arms so his vestments billow out like a butterfly, and says with a mischievous smile, "Glory be to God for Gloria!" The congregation bursts out laughing—and so do I. Suddenly, I feel okay. Laughter is a rescue.

I'm not talking about the Catholic position on abortion. Most people here have their own ideas, and thanks to honest Jesuit historians and to Catholics for a Free Choice (now called Catholics for Choice), they may well know that the Catholic Church not only didn't oppose abortion but actually regulated it until the mid-nineteenth century. It was made a mortal sin mostly for population reasons.[8] Napoleon III wanted more soldiers, and Pope Pius IX wanted all the teaching positions in the French schools—plus the doctrine of papal infallibility—so they traded. Also, Catholicism is hardly alone among patriarchal religions in controlling women's bodies. Patriarchy evolved as a way of giving men control over women's bodies and reproduction. It seems more hopeful to talk about what came **before** patriarchy—and could show us a way beyond it.

So I talk about original cultures that saw the presence of god in all living things—including women.

Only in the last five hundred to five thousand years—depending on where we live in the world—has godliness been withdrawn from nature, withdrawn from females, and withdrawn from particular races of men, all in order to allow the conquering of nature, females, and certain races of men. Though patriarchal cultures and religions have made hierarchy seem inevitable, humans for 95 percent of history have been more likely to see the circle as our natural paradigm. Indeed, millions still do, from traditional Native Americans here to original cultures around the world. The simple right to reproductive freedom—to sexuality as an expression that is separable from reproduction—is basic to restoring women's power, the balance between women and men, and a balance between humans and nature. So when Father Egan prays to a female as well as a male god—and invites women as well as men to speak from the church pulpit—he is taking a step toward restoring an original balance.

My homily seems to go over just fine. People nod at the idea that when God is depicted only as a white man, only white men seem godly. They laugh at the idea that priests dressed in skirts try to trump women's birth-giving power by baptizing with imitation birth fluid, calling us reborn, and going women one better by promising everlasting life. Indeed, elaborate concepts of Heaven and Hell didn't seem to exist before patriarchy; you just joined your elders or kept being reincarnated until you learned enough. There is the laughter of recognition.

Altogether I sense curiosity and openness, not hostility or opposition.

As people leave, there is a long line to shake hands, to share comments, and to thank—even to bless—Father Egan and me. He asks me to call him Harvey. I think we both feel bonded by this experience of both opposition and support.

Outside, the cars with pictures of fetuses are still circling, and bullhorns are still blaring. Minnesota is home to the Human Life Center, a think tank headed by the delightfully named Father Marx, who often warns that "the white Western world is committing suicide through abortion and contraception." His use of "white Western" is a big clue to the reasons for preserving patriarchy and controlling reproduction. But still, the parishioners streaming out of St. Joan of Arc don't seem alarmed. This isn't their first brush with local extremists. Harvey and I feel we have dodged a bullet.

In New York a few days later, I hear the news that Archbishop John Roach, Harvey's superior in the Catholic hierarchy, has reprimanded Father Egan and apologized in public for him. This is a big deal. It's all over the media, from the front pages of newspapers in Minnesota to national television.

The next time I see Harvey is two days later—on a TV screen. He is a disembodied head being interviewed in a Minneapolis studio by **CBS Morning News.** I am sitting in a studio in Washington, D.C. Neither our TV questioners nor the reprimanding archbishop ever quote anything I said, or cite any complaints from parishioners. The controversy is entirely directed at my being invited to give the homily at all.

I'm worried that I've endangered Harvey, but when I phone him, he seems to be his usual gentle and unrepentant self. From now on, he explains, he is supposed to invite speakers only from a list of names preapproved by the archdiocese. Later, I read his response to a reporter: "So far, they have found Mickey Mouse, Little Lord Fauntleroy, Peter Rabbit and Lawrence Welk." I laugh—and stop worrying.

Then a couple of weeks later, I'm in my apartment between travels, sitting peacefully with my cat on my lap, drinking my morning coffee, and I pick up **The New York Times.** Above the fold on the front page, a place usually reserved for wars and presidential elections, there is a headline:

POPE FORBIDS HOMILIES BY LAYPEOPLE

Nothing in my life quite prepares me for feeling directly addressed by the pope. I try to talk myself down—after all, many laypeople have given the homily; maybe I'm just being paranoid—and call a reporter who covers the Vatican. He says that at a minimum, Father Egan and I have provided what is known in the media, and perhaps also in the Vatican, as a news peg.

After that, Harvey is almost always present whenever I visit Minneapolis. He turns up because we really do like each other and I think also because he's protecting me. Whether it's a campus lecture or a YWCA benefit or a political rally, there he is, beaming from the sidelines with kindness, friendship, and his trademark enthusiasm. Though the controversy never quite goes away, he isn't in the least put off by it.

He also works around the pope's dictate by renaming the homily "a Sunday presentation" and inviting laypeople his congregation admires. He remains public about his support for "women and their participation in the liturgy," for artificial birth control, for the right of conscience that actually does exist within Catholicism, and for peace and justice movements around the world. Even far from Minnesota, Catholics tell me he provides hope amid the hierarchy.

When Harvey retires in 1986, St. Joan of Arc is still the most popular Catholic church in his and many other states, with a thousand people attending every mass. Father Egan continues to write about everything from the injustice of current wars to the past and future of Catholic mysticism. In the **Catholic Reporter,** he publishes an article titled "Celibacy, a Vague Old Cross on Priestly Backs," and explains that it started "only in 1139 when the church no longer wanted to be financially responsible for the children of priests." He opposes the so-called Human Life Amendment to the U.S. Constitution, even though the Catholic bishops advocate it. "Prohibition was a disaster," Harvey explains, and we shouldn't be pushing for "another Constitutional amendment based on a moral conviction."

In 2006, at the age of ninety-one, Harvey's unique life comes to an end. It's been twenty-eight years since he invited me to give the homily, yet whenever I'm in Minneapolis I always feel he's just around the corner. I miss him.

In his honor, I try to be as courageous and outrageous as he was. I add to speeches something I learned from historians of religious architecture but left out of my homily: the design of many patriarchal religious buildings resembles the body of a woman. Think about it: there is an outer and inner entrance (labia majora, labia minora) with a vestibule between (an anatomical as well as architectural term) and a vaginal aisle up the center of the church to the altar (the womb) with two curved (ovarian) structures on either side. The altar or womb is where all-male priests confer everlasting life—and who can prove that they don't?

This surrealism of patriarchy goes on after Harvey's death. In 2012 the Vatican announces an investigation—not of the sexual abuse of children by priests that has been exposed as epidemic, but of the Leadership Conference of Women Religious, a group that represents 80 percent of the nuns in North America. They are accused of asking for greater decision-making roles in the church for themselves and for women in general, of "remaining silent" on homosexuality and abortion, of spending too much time working against poverty and injustice, of promoting "radical feminist themes incompatible with the Catholic faith," and of supporting President Obama's health care legislation that includes birth control. Indeed, the success of that health care bill seems to have been the last straw. Some members of Congress cited support for the bill by nuns as giving them the courage to vote against the U.S. Conference of Catholic Bishops, which was the major force opposing the bill. The Vatican investigation declared that bishops "are the church's authentic teachers of faith and morals." As the Bible says, "Rebellion is as the sin of witchcraft."

Even I am surprised to find this is so literal. The name of the Vatican body investigating the nuns is the Congregation for the Doctrine of the Faith, the same body that conducted the Inquisition, which came to be known as the Holocaust of Women because as many as eight million women healers and leaders of pre-Christian Europe were killed by torture and burning at the stake over more than five hundred years. Chief among their sins was passing on the knowledge of herbs and abortifacients that allowed women to decide whether and when to give birth.

After a period of shock and conferring, the Leadership Conference of Women Religious issues a statement. It condemns "unsubstantiated accusations," offers to go to the Vatican for a dialogue, and observes that just by following the teachings of Jesus, many in the church might also be called "radical feminists." Also some of the nuns get their rebellious act together and take it on the road. They begin touring the country to highlight poverty and injustice and become known as the Nuns on the Bus. I start to see men and women of all descriptions wearing T-shirts that say, WE ARE ALL NUNS NOW!

If Harvey were alive, he would be wearing one, too.

A FEW YEARS LATER, I'm waiting for a friend on a snowbound street in Minneapolis. A skinny boy of twelve or thirteen, with a backpack almost as big as he is, is standing nearby. I realize he's trying to get up the courage to say something, so I say hello. All in a rush, he says he knows I was at St. Joan of Arc Church, it's where his family goes, he's part of a group there called Awakening the Dreamer, and it's trying to help indigenous tribes save the rain forest. He wants to go to Latin America one day, just like Father Egan did.

I look at this boy who wasn't born yet when I spoke there—maybe his parents weren't born yet either—and ask how he knows me or Father Egan. He says he read all about us on the big St. Joan of Arc website. I realize it's a new day.

It turns out that his family are Hmong refugees from Laos, people who were first displaced by the Vietnam War. Though Minneapolis has been mostly blond and Scandinavian in its immigrant past, it now has become the American city with the largest

288 MY LIFE ON THE ROAD

Hmong population. Indeed, I've read that a Hmong woman has just been elected to the city council.

I ask him why he cares about such a long-ago event. He says he's shy, his parents have a hard time with English, he is trying to help them and also to speak up in school. He read on the church website that I was the most protested speaker Joan of Arc ever had, and he wants to speak up for his family.

I tell him that he just took that power. Now no one can ever take it away. I also tell him that the rain forest is beautiful, like where his family came from, that Father Egan would be proud of him, and that I am proud of him, too. The first step toward speaking for others is speaking for ourselves.

As I watch him trudge off in the snow, I think for the millionth time: **You never know.**

WITH WILMA MANKILLER AND CHARLIE SOAP'S TRUCK,
TAHLEQUAH, OKLAHOMA, 1991.

VII.

What Once Was
Can Be Again

I USED TO THINK THERE WERE ONLY TWO POSSIBILI-
ties. The first was what many believed: that equality between males and females was impossible and
contrary to human nature. The second was what
many hoped: that equality would be possible in the
future for the first time. After the Houston Conference and spending more time with women and men
from Indian Country, I thought there might be a
third: this balance between females and males had
existed in the past, and for a few, it still did. There
were people to learn from.

When new people guide us, we see a new country.

I.

IT'S THE FALL OF 1995. I'M AT THE COLUMBUS, OHIO, airport, waiting at the baggage claim as instructed. I'm going to speak at a conference of the American Indian Science and Engineering Society, a national group that teaches Native students science and engineering by using Native examples—thus allowing them to excel without feeling they have to abandon their history and cultures. Since Native students often prosper in cooperative rather than competitive classrooms—as do a lot of female students, regardless of where they come from—I've been asked to talk about the feminist movement and efforts to change classrooms into learning circles. Actually, boys, too, often do better when they aren't always in a hierarchy, so the ideas of this group could improve education in general.[1]

After a few minutes of waiting, I notice a heavy-set man in a windbreaker leaning against the wall. I walk over and ask if he's waiting for me—and he is. Holding up a sign seemed like an invasion of privacy, he says, so he's been waiting patiently for the crowd to thin out.

On the long drive to the conference center, we pass a turnoff with a small sign: SERPENT MOUND. I ask what this is. He doesn't seem surprised, but he just explains that it's an ancient earthwork, one of the many around this country. Some are shaped like enormous birds and animals, others are circles or pyramids, some are as tall as a three-story building and surrounded by a hundred smaller mounds you can see only from the air. This one is a snake about three feet high and a quarter of a mile long; the oldest surviving mound of its kind, maybe two or three thousand years old.

I'm into my third decade of traveling around this country, and I know none of this. I tell him my family comes from southern Ohio, yet the Serpent Mound is news to me. As if to make me feel better, he says he has friends who went to England to see Stonehenge, and when he asked if they would like to see even older sites here, they said no. He says this not with an edge but with a smile.

Because I ask, he tells me that the mounds around this country were spiritual centers or astrological observatories or burial sites. Most are pyramids, with openings inside for viewing solstices and equinoxes, but others are flat mounds at global magnetic points where seeds were spread out to make them more fruitful. All were centuries in the making, with digging up and moving tons of earth. Sometimes those basins were turned into lakes or fish hatcheries. Burial mounds tell us the most, because they contain seashells from the Gulf of Mexico, or obsidian from Wyoming, or carved mica from the Carolinas, or even the teeth of Rocky Mountain grizzly bears inlaid with pearls—also bowls and jewelry made of silver and copper from Canada, turtle shells from the Atlantic, carved semiprecious beads from Central America, and textiles from everywhere. They tell how far the ancients traveled or traded.

By now I feel like I'm in an alternate reality. He says the mounds were such feats of construction that Europeans didn't believe people they regarded as savages could have ancestors who created them. One popular theory was that the Egyptians lived here—and then mysteriously left. Another was that the Chinese, the first sailors, had come and gone.

I ask if the mound builders were **his** ancestors. He says they might have been, but with all the mixed heritage in this country, they could be my ancestors, too. Nobody knows what they called themselves—the mounds are named after the places they were found: Adena, Hopewell, and so on. Most of the big mounds were along the Mississippi River. People on this continent then known as Turtle Island had cultures as advanced as any on earth.

Suddenly, it seems ridiculous that we just came from a city airport named for Columbus, a terrible navigator who insisted to his dying day that he was in India—which is why people here are called Indians. As the Native women in Houston said, "It could have been worse—he could have thought he was in Turkey." If you've been genocided and left out of history, as they explained, you need a sense of humor to survive. When I tell my host this, he looks at me as if I'm just beginning to get it.

Though I've been assuming this kind and patient man was sent to pick me up, I realize I don't know his role. He says mildly that he's one of the conference organizers. If I hadn't asked, he would have been content to remain a driver. So much for hierarchy.

As we pull into our destination, I ask how he keeps on working, despite ignorance like mine on one hand and all the commercial imitations on the other.

"In Indian Country," he says, "we have a different sense of time. I'm learning and you're learning—and more will."

WHEN I TELL THIS story to my friend Alice Walker, I discover that she too has always wanted to see the mounds. Like so many African Americans, Alice has Native Americans in her family tree. As William Loren Katz, a favorite historian of Alice's, once wrote, "Europeans forcefully entered the African blood stream, but Native Americans and Africans merged by choice, invitation and love."[2] Her friend Deborah Matthews, who grew up near these Ohio mounds and had a Cherokee great-grandmother, offers to show us what she learned in her childhood.

In the summer of 1997, I leave my home in New York, Alice and Deborah leave their respective homes in California, and we meet at the motel where Alice and I will be staying—though with the added comfort of meals in the nearby homey kitchen of Deborah's mother, a generous woman Alice calls by her middle name, Magnolia.

On the first day, Deborah shows us the mounds in her small hometown of Newark. One is a round, slightly raised grassy area about the size of a city block, with ancient curved edges still visible under bushes and refuse. Surrounded by working-class houses with families sitting on front porches in the August heat, it is an open space with kids playing near public restrooms. A second is Moundbuilders Golf Course at the Moundbuilders Country Club, just outside town. A third is the Great Circle Earthworks, which is protected as a state park. Its thirty acres are surrounded by a wall that even after two thousand years of erosion is still fifteen feet high. At the center are four mounds in the shape of a bird, its beak pointing toward the entrance. Deborah says excavations have revealed an altar inside the bird's body, and dowsing has identified energy lines along the top of the wall. She came here as a little girl on family outings. "If we ventured outside the wall," she remembers, "our elders would say, 'Just follow the circle and it will bring you back to us.'"

In Magnolia's kitchen, we eat homemade peach cobbler and talk about differences in the way countries treat their past. At Stonehenge in England, there are guards and tape-recorded tours. Modern Greeks picnic among the ruins and are intimate with their ancient history. Both can count themselves as descendants of past glories. Here, people arrived from another continent and, by war, disease, and persecution, they eliminated 90 percent of the residents. From 1492 to the end of the Indian Wars, an estimated fifteen million people were killed. A papal bull had instructed Christians to conquer non-Christian countries and either kill all occupants or "reduce their persons to perpetual slavery."[3] From Africa to the Americas, slavery and genocide were blessed by the church, and riches from the so-called New World shored up the papacy and European monarchs. Whether out of guilt or a justifying belief that the original occupants were not fully human, history was replaced by the myth of almost uninhabited lands.

Thinking about our schooling in different decades and parts of the country, all three of us in that kitchen discover that we were taught more about ancient Greece and Rome than about the history of the land we live on. We learned about the pyramid builders of Egypt but not the pyramid builders of the Mississippi River.

The next day Deborah drives us to Flint Ridge, an ancient quarry that once yielded flint for Native tools used in hunting, farming, and building. By local legend, Indians hurled themselves to their deaths from this ridge rather than be slaughtered by the enemy.

We need some healing, and find it at the Serpent Mound.

There it is, a grass-covered, undulating serpent stretching out for a quarter of a mile on a plateau above a valley. It seems to emerge from the earth, rather than to be built on it. From a globe or comet in its mouth to a tightly coiled tail, its direction was thought to be random until astronomers realized that the head points to the sunset at the summer solstice, and the tail to the sunrise at winter solstice. Radiocarbon dating traces its age back to at least two thousand years ago, not the few centuries originally thought. This is the largest of the effigy mounds surviving here, and also in the world. Like so many other mounds, it would have been destroyed to make room for construction if money hadn't been raised to save it, in this case with the help of a group of women at the Peabody Museum of Massachusetts.

There is a small wooden viewing tower, and pamphlets from the State of Ohio, but they focus on facts—for instance, the Serpent Mound is as long as four football fields—not on meaning. In **The Sacred Hoop,** Paula Gunn Allen, a Native poet, mythologist, and scholar, explains that Serpent Woman was one of the names of the quintessential original spirit "that pervades everything, that is capable of powerful song and radiant movement, and that moves in and out of the mind . . . she is both Mother and Father to all people and all creatures. She is the only creator of thought, and thought precedes creation."[4]

In Western mythology, she might be compared to Medusa, the serpent-haired Greek goddess whose name means Knowing Woman or Protectress. She once was all-powerful—until patriarchy came along in the form of a mythic young man who chopped off her head. He was told to do this by Athena, who sprang full-blown from the mind of her father, Zeus—a goddess thought up by patriarchy and therefore motherless. There is history in what is dismissed as prehistory.

In books we brought along, we read about earlier grave excavations here that revealed a young couple laid out side by side, wearing jewelry and breastplates, their noses shaped in copper to keep them after the fragile cartilage was gone. Their bodies were surrounded by buttons made of copper-covered wood and stone as well as more than a hundred thousand pearls.[5]

That night we join Deborah's mother, her eighty-six-year-old grandmother, and teachers and neighbors at a community potluck supper in the school gym. It's a welcome for us. With the slow-paced humor and warmth I've come to cherish, they talk about the history of small-town Ohio, and are delighted that we are interested. Deborah's grandmother has lived her entire life near Adena mounds that may be even older than the one we just saw. They reminisce about everything from romantic outings in the Great Circle Earthworks to the connection they feel to people they just call "the ancients." We tell them about the young couple in copper and pearls. All of us light a candle for them.

What I don't tell them is a feeling I don't understand myself. As a child, I went to Theosophical meetings with my mother, and to a Congregational church where I was christened. I've enjoyed many years of Passover seders, rewritten with scholarship and poetry to include women. But not one of them felt as timeless and true as Serpent Woman.

II.

COMING HOME FROM A ROAD TRIP IN THE LATE 1970s, I notice graffiti painted in big white letters over the Queens Midtown Tunnel: WHEELS OVER INDIAN TRAILS.

Soon I find myself looking for this graffiti whenever I come home. I wonder, **Who climbed so high above the traffic? One of New York's brash young street artists? Some Marlon Brando–esque guy in love with a culture not his own? A descendant of a tribe that once lived here?**

I assume this is not a message from a living culture. I don't yet realize that it is part of a journey that will change how I see the world and the possible.

Later when I'm sitting in my favorite place amid the tall outcroppings of igneous rock in Central Park, just a short walk from my apartment, I wonder, **Who rested in this same place long ago, before the Dutch and then the English arrived? Whose hand touched this stone, and who looked at the same horizon?** This vertical history feels more intimate and sensory than written history. It's been reaching out all along, I just wasn't paying attention.

WHEN I WAS YOUNGER and trying to become a writer by interviewing other writers, I got an assignment to profile Saul Bellow, the much-awarded novelist who chronicled Chicago in all its diversity. Since he didn't want to sit still for an interview, he took me on a day's tour of this city that was a character in all his writing. We started out in the claustrophobic rooms of a tenement preserved to show how generations of European immigrants lived, and a neighborhood shop that sold can openers and other cheap items in the front, and diamond rings in the back. Then we went to a bar where Native American steelworkers were sitting silently, drinking as the morning light filtered through venetian blinds. They were Mohawk, Bellow explained with a novelist's eye for a good story, and they had so little fear of heights that they could walk on steel beams seventy stories up while catching hot rivets in a metal sieve—sort of a death-defying jai alai. He admired their natural gift and looked at them as different. To me, they seemed as isolated as Mexican migrants working in California fields, or South African men working in diamond mines.

Years later, as if I'd sent out a call to the universe, I met women on a Mohawk reservation in Canada. They lived near a railway bridge that had given birth to this myth of fearlessness. They assured me that Mohawk men were just as afraid of heights as anybody else, but they needed the jobs. Maybe they were helped by a trail-walking habit of placing one foot directly in front of the other, and by a tradition of bravery in the face of danger, but so many had perished that Mohawk women asked their men never to go out on the same job together, to lessen the risk of group widowhood and fatherless children. If I hadn't been in that sad bar watching men numb themselves with alcohol—and met those women—I too would have believed in the myth of a fearless choice.

No wonder oral history turns out to be more accurate than written history. The first is handed down from the many who were present. The second is written by the few who probably weren't.

In my own schoolbooks, I remembered reading headings like "Indians Were Backward." Those sources ignored, or were ignorant of, a culture with agricultural techniques that gave the world three-fifths of the food crops still in cultivation in modern times,[6] developed long-strand cotton that made the mills of England possible, and attracted so many white settlers to Indian instead of European ways of life that Benjamin Franklin complained bitterly about it. As Jean-Jacques Rousseau wrote, "Indians enjoyed equality and plenty; Europeans were in chains."[7]

Often the myths about Indians depicted them as more violent than the white society around them, though "scalping" was initiated by the U.S. Army, in order to pay soldiers and settlers a reward for each Indian killed. In my childhood, Hollywood westerns presented a few noble savages as well as fearsome warriors (or rather non-Indian actors playing them), but pioneer women were portrayed as suffering a fate worse than death if captured. "Half-breeds" born of such liaisons were seen as wanting only to be accepted into white society, and, especially if they were females, they were doomed by an out-of-control sexuality.

In fact, much more typical were white women who experienced the communal work and higher status of a Native culture, and chose it over their own. For instance, Cynthia Ann Parker was an adopted Comanche who gave birth to the last free Comanche chief, was captured by Texas Rangers, and spent the last ten years of her life trying to return to the culture she loved.

As Benedict Anderson wrote in **Imagined Communities,** a witty and lethal exposé of fictions that justify nationalism, "All profound changes in consciousness . . . bring with them characteristic amnesias. Out of such oblivions . . . spring narratives."

Even graffiti above a tunnel can begin a journey that never ends.

LOOKING BACK AT THAT National Women's Conference in Houston. I realize how much I learned, not only there, but in the two years of travel and state conferences leading up to it. LaDonna Harris, a much-loved Comanche activist, was the only woman from what she called Tribal America among our commissioners, and she was also a rare link to Washington.[8] She had married Fred Harris, her high school sweetheart, who, with her help, became a U.S. senator from Oklahoma. Some people joked that she was the state's third senator because she was so active in organizing and educating on Native issues.

To create pride in Native young people and bring knowledge to the rest of the country, LaDonna also had founded Americans for Indian Opportunity, with an Ambassadors Program that trained young women and men to talk about their history and culture. This created more understanding in the mainstream plus confidence in new generations of emerging leaders, and this idea would be adapted by First Peoples in other countries. Still, as she told me, their first task was often to start from ground zero by explaining, "We're still here."

LaDonna herself reminded me of people I'd met in India who also came from cultures older than anything in my history books. Like them, she had double-consciousness, a term invented by W. E. B. Du Bois to describe the African American experience of being one's unique self on the inside, yet generalized by the racist gaze of outsiders. Somehow, LaDonna had turned this on its head. She lived fully in the modern world, yet included her Native consciousness within it and became a bridge for both. Being around LaDonna meant sensing a much longer span of history; also linking rather than dividing humans and nature; also valuing such timeless qualities as spirituality and humor. That last seemed so common to LaDonna and others in Indian Country that I wondered where the stoic and expressionless cigar store Indian had come from. In our many endless meetings with other commissioners, she, like so many of the Native people I'd met over the years, had a rare ability to find irony and humor in the midst of seriousness—and vice versa.

I understood that LaDonna's presence among the

thirty-five International Women's Year commissioners would send a signal to Native American women
around the country who otherwise might not feel
invited to state conferences. What I didn't understand was how rare this was. At less than 1 percent
of the population—at least, by the notorious under-
count of the U.S. Census[9]—the more than five
hundred tribes and nations made up the smallest,
poorest, and least formally educated group in the
United States. Nations were very diverse, varying in
size from the vast Navajo Nation that extended into
several states to reservations of less than twenty acres.
But across that diversity, they shared such common
struggles as dealing with a federal government that
had yet to honor one treaty in its entirety, gaining
control of the schooling and treatment of their own
children, protecting their land from exploitation for
oil, uranium, and other resources on it—and much
more. For instance, women on reservations suffered
the highest rate of sexual assault in the country, yet
the non-Native men who were the majority of their
assaulters were not subject to tribal police or juris-
diction, and were mostly ignored by the larger legal
system.

From quiet, understated, and sometimes hesitant
Native women who came to meetings and stayed
to talk, I learned about the generations of Indian
families who had been forced by law to send their
children to Christian boarding schools often funded
by tax dollars; never mind the separation of church
and state. The nineteenth-century founder of those

schools coined the motto "Kill the Indian, save the man." They deprived children of their families, names, language, culture, and even their long hair. Then they were taught a history that measured progress by their defeat. Often, these children were subjected to forced labor, malnutrition, and physical and sexual abuse. Later, after several schools were closed down, the land around them yielded graves of starved and abused children. Saddest of all, two centuries of child abuse in Indian boarding schools had sometimes normalized punitive child rearing and sexualized violence within Indian families. Childhood patterns are repeated because they are what we know. Even when the schools were humane, teaching Native languages and practicing Native religion was illegal, something that continued until the 1970s.

Listening to these stories reminded me of the words of the great Ghanaian novelist Ayi Kwei Armah: "For seasons and seasons and seasons, all our movement has been going against our self, a journey into our killer's desire."[10]

In Indian Country, there is a belief that one act of violence takes four generations to heal. Because many centuries of such acts have yet to be known or taken seriously by most Americans, much less healed, this nation may keep repeating its violent childhood—until we find the wound and heal it.

I began to sense that a big part of our problem is simple ignorance of what the oldest cultures have to teach. In Minnesota, a young woman from Women of All Red Nations, a group born of the activism of the 1970s that forms local women's circles and also speaks out on everything from land rights to health dangers, explained to me that Native nations were often **matrilineal:** that is, clan identity passed through the mother, and a husband joined a wife's household, not vice versa. Matrilineal does not mean **matriarchal,** which, like **patriarchal,** assumes that **some** group has to dominate—a failure of the imagination. Rather, female and male roles were distinct but flexible and equally valued. Women were usually in charge of agriculture and men of hunting, but one was not more important than the other.

Women were also quite able to decide when and whether to have children. Sometimes when Native women came up to talk to me after meetings, they listed traditional herbs used as contraceptives or abortifacients, whether or not they were still in use. They knew that in the 1970s the Indian Health Service of the U.S. government admitted that thousands of Native women had been sterilized without their informed consent. Some called it a long-term strategy for taking over Indian lands, and others said it was the same racism that had sterilized black women in the South. Both the traditionalists and the young radicals of the American Indian Movement called it "slow genocide." It also took away women's ultimate power.

I discovered that Native languages, Cherokee and others—like Bengali and other ancient languages— didn't have gendered pronouns like **he** and **she.** A human being was a human being. Even the concept of **chief,** an English word of French origin, reflected a European assumption that there had to be one male kinglike leader. In fact, **caucus,** a word derived from the Algonquin languages, better reflected the layers of talking circles and the goal of consensus that were at the heart of governance. Men and women might have different duties, but the point was balance. For instance, men spoke at meetings, but women appointed and informed the men who spoke.

I found plenty of non-Native testimony to this different way of life. For instance, in the early days of this nation, white women teachers in Native schools wrote about feeling safer in tribal communities than in their own. Ethnographers and journalists described the rarity of rape. Abuse of women was right up there with theft and murder as one of three reasons a man could not become a **sachem,** or wise leader. Anything that is prohibited must have existed, but it shocked Europeans by its rarity. I found testimonies like that of General James Clinton—no friend of the Indians he hunted down—who wrote in 1779, "Bad as these savages are, they never violate the chastity of any woman, [not even] their prisoner."[11]

In California, I sat at a lunch table with a professor of premonotheistic spirituality, plus several women from some of the tribes in this state that has more Native Americans than any other. All agreed that the paradigm of human organization had been the circle, not the pyramid or hierarchy—and it could be again.

I'd never known there **was** a paradigm that linked instead of ranked. It was as if I'd been assuming opposition—and suddenly found myself in a welcoming world; like putting one's foot down for a steep stair and discovering level ground.

Still, when a Laguna law student from New Mexico complained that her courses didn't cite the Iroquois Confederacy as the model for the U.S. Constitution—or explain that this still existing Confederacy was the oldest continuing democracy in the world—I thought she was being romantic. But I read about the Constitutional Convention and discovered that Benjamin Franklin had indeed cited the Iroquois Confederacy as a model.[12] He was well aware of its success in unifying vast areas of the United States and Canada by bringing together Native nations for mutual decisions but also allowing autonomy in local ones. He hoped the Constitution could do the same for the thirteen states. That's why he invited two Iroquois men to Philadelphia as advisers. Among their first questions was said to be: **Where are the women?**

Unlike the Native model, the Founding Fathers' Constitution allowed slavery and private property as well as the exclusion of women. But like its model, the Constitution upended every system of governance in Europe, from ancient Greece to the Magna Carta, by putting all power in the hands of the people, creating layers of talking circles from local to federal, separating military and civilian power, and doing away with monarchies and hereditary rulers.

It seemed to me that Americans could at least say thank you. Instead, there was a notion that democracy was invented in ancient Greece, despite the fact that it had slavery as well as excluding women from citizenship, had citizenship also limited by class, and much more.

As a Native spokeswoman said with irony when Indian nations were being lectured about democracy in the 1970s, "We, the Indian people, may be the only citizens of this nation who really understand your form of government . . . copied from the Iroquois Confederacy."[13]

III.

BEFORE HOUSTON, I'D BEEN PROUD OF THE DIVERSE experiences and geography represented on the board of the Ms. Foundation for Women. Afterward, I couldn't believe there was not one woman from Indian Country.

In that way, I came to work closely with four women who joined us in the 1980s and 1990s, and we've continued to work informally ever since. Each of them could have been a success anywhere, yet chose to stay within a way of life that was, by conventional standards, marginalized, impoverished, and in danger of disappearing. Each of them had one Indian and one non-Indian parent, and that, too, would have made conventional success easier.

Their choice to stay and struggle proved the value of warmth and relatedness, of balance and a sense of the natural world. All I knew was that being around them made me feel oddly understood and hopeful.

Rayna Green made our lively board meetings even more so. As a Cherokee writer, folklorist, and anthropologist for the American Indian Program at the Smithsonian Institution in Washington, D.C., she enriched our work and extended it to new places. So did her down-home sense of humor. Thanks to her, I began to learn about the Trickster, a common figure in Native mythologies, a boundary crosser who can go anywhere. Unlike the Jester and the Clown, who are at the bottom of a hierarchical pile and survive only by making the king laugh, the Trickster is free, a paradox, a breaker of boundaries who makes us laugh—and laughter lets the sacred in. In Native spiritualities, there is often a belief that we cannot pray unless we've laughed. Because the Trickster is sometimes female and is the spirit of free space and the road, I began to feel I'd found a totem of my own.[14]

For instance, whenever I or others at our board meetings explained some injustice at too great a length, or otherwise stated the obvious with an air of discovery, Rayna's humor restored proportion. When she cycled off the board after five years, she left behind a saying that I would only understand later: **Feminism is memory.**

With the help of Paula Gunn Allen, I finally did understand. "Feminists too often believe," she wrote, "that no one has ever experienced the kind of society

that empowered women and made that empower-
ment the basis of rules and civilization. The price
the feminist community must pay because it is not
aware . . . is necessary confusion, division and much
lost time."[15]

Her conclusion was simple and mind-blowing:
"The root of oppression is the loss of memory."

NEXT ARRIVED WILMA MANKILLER, someone I
admired but had never met. She was the first woman
to be elected deputy chief of the Cherokee Nation
and soon would be appointed to serve out the term
of principal chief. Two years later, in 1987, she would
go on to become the first woman ever elected principal chief in modern times.

Wilma's gift for helping people find confidence
in themselves—for creating independence, not
dependence—was exactly the wisdom that the Ms.
Foundation needed. If she could work this miracle
in Indian Country despite centuries of loss of life,
land, and respect, she could help diverse women and
girls find their strengths, too.

I'd heard about Wilma's hard and pioneering work
before she and I had lunch to talk about her joining the Ms. board, so I was surprised to find myself
in the presence of a quiet, warm, listening woman.
It was hard to believe she was eleven years younger
than I; her wisdom was so much older. I felt as if I
were being sheltered by a strong and timeless tree.
Just being with her made it hard not to be as authen-

tic and shit free as she was. Her humor didn't come along often, but when it did, it was as natural as the weather. For instance, when anyone asked about her name with honest curiosity, she would explain that **Mankiller** was a hereditary title for someone who protected the village. But you knew one too many people had asked her about it in a condescending way when she just deadpanned, "I earned it."

After many board meetings and over dinners, I learned that she was the sixth of eleven children born to a Dutch and Irish mother and a full-blooded Cherokee father. Her maternal grandparents had disapproved of this marriage, but her mother fell in love—and never looked back.

Wilma spent her first ten years on her paternal grandfather's land, called Mankiller Flats, in rural Oklahoma. This was his allotment at the end place of the Trail of Tears, the infamous forced march of the 1830s that deprived Cherokees of their Georgia homeland. More than a third of all the men, women, and children on this march perished from cold, starvation, and disease. Thanks to President Andrew Jackson's Indian Removal Act, Cherokee land was left to white farmers who used it to grow cotton with slave labor and to mine gold.

Mankiller Flats had no electricity or running water, but there was a creek with medicinal herbs growing along its banks, acres of woods to explore, a garden with enough fruits and vegetables to preserve for the winter, and games to play by lantern light with her brothers and sisters. Only when the white church ladies came to distribute donated clothing did Wilma understand that her family was seen as needy. She acquired a lifetime aversion to the phrases **bless your heart** and **poor dears.**

Then in one of Washington's many attempts to "mainstream" Native Americans through relocation and assimilation—and also to get them off valuable land—her parents were persuaded to move to San Francisco for "a better life." At ten years old, Wilma suddenly found herself in the rough life of an urban housing project—a particular surprise for a girl who had never seen a phone or indoor plumbing or that many people in one place. It was, as she remembered, "like landing on Mars." Despite being given a hard time at school for being different, and despite her family's need to survive on her father's minimum-wage job, they found community and support in an Indian center with other relocated families.

When her father became a longshoreman, Wilma began to learn about union organizing at the kitchen table. Such jobs were not for girls, so she went to a local college with the hope of becoming a social worker. Then, just before her eighteenth birthday, she fell in love with a young man from Ecuador who had come here to study. By twenty-one, she was a married woman with two daughters and a husband who expected her to be a stay-at-home wife.

When Wilma and I began to spend more time together as friends, she talked about looking over at her young husband and wishing with all her heart that she could be the traditional wife he wanted.

But she also longed to be part of the political activism exploding all around her in San Francisco in the 1960s. She kept studying for a degree and took part in the nineteen-month-long occupation of Alcatraz, an abandoned prison on a federally owned island that was supposed to revert to Indian ownership. This experience of activism and community made her feel reconnected to her own life at last.

In 1974 Wilma and her husband went their separate ways. She continued college and found support among other single mothers, but still felt far from her own land. In the summer of 1976, she left her comfortable home, bought a red car with the last of her money, and set off with her two teenage daughters for Oklahoma and Mankiller Flats.

The family house had burned down years before, but they camped in their car by a lake near the ancestral land that her father had refused to sell, no matter how broke he was. Wilma and her daughters swam, caught fish, and harvested wild foods as she had done as a child. They learned to tell time by the sun, played Scrabble by lantern light, and listened to music from a portable radio by the campfire. Far from feeling insecure with no money and no home, Wilma said she felt free for the first time since she had left there. It made me realize how deep her connection to the land was.

Later, she found an abandoned house nearby, made it into a makeshift home, and applied for an entry-level job at the Cherokee Nation in Tahlequah. Several rejections later, she was hired as a writer of funding proposals. She not only worked harder than anyone else but began to prove her unique gift as an organizer. By respecting and expecting self-authority in others, she drew people out of passivity and despair. It was the beginning of her long and rocky path to leadership.

Three years later Wilma was driving on a deserted country road and suffered a head-on collision with another car. Her body was crushed, and she barely survived. She wasn't told until later that the driver of the other car was a woman friend—who had died instantly.

Wilma was in a wheelchair for what was supposed to be the rest of her life. Only after seventeen surgeries—plus a bout with myasthenia gravis, a weakening neuromuscular disease—did she walk again. Even then, she had to wear a metal brace from knee to ankle on one leg, suffered swelling and pain, and needed specially constructed shoes.

All this had happened long before we met. Her flowing skirts concealed the brace, and her calm concealed the pain. I never would have guessed any of it.

Together with Charlie Soap, a full-blooded Cherokee who also worked for the nation—and who was fluent in Cherokee, as Wilma was not—she took on what was seen as an impossible project: trying to make positive change for the residents of Bell, an isolated rural community of three hundred families. It was such a place of poverty and despair that even people who escaped were ashamed to say they ever lived there.[16]

Because Wilma was patient, respectful, listened, and understood that people could only gain confidence by making decisions for themselves, she slowly persuaded families to trust her enough to come to a community meeting and decide what they needed most. Wilma thought it might be a school, but they chose something that would help everyone, young and old: running water. They had been surviving with one pump by carrying pails every day. To connect to the main water supply would mean digging eighteen miles of deep ditches, laying large pipes, and adding two miles of smaller ones to every house. Wilma told them she would raise the money and find the equipment—if they did the work themselves.

No one had thought this was even a possibility, but Wilma's faith in them raised the hope that they could help themselves. Entire families, from children to the elderly, did the work of digging and laying pipe. It took fourteen long and hard months, but in the end there were two successes: running water and a community with confidence instead of despair. It was such a feat that CBS News covered it, people around the country were inspired, and so were viewers in the underdeveloped parts of the world that Bell so resembled.[17] In times to come, this story of Wilma and Bell would be made into a feature movie, **The Cherokee Word for Water.**

Charlie and Wilma bonded over this long struggle, and in 1986, the same year she joined the Ms. board, they were married.

Once after a painful Ms. Foundation meeting, with too many proposals from rape crisis centers and too little money to give them, Wilma told me the story of something she hadn't dealt with herself. In a movie house near her housing project in San Francisco, she was sexually assaulted by a group of teenage boys. She had talked with them because she felt flattered that anyone wanted to talk to her— and then was betrayed. She didn't tell her parents or her friends. She didn't go into much detail with me either. The experience still felt both too serious and not serious enough. Only sitting in a circle of women, listening to similar stories, allowed her to realize that she wasn't alone, it wasn't her fault, she could speak up.

From then on I realized she had said yes to joining us for a reason, conscious or not. I thought of this again when she and Charlie and I spent a winter holiday in Mexico with Alice Walker. At the very end of our stay, Wilma said to us quietly, "This is the first time in my life that I've been with people who didn't need anything from me." It gave me a glimpse of the price Wilma had paid for leadership among a people who had been so long prevented from leading themselves.

In 1987 she ran to be elected principal chief of the Cherokee Nation, a very controversial thing to do. There had never been an elected female Cherokee chief in modern times, and many Cherokees had come to assume that male leadership was as inevitable as Christianity and store-bought food. In the long past, the Cherokee Nation's council of female elders had chosen leaders and even decided if wars should be fought. Treaties with Washington had to be signed by female as well as male elders, something officials there mercilessly ridiculed as "Petticoat Government." Some modern Cherokees still feared this ridicule, or thought a woman couldn't represent the Nation in Washington, or both.

Her election campaign had all the complexities of any statewide campaign, plus the necessity of reaching enrolled Cherokee voters in states outside Oklahoma and in foreign countries. I found myself in the familiar role of helping with fund-raisers and even a television commercial. But in the end, Wilma won because of her record of helping people to help themselves, as she had in Bell, and also because Cherokee traditionalists, who had rarely voted before, saw her leadership as a return to the balance and reciprocity of the past.

After that, I watched as she quietly, person by person, one rural community at a time, one Washington lobbying battle at a time, helped people build their own water systems, youth programs, and a health care delivery system that was a model for other rural areas. Gradually she brought the Cherokee Nation from being mostly dependent on government allotments to being mostly independent through communally run businesses. In order to honor other Native women leaders, she interviewed many for her book, **Every Day Is a Good Day: Reflections by Contemporary Indigenous Women.**[18]

In 1991 she was reelected with an unprecedented 82 percent of the vote. In 1994 President Bill Clinton invited leaders from all the Native nations to meet in Washington, a first in history. This almost totally male group elected Wilma as one of its two spokespeople.

Six years after that, I went to the White House with Wilma and watched as President Clinton and Hillary Clinton presented her with a Medal of Freedom, the highest civilian honor.

As she stood there, strong, kind, and not at all intimidated by another chief of state, I was not the only one in the audience who thought, **She could be president.** I also thought, **In a just country, she would be.**

In Wilma's last year on the board, she overlapped with Rebecca Adamson, a shy, slender, magnetic woman who was a self-educated expert on grassroots economics. Younger and more diffident than Rayna and Wilma, she seemed to defeat her shyness by sheer force of will. Her gift for understanding everything from the most humble detail to the most challenging economic theory reminded me of that 1930s ideal, the working-class intellectual.

Unlike Rayna and Wilma, Rebecca had grown up totally outside Indian Country. She was saved by summers in the Smoky Mountains, where her Cherokee grandmother lived. There, Rebecca discovered a way of life that felt like home. Finally, she quit university to become the first staff member hired by the Coalition of Indian Controlled School Boards, a group with the huge goal of reforming schools that were abusing or shaming Indian children, whether they were run by religions, the Bureau of Indian Affairs, or local school boards. In Rebecca's experience, this right to schools that didn't shame and abuse was to become to Indian Country what registering and voting in the South was to African Americans—the beginning of a larger movement. Given the parallels of prejudice and power, Rebecca had her life threatened more than once.

By the time I met her, she had finished college part time, earned an advanced degree in economics, and was advising the UN International Labor Organization plus indigenous groups in other countries. She had a gift for being understandable—a sure sign of a good organizer—and wrote an essay on reservation life with the concise title "Land Rich, Dirt Poor." She also put her organizing goal into a four-word slogan for T-shirts: DEVELOPMENT—WITH VALUES ADDED.

I wouldn't fully understand how deep "values added" went until Rebecca asked me to come to a two-day meeting of activists near the Pine Ridge Reservation in South Dakota. My role was to bring knowledge of Gandhian village-level economics, plus the low-income and welfare women who had created their own family-friendly small businesses with the support of the Ms. Foundation. Otherwise, I had no idea what to expect.

Our meeting took place in the small tribally owned motel next to South Dakota's Badlands. The goal was to figure out how to create communal economic success in an individualistic economic world.

For two full days and late into the nights, this casual, serious, idealistic, practical discussion went on. I noticed how carefully everyone listened and how little ego seemed invested in speaking. Every once in a while, Larry Emerson, a Navajo educator, and Birgil Kills Straight, the Lakota traditionalist from the Oglala Sioux Nation who had first hired Rebecca in the school movement, would speak, sometimes illustrating their comments on the blackboard; then they'd just listen again. Neither seemed to need to talk a lot, to show how much he knew, to approve or disapprove what others said, or to be in control. It took me a while to realize, **These men talk only when they have something to say.** I almost fell off my chair.

In those meetings, I learned that even economic diagrams needn't be linear. Ours was a nest of concentric circles, and an enterprise was measured by its value to each circle, from the individual and family to the community and environment. I realized that Rebecca and her colleagues were trying to do nothing less than transform the System of National Accounts, the statistical framework here and in most countries for measuring economic activity. For instance, the value of a tree depends on its estimated value or sale price, but if it is sold and cut down, there is no accounting on the debit side of the ledger for loss of oxygen, seeding of other trees, or value to the community or the environment. This group was inventing a new way of measuring profit and loss.

By the end of our days together, I understood economics in a whole new way. A balance sheet really could be about balance.

FAITH SMITH, AN OJIBWA educator from Chicago, followed Rebecca onto the board. Quiet, intense, and classically beautiful, Faith represented the half of Native people who live in cities and have a multitribe experience. To give urban Native students a college that included their own history, she helped to found the Native American Educational Services College, a small, private, Indian-controlled, degree-granting institution where students ranged in age from seventeen to seventy.

She told me that only 10 percent of Native students who enter mainstream institutions stay long enough to get a degree, partly because they are in an academic version of the world that doesn't include their experience or even their existence. However, this college was graduating 70 percent of those who entered and sending 20 to 30 percent on to graduate schools.

When I went to see Faith at the college in Chicago, we had lunch with students who told me that, in other schools, they felt forced to choose between an education that excluded them and a community that included them. Here, they could have both.

Lunch was a lesson in itself. The students explained that food was a generational marker. Their grandparents and others born before World War II had lived in the country and eaten traditional Native foods, the kind that had caused colonists to write home about how much taller, stronger, and healthier Indians were. Then came generations of people living on reservations, dependent on government rations of refined sugar, lard, and white flour, and also with trading posts that dealt in alcohol. Health declined, and alcoholism and diabetes went up. Every student now eating healthy food in that sunny multipurpose classroom had at least one friend or family member who was on dialysis. Taking relatives to hospitals and clinics had become a family ritual.

I could see Faith was an example in many ways. For instance, she was president of this college, yet she paid herself the same as the teachers and the janitor whenever cash flow became an issue. Her physical self was important, too. Overworked but healthy and slender, she was a living, breathing example of the possible. A sign on the lunchroom wall brought it home:

YOU CANNOT THINK YOURSELF INTO RIGHT LIVING.
YOU LIVE YOURSELF INTO RIGHT THINKING.
—Native Elders

IV.

WHENEVER I WAS ON NEW TURF, I ASKED ABOUT the vertical history of people who had lived there in the long past or who might still be there. I tried never to give a speech without including Native examples, just as we do other groups in this diverse country. It was like casting bread upon the waters. It almost always came back buttered—with new knowledge.

• On a book tour in my own college town of Northampton, Massachusetts, I try out my question about original cultures. A very old and scruffy-looking white guy at the back of the bookstore says he's heard there are abandoned fields nearby that have an odd pattern of large bumps in the earth every few feet, like a giant rubber bathmat. They've been there since time immemorial and are supposed to be an Indian method of planting.

I enlist the help of a Smith College librarian. We discover the bumps are **milpa,** small mounds of earth on which complementary crops were planted. Unlike linear plowing, which encourages water runoff and soil erosion, the circular pattern traps rainfall. Each mound is planted with a cluster of the Three Sisters that were the staples of Indian agriculture: corn, beans, and squash. The corn provided a stalk for the beans to climb, while also shading the vulnerable

beans. The ground cover from the squash sta-
bilized the soil, and the bean roots kept the soil
fertile by providing nitrogen. As a final touch,
marigolds and other natural pesticides were
planted around each mound to keep harmful
insects away. Altogether it was a system so perfect that in some Central American countries
too poor to adopt linear plowing with machin-
ery, artificial pesticides, and monocrops of agri-
business, the same **milpa** have been producing
just fine for four thousand years.[19] Not only
that, but **milpa** can be planted in forests without clear-cutting the trees; at most, by remov-
ing a few branches to let sunlight through on a
mound. This method was a major reason why
three-fifths of all food staples in the world were
developed in the Americas.

• I'm in Oklahoma City for a Women of the
Year lunch honoring women business leaders.
This is not a city where it seems like a good idea
to ask about Indian Country. It is so conservative that its major newspaper prints Bible quo-
tations on the front page. Also I'm distracted
by making fund-raising calls on which depends
the fate of **Ms.** magazine. Its brief and acciden-
tal owner is threatening to close it unless we
come up with the purchase price pronto—a
form of extortion, since he knows its staff cares
too much to let it go.

After lunch a middle-aged woman with an

American flag in her lapel tells me that she is haunted by a story her grandmother told her. An Oklahoma mining company was founded in the 1930s for the sole purpose of burrowing into and looting Indian burial mounds. Local newspapers compared its "finds" to the treasures of Egyptian tombs, a description that enticed souvenir hunters but made the burial mounds seem even more remote from local Native families whose ancestors had been interred there. This company traveled the country selling looted artifacts—flint knives as big as swords, copper bowls, pipes made to look like animals, shells carved into jewelry, pearls—everything for a few dollars or even pennies. Since they assumed there was little market for cloth or wood items, they piled them up and burned them.

Only after a couple of years did the Oklahoma legislature bow to outrage from archaeologists and Native families by passing a law against this looting. In revenge, the mining company strung dynamite through the mounds and blew them up.

I will remember this day in Oklahoma for the vengefulness of that dynamite and the importance of that grandmother's story. When I return to my hotel room, there is another reason. A woman I have not met but who cares about the fate of **Ms.** magazine calls to say that she will help us buy it out of bondage. Her **yes** puts us over the top. As the last of a dozen women investors, she makes its continuation possible.

She also remarks on what a coincidence it is to find me in Oklahoma City, where her family comes from, and where she grew up. She is the feminist granddaughter of that very conservative family that owns the Oklahoma City newspaper with the Bible verses on the front page. She fled Oklahoma but took with her the spirit of the land, not the newspaper.

• In Arizona where I've been speaking, I'm invited to Thanksgiving dinner by Leslie Silko, a Laguna Pueblo novelist and filmmaker whose writing seems to link all eras and living things. I know her only from spending one odd weekend with her and her screenwriting partner, Larry McMurtry, at a hotel near the Dallas/ Fort Worth airport. We had met to talk about working on a possible film project together, but never could solve the problem of how to do the script. As compensation, we bought exotic cowboy boots.

Dinner is with Leslie and her mother at home, a small sun-bleached wooden house that looks as if it grew out of the desert. After dinner, Leslie gives me the memorable gift of a ride on one of her Indian ponies. Among the things I discover, as we amble along at the ponies' own pace, is that the Serpent Woman of the Midwest is called Spider Woman here in the

Southwest—but she is the same source of creation and energy. I remember Spider Woman from the first page of Leslie's novel **Ceremony**. She is the Thought Woman who names things and so brings them into being. Until then, I had imagined myself alone in believing that spiders should be the totem of writers. Both go into a space alone and spin out of their own bodies a reality that has never existed before.

Until this ride, I'd felt good in nature only if it was near the ocean. Perhaps because an ocean beach had always been our goal during the travels in my childhood, or perhaps because my experiences of midwestern green expanses had been cold and lonely, the ocean was the only part of nature that I, a city and village person, really enjoyed.

But this was different. The great expanse of ivory-to-beige-to-rose sand, the seeming nothingness that turned out to be a delicate universe of plant life as soon as you looked closer—all this was laid out before us as we rode in the late afternoon light.

I tried to explain all this to Leslie, a little ashamed of confessing any discomfort in nature to this woman who was so at home in it, yet mystified as to why I was undepressed and unreminded of midwestern childhood sadness here, so far from any ocean.

"Well, of course," Leslie said. "The desert used to be the ocean floor."

Suddenly, I had a moment of seeing this land as a living being in its own time span, as she did.

Clearly, Columbus never "discovered" America, in either sense of that word. The people who knew it were already here.

V.

WILMA DID NOT RUN FOR A THIRD TERM AS PRINCIPAL chief; she had received a diagnosis of cancer and needed chemotherapy. I knew she dreaded the regular visits to the hospital for weeks of outpatient infusions. She had already spent way too much of her life in hospitals, and she was not as invulnerable as she seemed. Her two daughters had been with her faithfully in past health crises, but they had jobs and lives in Oklahoma. I asked Wilma if she would let me stay with her in Boston, instead of going on a scheduled trip to Australia that I could easily do another time—hoping but not believing that she, always the strong one, would say yes—but she actually did. Of all the gifts she had given me, that was the greatest.

Wilma and I stayed in a big old-fashioned house that friends of hers had left for the summer. Every morning we went to the hospital, where chemicals were dripped slowly into her veins, then we came home to watch movies we had rented, including every episode of Helen Mirren's **Prime Suspect**, a depiction of female strength and complexity that Wilma loved.

For me, those weeks in Boston, with Wilma, became a lesson in her ability to be "of good mind," in her phrase, which also meant a people's ability to survive. Her hope was to preserve what she called The Way, to keep it alive, for that future moment when the current obsession with excess and hierarchy imploded. Wilma said many Native people believed that the earth as a living organism would just one day shrug off the human species that was destroying it—and start over. In a less cataclysmic vision, humans would realize that we are killing our home and each other, and seek out The Way. That's why Native people were guarding it.

This seemed impossibly generous. It also seemed just plain impossible. Too many Native people have themselves forgotten or forsaken The Way, with too few chances to relearn it. This worldview has more layers than I know, but it seems to start with a circle in which all living things are related, and with a goal of balance, not dominance, which upsets balance.

In our weeks of talk, movies, and friendship, I watched as Wilma turned a medical ordeal into one more event in her life, but not its definition. I believe she was teaching me an intimate form of The Way. In her words, "Every day is a good day—because we are part of everything alive."

That wasn't Wilma's only gift to me. Often over the last dozen years, I've joined her in Oklahoma at the end of the summer for the Cherokee National

Holiday: days filled with ceremonial dances, feasting on traditional and not-so-traditional foods, buying creations of artists and craftspeople in booths that ring the campground, and meeting members of other nations who come as dancers and guests. It was there that I finally fulfilled the dancing prophecy of the women who gave me that ceremonial red shawl in Houston so many years before.

ON A HUGE GRASSY FIELD surrounded by low bleachers and tall klieg lights, dozens of traditional dancers were circling slowly in the summer night. Each participant or group was dressed and dancing in a traditional style of a tribe and a part of the country, but each person was unique, too. There was no program to explain the order of the dancers. Each seemed focused internally, not on the audience. Prizes would be given out eventually, but no one seemed aware of being judged.

This balance between tribe and individuality, community and uniqueness, was a surprise in a world that makes us think we have to make a choice between them.

After this public Holiday, Wilma and Charlie invited me to join them in the all-night Cherokee Stomp Dance that follows. Even after 1978, when the American Indian Religious Freedom Act finally lifted the legal ban on sacred rituals, this ceremony, which had gone on for millennia, remained safe and secret, or at least private. Outsiders had to be invited to go—or even to know **where** to go.

We drove down dark rural roads with no signs or lights to mark their twists and turns, then parked in an unmarked field amid dozens of cars and pickup trucks. Walking toward a large flickering light rising into the sky, I gradually saw that it came from a bonfire that was even taller than the men and women moving around it. On our side were rough wooden shelters and dozens of long picnic tables, all lit with lanterns or bare bulbs hanging from the trees. They were laden with enough food to last the night. There were old-fashioned cauldrons of stew, platters of fried chicken, dozens of deep-dish fruit pies, and mounds of fry bread made with the white flour, lard, and sugar that government rations had turned into a time-honored and unhealthy treat. Alcohol was not allowed in this sacred space, but there were coolers of soft drinks and urns of coffee. Family groups were eating or talking quietly—not hushed, as in a church, but not loud or boisterous either. People were watching the dancers from lawn chairs, some far from the fire and wrapped in blankets against the chill, others closer and just resting before rejoining the dancing. On the other side of the huge bonfire, I could see a shadowy group of men chanting deep-toned call-and-response songs.

Dancers spiraled around the huge bonfire, the innermost circle barely moving and the outermost one increasing in speed like a whip until only the young and strong could keep up. Charlie invited me to join with him, and it was daunting, like trying to get on a moving train. Once inside, I realized that the dancers were not so much stomping as caressing the earth with each sliding step. So many together made a deep **whooshing** sound. We formed a curved line, like a huge living nautilus shell, with women elders at its heart around the fire. I knew from Wilma that their heavy leggings were sewn with small tortoise shells, and each shell was filled with tiny pebbles, so as their feet and rattling shells hit the ground, there was a sound I'd never heard before, yet it was right and familiar. Women elders were keeping the rhythm of life.

I knew that Wilma should be dancing with these women elders at the center near the fire. But could she?

I sat with her at the outer edge of the firelight as she prepared for a ritual that has survived centuries of land loss, warfare, lethal epidemics, outlawed languages and spiritual practices, and other attempts to take away home, culture, pride, family, and life itself. I watched as Wilma wrapped thick strips of cloth from knee to ankle, covering the steel brace that she could not walk without, adding the weight of tortoise shells and stones by her own choice. She moved out of the dark, past the dancers at the speeding end of the spiral, into the inner circle of women moving around the fire.

And then she danced.

IT'S A FEW YEARS LATER, and I know that Wilma
still has health problems. Lately, she has had a series
of tests for fatigue and back pains. But I assume she
will overcome these obstacles because she always
has. I have been with her through dialysis because
of kidney disease inherited from her father, a kidney transplant, cancer brought on by immune sup-
pressants to maintain the transplant, chemotherapy
and a second transplant, then a second bout with
cancer.

For a long time, we've wanted to write a book
together. Now we've made plans to set aside the
month of May 2010 to spread out our notes and
research on her kitchen table and start writing about
traditional practices in original cultures that modern
ones could learn from. She has even less time for
writing than I do, so we're excited about it. Also,
if we have one more start-up left in us, it will be a
school for organizers. Wilma can pass on her gift for
creating independence; I can explain why stories and
listening are part of change that comes from the bottom up. Organizers from this and other countries
can come to teach and brainstorm solutions to one
another's problems.

In March I'm at a conference at my own college,
where I always imagine my former self on campus,
a little scared and out of place. Yet now I'm about to
be seventy-six and planning to live to a hundred. I'm

doing work I love, with friends I love. What could be better than that?

Then I get an unusual message from Wilma: **Can I come now instead of waiting for May?**

I know what this means. I cancel conference and birthday plans. On the phone with Charlie, I learn that Wilma has been diagnosed with fourth-stage pancreatic cancer. It is one of the least curable and most painful forms.

Two plane flights and a long drive later, I arrive at Wilma and Charlie's house on Mankiller Flats. Her caregiving team is assembling. Besides Charlie, there are Gina and Felicia, her two daughters, who come and go from their nearby homes; Dr. Gloria Grim, a young physician who heads the Cherokee Rural Health Clinics that Wilma started; also two of Wilma's longtime women friends, one a nurse. They have had a lifetime pact to come and stay whenever one of Wilma's many health crises seems likely to be her last.

Wilma herself is lying in a hospital bed next to the big four-poster she shares with Charlie, so they will still be in the same room. She is calm, honest, laconic, even funny, and as clear as any doctor about what is happening inside her body. She can tell I haven't accepted any of this yet. As if to comfort me, she says most Americans want to die at home, but many spend their last weeks in a hospital without friends and family. I ask her if she's now organizing a campaign for the right to die at home. This makes her laugh, and I buy some time.

All I can think of is her description of her near-death experience after the head-on car crash years earlier. She told me it felt as if she were flying through space, faster than any living thing could fly, feeling warm and loved in every pore of her being, as if she were one with the universe, then realizing: **This is the purpose of life!** Only the thought of her two young daughters made her turn back.

I've always remembered that and hoped other people I love would share this last feeling. One day I hope I will, too. But I can't think about such a moment for Wilma now. I can't wish it for her, because then she will be gone. She shows me a statement she is making about her illness, explaining that she is "mentally and spiritually prepared for the journey." She's definitely more ready than I am.

That night I'm bolted awake by hearing Wilma cry out in pain. I find Charlie warming blankets on a potbellied stove. As a traditional healer, he not only knows the uses of herbs but has an instinct for the untried. He has devised a system of spreading heated blankets over Wilma's body, and it does seem to relieve the pain. This terrifying sequence is repeated several times.

The next day I ask the young Dr. Grim, who could not be more different from her name, what can be done about the pain. She says Wilma knows that morphine and other opiates would help, but taking enough to cut the pain would also dull her consciousness. She wants to be fully present for as long as she can.

In the next few days, relatives, friends, and colleagues come from miles around to pay their respects. They sit near her, reminisce about the past, argue politics for the future, and bring pies, cakes, and casseroles for ever-increasing numbers of visitors. Children bring flowers, or sing a song from church or school, or just watch television. Some stare at Wilma and their parents in a way that says they will never forget. As some of the older visitors leave, they say, "I'll see you on the other side of the mountain."

I've never seen such honesty about dying.

People closest to the family do the small and continuous tasks: laundry, bringing in firewood, feeding Wilma's indoor dog and outdoor cats. Soon, they include our mutual friends of many years, Kristina Kiehl and Bob Friedman, who fly in from San Francisco. Kristina invents a way of washing Wilma's hair in bed since she can no longer stand in the shower. Bob takes over the continual task of washing dishes for the many people who gather in the big kitchen, talking softly.

At night Wilma calls out in pain. Then it begins during the day, too. I can't bear it. I go into full research mode and phone every physician I know. I learn that there are several kinds of drastic nerve blocks that could diminish her pain and leave her mind clear. But such procedures can be done only in a hospital.

Wilma's caregiving team has a conference with Dr. Grim, who says a local ambulance could take her to and from the hospital—more than two hours or so each way. We talk to Wilma. She thinks about it. The ambulance comes and parks in the yard just in case. She decides she might die in transit, or become too hooked to tubes to leave the hospital, and she wants to be at home in Indian Country. She thanks us for giving her a choice. To me, she says with some of her old humor, "You're an organizer to the end."

It also reminds me of an organizing principle: **Anybody who is experiencing something is more expert in it than the experts.** From that moment on, I accept Wilma's wisdom.

Seeing that I need a task, Wilma's daughters assign me the duty of making sure each visitor's contribution is recorded on a list in the kitchen. I write names down next to rhubarb and peach pies, vats of sweet iced tea, and trays of cornbread. A high school student carries in crates of bottled water, and a silent man in overalls mows the lawn just because it needs it. Wilma's family wants to be able to thank each person, hence the list. Once again the individual honors the community, and vice versa. I finally understand why Winterhawk, Charlie's son by an earlier marriage, turned down a scholarship to Dartmouth and stayed here instead. It was not just land that brought Wilma home; it was also community.

At the long kitchen table, knowing Wilma creates a bond among us, and strangers talk. The husband of her dear friend who died in the car crash has been here for days, and explains that Wilma helped to raise their daughter. Gail Small, Wilma's friend and one of the activists she admires and profiled in her book

Every Day Is a Good Day, has come all the way from the Northern Cheyenne Nation in Montana. There, Gail has waged a lifetime battle to keep extractive and exploitive energy companies from destroying the land, and to keep religious schools from abusing the next generation. As she says, "Children were sexually molested by priests and nuns, then came home to spread the cancer themselves." She started not only an environmental group called Native Action, but also a high school on the reservation.

Oren Lyons has come from his home in upstate New York, the headquarters of the governing body of the six nations of the Iroquois Confederacy, or Haudenosaunee. It is the oldest continuous democracy in the world.[20] Whenever Wilma or I used to ask him something serious, he always answered, "I have to consult with my women elders first." In fact, it was the equality of women in those nations that inspired white women neighbors to begin organizing the suffrage movement.

Wilma's own mother is there every morning, having walked from her house just down a dirt road. She tells me that Wilma took her to Ireland to see her own hereditary land for the first time. We both know that she will outlive her daughter.

I've promised to bring Wilma conversations from her kitchen table, since she is unable to have them herself. Over the two weeks I've been here, this house has become like a ship at sea for me; nothing else exists. I tell her that, thanks to her, I've come to understand the power of community. There is silence. I fear her good hours are gone. Then she smiles and says, "You'll never be the same."

Later, a medical attendant arrives, and I know she has decided to accept morphine. Since this is real life, not a novel, there is no sharp line, no definitive good-bye. Wilma just seems to pull away from us, like an ocean tide receding from all of us left standing on the beach.

The moment after is utterly different from the moment before. Now I understand why people believe the soul departs with the last breath. Everything looks the same, yet everything is different. We stand in the room around Wilma's bed. She is no longer there.

Respectful attendants come with a stretcher on wheels, open the French doors, and move her slowly across the porch where she loved to sit, and onto her beloved land one last time.

Later, her ashes will be returned to the banks of the spring where Charlie's medicinal herbs grow. This is where she wanted to be.

IT'S THE BEAUTIFUL SATURDAY MORNING of April 10, 2010, and we are sitting outdoors at the Cherokee Cultural Grounds. Though it's only four days after Wilma's death, 150 tribal, state, and national leaders, including President Clinton and President Obama, have sent messages, and about fifteen hundred people have gathered to hear friends and family share personal memories. It's the best kind of memorial because each of us will leave knowing Wilma a little better than we did when we arrived.

Among her last requests was that everyone wear or carry something in her improbable favorite color: bright pink. A symbolic drink made of strawberries is served. Strawberries are called **ani** in Cherokee and are supposed to help her make her way through the sky to the ancestors.

For me, this is the beginning of years of picking up the phone—and realizing I can't talk to her; of thinking about our book—and knowing we can't write it together; of hearing something that would make her laugh—yet I can't tell her.

My friend Robin Morgan, author of a lovingly researched novel about pagan times,[21] has called to tell me that Wilma is being honored in many countries around the world as a Great One. Pagan and Native cultures share many beliefs, and one is that lighting signal fires at high points in the landscape will light the path of a Great One home. As Wilma's friends put it, she is finally going to the other side of the mountain.

At the end of my own tribute to Wilma, I tell the people gathered here in rural Oklahoma that in no fewer than twenty-three countries, signal fires have been lighted for Wilma, and are now lighting her way home.

Back at Wilma and Charlie's house, Charlie carries out her last request, one she was and wasn't laughing when she made. She asked him to take the metal leg brace that she had had to wear all the years after the car crash, place it in a field, and blast it with a shotgun. He does just that.

IT IS NOW FIVE YEARS AFTER Wilma's death, and I'm more than ever learning from and about original cultures—on my own continent, in India, and in countries of Africa, where we all came from. Our current plight is not made inevitable by human nature. What once was could be again—in a new way.

I once asked Wilma if one day my ashes could be with hers, and she said yes. In the future they will be. Even though my ancestors were forced to escape their homes and come here, I feel I've found my land.

If I could say one thing to Wilma, it would be this:

We're still here.

Coming Home

As I write this, I'm fifteen years older than my father was when he died.

Only after fifty did I begin to admit that I was suffering from my own form of imbalance. Though I felt sorry for myself for not having a home, I was always rescued by defiance and a love of freedom. Like my father for instance, I'd convinced myself that I wasn't earning enough money as a freelancer to file income tax returns, something I had to spend months with an accountant to make up for. Like him, I'd saved no money, so there was a good reason for my fantasy of ending up as a bag lady. I handled it just by saying to myself, **I'll organize the other bag ladies.**

Finally, I had to admit that I too was leading an out-of-balance life, even if it was different in degree from my father's. I needed to make a home for myself; otherwise it would do me in, too. Home is a symbol of the self. Caring for a home is caring for one's self.

Gradually, the rooms that I had used mostly as an office and a closet were filled with things that gave me pleasure when I opened the door. I had a kitchen that worked, a real desk to spread papers on, and a welcoming room where visiting friends could stay, something I'd always wanted as a child when I was living with my mother in places too sad to invite anyone. Though it was a little late after fifty, I even began to save money.

After months of nesting—and shopping for such things as sheets and candles with a pleasure that bordered on orgasmic—an odd thing happened: I found myself enjoying travel even more. Now that being on the road was my choice, not my fate, I lost the melancholy feeling of **Everybody has a home but me.** I could leave—because I could return. I could return—because I knew adventure lay just beyond an open door. Instead of **either/or,** I discovered a whole world of **and.**

Long before all these divisions opened between home and the road, between a woman's place and a man's world, humans followed the crops, the seasons, traveling with their families, our companions, our animals, our tents. We built campfires and moved from place to place. This way of traveling is still in our cellular memory.

Living things have evolved as travelers. Even migrating birds know that nature doesn't demand a choice between nesting and flight. On journeys as long as twelve thousand miles, birds tuck their beaks under wings and rest on anything from ice floes to the decks of ships at sea. Then, once they arrive at their destination, they build a nest and select each twig with care.

I wish the road had spared my father long enough to show him the possibilities of **and** instead of **either/or.** If he'd been around when I finally created a home, I might have had something to teach him, as well as time to thank him for the lessons he taught me.

I wish my mother hadn't lived an even more polarized life of **either/or.** Like so many women before her—and so many even now—she never had a journey of her own. With all my heart, I wish she could have followed a path she loved.

I pause for a moment as I write these words. My hand, long-fingered like my father's, rests on my desk where I do work I love, in rooms that were my first home—and probably will be my last. I'm surrounded by images of friends and chosen objects that knew someone's touch before mine—and will know others after I am gone. I notice that my middle finger lifts and falls involuntarily, exactly as my father's did. I recognize in myself, as I did in him, a tap of restlessness. It's time to leave—there is so much out there to do and say and listen to.

I can go on the road—because I can come home. I come home—because I'm free to leave. Each way of being is more valued in the presence of the other.

This balance between making camp and following the seasons is both very ancient and very new. We all need both.

My father did not have to trade dying alone for the joys of the road. My mother did not have to give up a journey of her own to have a home.

Neither do I. Neither do you.

At home in New York City, 2010.

COURTESY OF ANNIE LEIBOVITZ

NOTES OF GRATITUDE

——

WHEN A BOOK HAS TAKEN SHAPE OVER TWO decades, there are a lot of people to thank.

Ann Godoff at Random House was the first to believe in an on-the-road book by a traveling feminist organizer. Then Kate Medina became my editor, and if there were an Olympics for kindness, support, and patience, she would win it.

Hedgebrook, the women writers' retreat on Whidbey Island, Washington, gave me solitude, a magical cabin, and time to discover and write the story of my father.

Because I depended on memory as a curator of stories—the road is way too intense for journal keeping—I turned to the Sophia Smith Collection at Smith College to supply places and times, and to Google to deliver everything my memory did not.

I was lucky to have houseguests who volunteered as readers—especially Lenedra Carroll, who read it all, and also Agunda Okeyo. New York friends Kathy Najimy and Debra Winger read chapters. My friend Irene Kubota Neves, a journalist and an age peer,

read and commented on every word, and even rescued some from the cutting-room floor.

Through all of this, Robert Levine, my friend and
literary agent, kept his faith that a book would get
done, and gave the publishers faith, too.

As the years stretched on, I could devote time each
summer to writing, then I was traveling the rest of
the year and starting over again the next summer.
Stories were soon creating more than one book.

Though I was often rescued by my colleague Amy
Richards, who read and gave me advice, there was
still way too much. Finally, Suzanne Braun Levine,
the first editor of **Ms.** magazine, who knows how
to cut like a sculptor, joined Amy. Together, they
turned Way Too Much into Just Enough. As they
pointed out, I could keep on publishing road stories
on a website. (Go to gloriasteinem.com.)

I've also had the pleasure of watching Amy, my co-
worker through three books and more than twenty
years, become a writer of more books than I, a giver
of more lectures than I, and a creative organizer here
and in other countries. There is no one who could
make me feel better about the present and more
hopeful about the future.

Finally, I thank Robin Morgan for reminding me,
even when the road was causing me to write the least,
that there is no better moment in life than finding
the right word.

NOTES

———

INTRODUCTION: ROAD SIGNS

1. Marilyn Mercer, "Gloria Steinem: The Unhidden Persuader," **McCall's,** January 1972.
2. Robin Morgan, **The Word of a Woman: Feminist Dispatches, 1968–1992** (New York: W. W. Norton, 1992), pp. 275–77.
3. Margaret Atwood, "Headscarves to Die For," **New York Times Book Review,** August 15, 2004.
4. Because only women's ova pass on mitochondrial DNA and only men's sperm pass on the Y chromosome, the mix in a current population indicates who came from afar and who didn't. Natalie Angier, "Man vs. Woman: In History's Travel Olympics, There's No Contest," **New York Times,** October 27, 1998; she is quoting from a study by the Harvard School of Public Health and Stanford University, reported in Mark T. Seilelstad, Eric Minch, and L. Luca Cavalli-Sforza, "Genetic Evidence for a Higher Female Migration Rate in Humans," **Nature Genetics** 20 (November 1998).

5. Douglas Martin, "Yang Huanyi, the Last User of a Secret Women's Code," **New York Times**, October 7, 2004.

CHAPTER I: MY FATHER'S FOOTSTEPS

1. Bruce Chatwin, **The Songlines** (New York: Penguin Books, 1987), p. 161.

CHAPTER II: TALKING CIRCLES

1. Besides advertising campaigns and Hollywood movies that romanticized car ownership, Detroit lobbied for legislation against—and sometimes bought up and destroyed—public transportation, from the streetcars of eastern cities to the trains of the California coastline. In a parallel effort, the construction industry sold isolated houses over communal housing. See T. H. Robsjohn-Gibbings, **Homes of the Brave** (New York: Alfred A. Knopf, 1954).

2. To hear exactly why—in very smart and angry observations of men on the Left that may still ring true—read the classic "Goodbye to All That" by Robin Morgan. Originally written for **Rat Subterranean News** in 1970, it has since been reprinted in **The Word of a Woman: Feminist Dispatches, 1968–1992** (New York: W. W. Norton, 1992).

3. In checking history, I found that just before the

march began, Josephine Baker, dressed in the uniform of the French Resistance, spoke about the racism that caused her move to France. Daisy Bates was the only woman officially listed as a speaker at the march. She was substituting for Myrlie Evers, widow of Medgar Evers, who had been murdered in Mississippi just a month before, but Bates was unable to reach the Lincoln Memorial through the traffic. Male civil rights leaders marched on Pennsylvania Avenue with the press, while female leaders marched on Independence Avenue. Anna Arnold Hedgeman was the only woman on the planning committee for the 1963 march. She consistently demanded that women be speakers on the program. For her inside account, see her 1964 autobiography, **A Trumpet Sounds: A Memoir of Negro Leadership** (New York: Holt, Rinehart and Winston, 1964). Also see Keli Goff, "The Rampant Sexism at March on Washington," **The Root,** August 22, 2013.

4. Danielle McGuire, **At the Dark End of the Street: Black Women, Rape and Resistance—A New History of the Civil Rights Movement, from Rosa Parks to the Rise of Black Power** (New York: Knopf, 2010).

5. Valerie Hudson, Bonnie Ballif-Spanvill, Mary Caprioli, and Chad Emmett, **Sex and World Peace** (New York: Columbia University Press, 2012).

6. Vincent Shilling, "8 Myths and Atrocities About

Christopher Columbus and Columbus Day," **Indian Country,** October 14, 2013. For more about Columbus's atrocities, see Howard Zinn, **A People's History of the United States** (New York: Harper Perennial, 2005).

7. Gloria Steinem, "The City Politic: A Racial Walking Tour," **New York,** February 24, 1969.

8. Gloria Steinem, "Why Women Voters Can't Be Trusted," **Ms.,** 1972. Virginia Slims sponsored the American Women's poll by Louis Harris Associates, the first national survey of women's opinions on women's issues.

9. Ron Speer, "Gloria's Beauty Belies Her Purpose," **St. Petersburg Times,** December 3, 1971.

10. **As If Women Matter: The Essential Gloria Steinem Reader,** ed. Ruchira Gupta (New Delhi: Rupa Publications India, 2014).

11. The Equal Rights Amendment states: "Equality of rights under the law shall not be denied or abridged by the United States or by any state on account of sex."

12. At a 1979 American Psychological Association conference, Sonia Johnson, a leading Mormon feminist, gave a speech titled "Patriarchal Panic: Sexual Politics in the Mormon Church," charging the Church of Jesus Christ of Latter-Day Saints with ignoring the separation of church and state by opposing the ERA with an illegal use of church money and power. She was excommunicated.

13. Once we were in Houston, it turned out that other states had slightly overrepresented African Americans, so the national body still reflected the nation. Instead of a time-consuming process of challenging the seating of Mississippi, which was reportedly what the Klan had in mind, the Black Women's Caucus organized a floor demonstration to let delegates know that Mississippi wasn't properly represented—and then moved on. Klan delegates were left with nothing to do but echo Imperial Wizard Robert Shelton's vow "to protect our women from all the militant lesbians." See Caroline Bird and the National Commission on the Observance of International Women's Year, **What Women Want: From the Official Report to the President, the Congress and the People of the United States** (New York: Simon and Schuster, 1979).

14. National Commission on the Observance of International Women's Year, **The Spirit of Houston: An Official Report to the President, the Congress and the People of the United States** (Washington, D.C.: U.S. Government Printing Office, 1978), p. 157.

15. Ibid. The Houston Women's Conference and the fifty-six conferences that led up to it gave birth to a majority national agenda and to state and national organizations. See also Bird, **What Women Want.**

16. Bird, **What Women Want,** p. 37.

CHAPTER III: WHY I DON'T DRIVE

1. Pete Hamill, "Curb Job," a review of **Taxi!** by Graham Russell Gao Hodges, **New York Times Book Review,** June 17, 2007, p. 19.
2. Gail Collins, **When Everything Changed: The Amazing Journey of American Women from 1960 to the Present** (New York: Little, Brown and Company, 2009).
3. Christine Doudna, "Vicki Frankovich," **Ms.,** January 1987.

CHAPTER IV: ONE BIG CAMPUS

1. Gerda Lerner, **The Creation of Patriarchy** (New York and Oxford: Oxford University Press, 1986), p. 225.
2. Caroline Heldman and Danielle Dirks, "Blowing the Whistle on Campus Rape," **Ms.,** February 2014.
3. As far as I know, no one ever burned a bra. At the 1968 Miss America Contest in Atlantic City, several hundred feminists protested on the boardwalk by putting girdles, steno pads, aprons, dust mops, and other symbols of the "feminine" role into a trash can and threatening to burn them; it was an echo of Vietnam draft resisters burning draft cards. However, they couldn't get a fire permit and never burned anything.
4. Ira C. Lupu, "Gloria Steinem at the **Harvard**

Law Review Banquet," **Green Bag,** Autumn 1998.
5. Ibid., pp. 22–23.

CHAPTER V: WHEN THE POLITICAL IS PERSONAL

1. Actually, this was old journalism. Before the advent of the telegraph, writers used the essay and other literary forms to let the reader see through the eyes of the writer. The many books by the young Winston Churchill were collections of his journalistic essays reported from Cuba, India, and Africa. Then the telegraph required facts first—who, what, why, when, where—then elaborating on them with each paragraph in pyramid form. But simultaneous electronic transmission allows writers freedom again. Facts should be checked, but stories can again be told.
2. Gloria Steinem, "Trying to Love Eugene," **New York,** August 5, 1968.
3. For an account of exactly how the Republican Party gradually ejected women who supported equality, see Tanya Melich, **The Republican War Against Women: An Insider's Report from Behind the Lines** (New York: Bantam Dell, 1998).
4. As I was writing this, I turned on the radio, and there was Barry Farber, who is now a digital talk radio host and a "birther," that is, someone who believes President Obama was not born in Hawaii and therefore took office illegally.

---

5. Betty Friedan, "Up from the Kitchen Floor," **New York Times Magazine,** March 4, 1973.

6. Chisholm was the first African American, male or female, to run for the presidency in a major party. It is instructive that she claimed to have experienced sex as an even bigger barrier than race in politics.

7. This would be proven later when Republican presidential candidate John McCain chose Sarah Palin as his vice-presidential running mate. Her support came more from male than from female voters—overwhelmingly white in both cases.

8. Renamed "Right Candidates, Wrong Question," **New York Times,** February 7, 2007.

9. MSNBC's **Morning Joe,** January 9, 2008, appearance.

10. Conducted by the National Opinion Research Center at the University of Chicago for **The New York Times,** Associated Press, **The Washington Post, The Wall Street Journal,** CNN, **St. Petersburg Times, The Palm Beach Post,** Tribune Company, **Los Angeles Times, Chicago Tribune, Orlando Sentinel,** and **The Baltimore Sun.**

11. More from the Parable of the Nail: If Gore had been elected instead of Bush, we wouldn't have had a second, optional war in Iraq; or abstinence-only sex education enforced by federal funding for public schools; or the highest unwanted pregnancy rate in the developed world; or an executive order giving billions in tax dollars

to "faith-based" centers of right-wing political power; or the global gag rule that deprives poor countries of all U.S. aid if they even offer information about abortion, even with their own funds; or corporate profiteering on privatized wars abroad as well as privatized prisons at home; or a higher percentage of the U.S. population in prison than in any other country in the world; or corporate CEOs whose salaries rose from thirty times that of the average worker before the right-wing backlash took over Washington to an average of 475 times; or an unregulated financial industry that led to a worldwide economic meltdown—and so much more.

CHAPTER VI: SURREALISM IN EVERYDAY LIFE

1. In 2013 three thousand truckers—angered by low wages, high fuel prices, and a government shutdown in Washington—planned to stage a slowdown on the highways around D.C., plus a peaceful rally within it. Though it's mostly misdirected at President Obama, and rain masks the slowdown's effectiveness, it's a flexing of political muscle that sobers police and makes protesters with no trucks envious.

2. As I write this almost a half-century later, employers have to pay servers only $2.10 an hour if they do or might get tipped, according to federal law. Groups of such workers, almost totally women, are organizing for coverage by minimum wage

laws. U.S. Department of Labor, "Minimum Wages for Tipped Employees," January 1, 2015, http://www.dol.gov/whd/state/tipped.htm.

3. Jo Freeman, "Trashing: The Dark Side of Sisterhood," **Ms.**, April 1976.

4. Rachel K. Jones, Jacqueline E. Darroch, and Stanley K. Henshaw, "Patterns in the Socioeconomic Characteristics of Women Obtaining Abortions in 2000–2001," Alan Guttmacher Institute, **Perspectives on Sexual and Reproductive Health** 34, no. 5 (September–October 2002).

5. It never did get published. I didn't yet understand that dividing news into "hard" and "soft" was one more idea that gender is a reality instead of a political creation.

6. Gloria Steinem, "Ho Chi Minh in New York," **New York,** April 8, 1968.

7. "Gloria Steinem's Sermon Protested," **Lodi News-Sentinel,** September 21, 1978.

8. The church regulated abortion until 1860 or so. For instance, a female fetus could be aborted for up to eighty days, and a male fetus for up to forty days, because it was thought that the male, being superior, quickened earlier. The question of ensoulment or when life begins was restricted to when to baptize. John T. Noonan, ed., **The Morality of Abortion: Legal and Historical Perspectives** (Cambridge, MA: Harvard University Press, 1970).

CHAPTER VII: WHAT ONCE WAS CAN BE AGAIN

1. Alice Kohn, **No Contest: The Case Against Competition** (Boston: Houghton Mifflin, 1992).

2. William Loren Katz, **Black Indians: A Hidden Heritage** (New York: Atheneum, 1986), p. 2.

3. Pope Nicholas V, Papal Bull **Dum Diversas,** June 18, 1452.

4. Paula Gunn Allen, **The Sacred Hoop: Recovering the Feminine in American Indian Traditions** (Boston: Beacon Press, 1992), pp. 13–15.

5. Stuart J. Fiedel, **Prehistory of the Americas** (Cambridge: Cambridge University Press, 1987), p. 238; and Robert Silverberg, **The Mound Builders** (Columbus: Ohio University Press, 1986), pp. 280–89.

6. Jack Weatherford, **Indian Givers: How the Indians of the Americas Transformed the World** (New York: Fawcett Columbine, 1988), pp. 59–97.

7. Quoted by John Mohawk et al., **Exiled in the Land of the Free: Democracy, Indian Nations and the U.S. Constitution** (Santa Fe, NM: Clear Light, 1992), p. 69.

8. For a documentary about the life and work of LaDonna Harris, see **Indian 101,** a film by Julianna Brannum; http://www.indian101themovie.com.

9. Here is one example of many: "Walter Ashby

was the first registrar of Virginia's Bureau of Vital Statistics, which recorded births, marriages and deaths. He accepted the job in 1912. For the next thirty-four years, he led efforts to purify the white race in Virginia by forcing Indians and other nonwhites to classify themselves as blacks. It amounted to bureaucratic suicide." Warren Fiske, "The Black-and-White World of Walter Ashby Plecker," **Virginian Pilot,** August 18, 2004.

10. Ayi Kwei Armah, **Two Thousand Seasons** (Portsmouth, NH: Heinemann International Literature and Textbooks, 1979).

11. Quoted by J. N. B. Hewitt, "Status of Women in Iroquois Polity before 1784," **Annual Report to the Board of Regents of the Smithsonian Institution for 1932** (Washington, D.C.: U.S. Government Printing Office, 1933), p. 483.

12. For an overview of Native American cultures as the main source of democracy and democratic structures, see Weatherford, **Indian Givers,** pp. 133–50.

13. "Native Women Send Message," **Wassaja** 4, no. 8 (August 1976), p. 7.

14. In the Yoruba culture of Africa, there is a Trickster called Eshu, and in India, the always-playful Krishna—and many more. To focus on Native American mythology and also find these parallels, see Lewis Hyde, **Trickster Makes This World: Mischief, Myth, and Art** (New York: Farrar, Straus and Giroux, 1998).

15. Allen, **The Sacred Hoop**.
16. Wilma would ultimately help in breaking the cycle of dependence to bring indoor running water to Bell, an isolated community of three hundred or so mostly Cherokee families in the backwoods of Oklahoma. Filmmaker Kristina Kiehl's **The Cherokee Word for Water** (2013) is a dramatization of the story of Bell and a testament to Wilma's leadership and sense of community.
17. Europeans didn't believe that the inhabitants they killed and conquered could be descendants of those who developed agriculture, pharmacology, the world's largest system of earthworks, and democracy itself. Some said the Egyptians must have come here, then left again. In my lifetime, estimates of the length of time since migratory cultures settled this land have increased from 9,000 to 12,000 to 30,000 years. "The Untold Saga of Early Man in America," **Time,** March 13, 2006.
18. Wilma Mankiller, **Every Day Is a Good Day: Reflections by Contemporary Indigenous Women** (Golden, CO: Fulcrum, 2004).
19. Weatherford, **Indian Givers,** pp. 82–84.
20. Ibid.; see chapter 7, "Liberty, Anarchism, and the Noble Savage."
21. Robin Morgan, **The Burning Time** (Brooklyn, NY: Melville House, 2012).

INDEX

———

The abbreviation GS = Gloria Steinem
Page numbers of photographs appear in bold.

Mankiller Flats, Oklahoma
abortion protesters, 161–65
Cherokee, 311–21
Cherokee National Holiday, 331–34
Comanche activist in, 303
driving from Texas to, 257
GS speaking in, 161–65
Oklahoma City, 326–28
bombing, 102
O'Neill, Eugene, xxviii
Organizing, 113, 288
abolitionists and suffragists, 186
bee-and-flower model of, 138
Gandhian tactics for women's movements, 53
Gandhian wisdom for, 51
GS as itinerant organizer, xix, xxvi, xxvii, 54–55, 65, 76–79, 81–82, 122–24, 169–71, 186, 205, 247–48, 263–64, 287–88, 339
Huerta on mantra of, 161
importance of organizing in person, 170–171
in India, 49–51, 53
for National Women's Conference, 76–80, 88, 122
Poo and, 73
principle for, 339
as surrealistic, 263
TWU students and, 150–151, 152–153

Palin, Sarah, 259, 360n7
Papal bull promoting slavery and genocide, 294
Paper Moon (film), 22
Parable of the Nail, 234–242, 360–361n11
Parker, Cynthia Ann, 303
Parker, Dorothy, 63
Parks, Rosa, 60

ABOUT THE AUTHOR

GLORIA STEINEM is a writer, lecturer, political activist, and feminist organizer. She was a founder of **New York** and **Ms.** magazines. She is the author of **Moving Beyond Words, Revolution from Within,** and **Outrageous Acts and Everyday Rebellions,** all published in the United States, and, in India, **As If Women Matter.** Her writing also appears in many anthologies and textbooks. She co-founded the National Women's Political Caucus, the Ms. Foundation for Women, the Free to Be Foundation, and the Women's Media Center in this country. As links to other countries, she helped found Equality Now, Donor Direct Action, and Direct Impact Africa. For her writing, Steinem has received the Penney-Missouri Journalism Award, the Front Page and Clarion awards, the National Magazine Award, the Lifetime Achievement in Journalism Award from the Society of Professional Journalists, the Society of Writers Award from the United Nations, and the University of Missouri School of Journalism Award for Distinguished Service in Journalism. In 1993, her concern with child abuse led her to co-produce an Emmy Award–winning TV documentary for HBO, **Multiple Personalities: The Search for Deadly Memories.** She is currently working with the Sophia Smith Collection at Smith College on documenting the grassroots origins of the U.S. women's movement, and on a Center for Organizers in tribute to Wilma Mankiller, principal chief of the Cherokee Nation. Steinem has been the subject of three television documentaries, including HBO's **Gloria: In Her Own Words,** and she is among the subjects of the 2013 PBS documentary **Makers,** a continuing project to record the women who made America. After graduating Phi Beta Kappa from Smith College in 1956, she spent two years in India on a Chester Bowles Fellowship, and was influenced by Gandhian organizing. She has been awarded numerous honorary degrees, including the first doctorate of human justice awarded by Simmons College, the Bill of Rights Award from the American Civil Liberties Union of Southern California, the National Gay Rights Advocates Award, and the Ceres Medal from the United Nations. In 2013, President Obama awarded her the Presidential Medal of Freedom, the highest civilian honor. Rutgers University is now creating the Gloria Steinem Endowed Chair in Media, Culture and Feminist Studies. Steinem lives in New York City and spends about half her time traveling in this and other countries.